语篇反馈研究
| 基于社会认知理论 |

Constructing and Interpreting Non-error Feedback:

From the Perspective of Sociocognitive Theory

卞晓云 / 著

中国出版集团
中译出版社

图书在版编目（CIP）数据

语篇反馈研究：基于社会认知理论 = Constructing and Interpreting Non-error Feedback:From the Perspective of Sociocognitive Theory：英文 / 卞晓云著.—北京：中译出版社，2023.2
ISBN 978-7-5001-7246-8

I.①语… II.①卞… III.①英语－写作－教学研究－高等学校 IV.①H319.36

中国版本图书馆CIP数据核字（2022）第222980号

出版发行：中译出版社
地　　址：北京市西城区新街口外大街28号普天德胜大厦主楼4层
电　　话：（010）68359827，68359303（发行部）　68359725（编辑部）
邮　　编：100044
电子邮箱：book@ctph.com.cn
网　　址：http://www.ctph.com.cn

出 版 人：乔卫兵
总 策 划：刘永淳
策划编辑：范祥镇　钱屹芝
责任编辑：钱屹芝
文字编辑：杨佳特
营销编辑：吴雪峰　董思嫄
封面设计：潘　峰

排　　版：北京中文天地文化艺术有限公司
印　　刷：北京玺诚印务有限公司
经　　销：新华书店

规　　格：710 mm×960 mm　1/16
印　　张：23.5
字　　数：438千字
版　　次：2023年2月第1版
印　　次：2023年2月第1次

ISBN 978-7-5001-7246-8　　　　定价：78.00元

版权所有　侵权必究
中 译 出 版 社

List of Tables

Table 3.1	Participant Profile: Teacher T	87
Table 3.2	Participant Profile: The Students	88
Table 3.3	Research Methods	89
Table 3.4	Resulting Data Set	99
Table 3.5	Types of Data and Examples	101
Table 3.6	Labelling Teacher T's Think-Alouds: A Sample	104
Table 3.7	Labelling Student A's Think-Alouds: A Sample	104
Table 3.8	Cognitive Acceptance Categories and Their Indications	106
Table 3.9	Segmenting and Labelling Feedback Focus: A Sample	109
Table 3.10	Segmenting and Labelling Feedback Delivery Approaches: A Sample	110
Table 3.11	Handling Teacher/Student Interview Data: Topic Coding	113
Table 4.1	Teacher Feedback: Its General Distribution	130
Table 4.2	Teacher T's Non-error Feedback and EA Feedback	130
Table 4.3	Teacher T's Non-error and EA Feedback: Cross-task Changes	132
Table 4.4	Teacher T's Non-error and EA Feedback: Cross-student Changes	133
Table 4.5	Teacher T's Feedback Delivery Approaches: From the Perspectives of Orientation and Language Channel	137

Table 4.6	Teacher T's Feedback Delivery Approaches: From the Perspective of Scaffolding Degree	139
Table 4.7	Cross-assignment Changes: From the Perspective of Orientation	140
Table 4.8	Cross-assignment Changes: From the Perspective of Scaffolding Degree	141
Table 4.9	Cross-student Changes: From the Perspective of Orientation	142
Table 4.10	Cross-student Changes: From the Perspective of Scaffolding Degree	143
Table 4.11	Teacher T's Cognitive, Behavioral, and Affective Engagement	150
Table 4.12	The Cognitive Decision-Making Process Teacher T Involved in	151
Table 5.1	Student A's Acceptance and Incorporation of EA Feedback	179
Table 5.2	Student B's Acceptance and Incorporation of EA Feedback	185
Table 5.3	Student C's Acceptance and Incorporation of EA Feedback	191
Table 5.4	The Students' Engagement with EA Feedback	195
Table 5.5	Students A, B, and C's Cognitive Engagement with EA Feedback	197
Table 6.1	Effectiveness of the Construction and Interpretation of EA Feedback	228
Table 6.2	Helpfulness of EA Feedback	236

List of Abbreviations

EA	expository argumentation
EFL	English as a foreign language
ESL	English as a second language
L2	second language
L1	first language
RQ	research question
JSLW	*Journal of Second Language Writing*
LW	learning-to-write
WL	writing-to-learn

Table of Contents

List of Tables ··· I

List of Abbreviations ·· III

Chapter 1 Introduction ··· 1

    1.0   Introduction: An Overview ······································· 1

    1.1   Problem Statement ·· 2

    1.2   The Rationales Behind the Study ······························· 6

    1.3   Overview of Research Methodology ························· 12

    1.4   Significance of the Study ·· 13

    1.5   Organization of the Book ·· 15

Chapter 2 Issues in Teacher Feedback ································ 16

    2.0   Introduction ··· 16

    2.1   Development of Teacher Feedback: Questions ············ 16

    2.2   Theoretical Perspectives on Teacher Feedback and Its Importance ··· 23

    2.3   Research on Teacher Feedback ································ 44

    2.4   Research Gaps and Emergent Issues ························· 68

    2.5   Chapter Summary ·· 72

Chapter 3 Research Design — 73

- 3.0 Introduction — 73
- 3.1 Research Design: The Rationale — 73
- 3.2 Research Design: Defining the Term "Case Study" — 74
- 3.3 Research Design: Key Issues — 80
- 3.4 Chapter Summary — 116

Chapter 4 The Construction of Non-error Feedback — 117

- 4.0 Introduction — 117
- 4.1 What the Teacher Brought to the Feedback Process: Contextual Information — 118
- 4.2 The Entire Feedback-Constructing Process the Teacher Went Through: Contextual Information — 129
- 4.3 The EA Issues the Teacher Actually Focused on — 129
- 4.4 Teacher Decision-Making: How the Teacher Decided Which EA Issues to Focus on — 133
- 4.5 The Feedback Delivery Approaches the Teacher Used — 136
- 4.6 Teacher Decision-Making: How the Teacher Decided on Feedback Delivery Approaches — 144
- 4.7 Chapter Summary — 164

Chapter 5 The Interpretation of Non-error Feedback — 168

- 5.0 Introduction — 168
- 5.1 What the Students Brought to the Feedback Process: Contextual Information — 169
- 5.2 Student A's Acceptance and Incorporation of EA Feedback — 177
- 5.3 Student B's Acceptance and Incorporation of EA Feedback — 184

5.4 Student C's Acceptance and Incorporation of EA Feedback 190
5.5 How the Students' Acceptance and Incorporation of EA Feedback were Decided 194
5.6 Chapter Summary 223

Chapter 6 The Feedback Process: Its Effectiveness and Helpfulness ... 227
6.0 Introduction 227
6.1 Effectiveness of the Feedback Process 227
6.2 Helpfulness of the Feedback Process: Student Changes 234
6.3 More Helpfulness of Non-error Feedback 235
6.4 Chapter Summary 242
6.5 Summary of All Findings 243

Chapter 7 Discussion and Conclusion 245
7.0 Introduction 245
7.1 Aims and Methodology of the Study 245
7.2 Summary of Key Findings 246
7.3 Contributions of the Findings 249
7.4 Limitations and Future/Further Research 302
7.5 Final Remarks 306

References **308**

Appendices **334**
Appendix A: Teacher Background Interview Guide 334
Appendix B: Student Background Interview Guide 336
Appendix C: Think-Aloud Protocol in the Training Session 338
Appendix D: Teacher Retrospective and Ongoing Interviews Guide 340
Appendix E: Student Retrospective and Ongoing Interviews Guide 342

Appendix F: Teacher/Student Final Interview Guide ·················· 344

Appendix G: Teacher Think-Aloud Data Codebook ····················· 346

Appendix H: Student Think-Aloud Data Codebook ····················· 350

Appendix I: Student Writing with Teacher Comments ················· 357

Appendix J: Student Writing with Teacher Comments and Student-Written Notes ··· 360

Appendix K: Writing Prompts ··· 364

Chapter 1   Introduction

1.0   Introduction: An Overview

Teacher written feedback on second language (L2) students' writing (hereinafter mainly referred to as "**teacher feedback**" for short) has been a subject of researchers' interest since the 1980s (Bitchener & Ferris, 2012; Ferris, 2003). However, research into it has mainly focused on the surface-level errors of student writing and there has only been a small body of research addressing teacher feedback on non-error issues such as the organization and content of student writing (Ferris & Hedgcock, 2014; Goldstein, 2001, 2006, 2016). This book directs its attention to non-error feedback and prioritizes **Chinese EFL (English-as-a-Foreign-Language) teachers' feedback on the argumentation-related issues in expository writing** (hereinafter referred to as **feedback on "expository argumentation"** or "**EA feedback**" for short, e.g., teacher feedback on supporting evidence). By defining teacher feedback from the sociocognitive perspective and focusing on EA feedback, this book reports a study on the process during which teachers construct EA feedback and students interpret that EA feedback (hereinafter mainly referred to as "**the feedback-and-interpretation process**" for short). Reporting this study in this book aims to extend the empirical, theoretical, and knowledge base of teacher written feedback.

Specifically, the following three research questions (hereinafter referred to as "**RQ(s)**" for short) were addressed in the study this book reports:

- RQ1: When constructing feedback, how does the Chinese EFL teacher decide what EA concerns to focus on and how to deliver EA feedback?
- RQ2: When processing the teacher's EA feedback, how does the Chinese EFL student decide the extent to which it is accepted and incorporated?
- RQ3: According to the student and the teacher, to what extent does the process of constructing and interpreting EA feedback help students improve, if it is considered effective?

This introductory chapter provides an orientation to the study this book reports. It begins with stating the research problem (1.1). Then, the practical, theoretical, and empirical rationales for the three RQs are explained (1.2.1–1.2.3). Following the rationales that motivated the RQs is a description of the research methodology (1.3), an explanation of the significance of the study this book reports (1.4), and an outline of the organization of this book and the composition of chapters (1.5).

1.1 Problem Statement

In the context of L2 writing instruction, the provision of written feedback continues to be an activity widely practiced by teachers (Ferris, 2003; Hyland, 2003; Yu, Jiang, & Zhou, 2020). From the perspective of teachers, they usually do not feel that they have done justice to students' writing efforts until they have written substantial comments on students' papers (Hyland, 2003). It is believed that many teachers often spend more time providing feedback than preparing for or conducting classroom sessions (Ferris & Hedgcock, 2014).

Students also consider their teachers' feedback crucial to their improvement as writers. (Hyland, 2003; Zhang & Hyland, 2022)

Sharing this central concern of teachers, L2 scholars have done a great deal of thinking and research about teacher feedback since the 1980s. This can be seen by the emergence of a large number of published books that are wholly or partially devoted to teacher feedback over the past four decades (e.g., Bitchener & Ferris, 2012; Bitchener & Storch, 2016; Ferris, 2003, 2013; Ferris & Hedgcock, 2014; Flowerdew & Peacock, 2001; Goldstein, 2005; Hyland & Hyland, 2006b; Lee, 2017; Manchón & Matsuda, 2016; Silva & Matsuda, 2001). Moreover, according to Murphy and de Larios (2010, p.i), over 85% of the manuscripts received by *The Journal of Second Language Writing (JSLW)* from 2007 to 2010 dealt with the topic of feedback. Certainly, these manuscripts might be concerned with different types of feedback (e.g., teacher feedback, peer feedback, self-feedback, teacher-student conference); but as teacher feedback is a persistent teacher practice, there must be a high percentage of these manuscripts pertinent to it. Furthermore, teacher feedback has become one of the most accessed topics by graduate students (Tardy, 2014). In general, investigating L2 teachers' feedback has already been established as an important area of inquiry (Silva, Thomas, Park, & Zhang, 2014).

Despite the general recognition of the importance of teacher feedback, there are two notable issues that merit immediate attention in the arena of teacher feedback. First, the term *"teacher written feedback"* has not yet been clearly defined (Hattie & Timperley, 2007). By reviewing feedback literature, it can be found that since the publication of Truscott's 1996 controversial and compelling article that harshly criticized teachers' corrections of linguistic errors in student writing (i.e., error/corrective feedback), error feedback has received so much of researchers' attention that "teacher response to errors is more commonly referred to now as feedback" (Ravand & Rasekh, 2011, p.1136).

The following example illustrates how teacher feedback is understood as error feedback by default and it is necessary to explain what teacher feedback really means. When Zhang, Yan, and Liu (2015) reviewed the research presentations that appeared at the 7th International Conference on English Language Teaching in China in 2014, they only reported error feedback studies presented at that conference. It is evident in this example that Zhang, Yan, and Liu tacitly equated "teacher feedback" with "error/corrective feedback" and used these two terms interchangeably. However, the conference program available online indicated that at that conference there were presentations of studies on non-error feedback. Having a clearly defined teacher feedback is a helpful way to understand why presentations about non-error feedback at that conference were not reviewed by Zhang, Yan, and Liu.

Second, studies on teacher feedback mainly cover issues about the surface-level errors of student writing and few have thoroughly studied non-error feedback on content and organization issues. According to Goldstein (2001), since Zamel's (1985) first study about content-focused feedback, as of 2001 there were only 15 readily available studies on non-error feedback, or "text-level feedback" (i.e., feedback on content and rhetoric, Goldstein, 2006, p.185). Indeed, in the years that followed (2001–present), published feedback research focusing on non-error feedback has remained sparse. In 2006, Goldstein concluded once again: "a small body of research has developed addressing issues pertaining to teacher feedback and revision at the text level" (p.185). Today, published feedback research beyond surface errors continues to be far from adequate (Ferris & Hedgcock, 2014; Goldstein, 2016).

Certainly, researchers' attention to error feedback is deserved. According to Manchón (2011), one purpose of L2 writing is to learn the language. As such, researchers' attention to error feedback can help L2 teachers deal with the linguistic accuracy of student writing and promote students' language acquisition. However, researchers' strong interest in error feedback does not mean that research into non-error "text-level" feedback is unimportant and unnecessary. As a matter of fact, there is a need for an extensive and thorough investigation of non-error feedback. Two reasons can explain this point. First, when L2 students' writing practice occurs, it also serves the purpose of learning to master writing skills and competence in dealing with issues beyond the level of language (i.e., learning-to-write; Manchón, 2011). Accordingly, research on non-error feedback is needed so as to provide L2 writing teachers with important insights regarding how to help students achieve the goals of learning-to-write and build writing abilities. Second, there is empirical evidence that as many as 85% of teachers' comments were focused on students' ideas and organization (e.g., Ferris, 1997; Ferris, et al., 1997). As such, L2 teachers need research on non-error feedback to help them improve their responding practices.

To summarize the problems stated above, it is worthwhile studying L2 teachers' written feedback and exploring it empirically. As to the research, there are two urgent concerns for researchers to address:

1) the conceptual problem associated with the term *"teacher written feedback"*, and
2) the paucity of research into non-error feedback.

The study this book reports provided a remedy for these two major problems in feedback research and practice. As mentioned in Section 1.0, there are three RQs addressed in the study this book reports. The following section (1.2) explains the rationales behind the RQs under three subheadings: practical rationales, theoretical rationales, and fivefold empirical rationales.

1.2 The Rationales Behind the Study

1.2.1 Practical Rationales: Personal Responding Experience

The practical impetus for the study reported in this book came from the author's personal first-hand experiences of providing written feedback on the expository writing produced by the Chinese EFL first- and second-year university students. What follows is the story of how I, the author, was motivated by my previous responding experience to do the study this book reports.

In fact, this book is converted and adapted from the PhD thesis I wrote when I pursued my doctoral study in New Zealand. Before I left to pursue the doctorate in New Zealand, I had already taught *College English* in China for about ten years. In China, *College English* is a compulsory, integrated skills course offered by almost every university during non-English language major students' Sophormore and/or freshmen years. To complete the course and receive credit, apart from reading, speaking, and listening skills, my students (generally with low or mid-intermediate English proficiency of a level corresponding to IELTS scores around 5.0–5.5) needed to demonstrate that they had gained good control over expository writing.

In the Chinese EFL educational context, English expository writing is the genre most frequently learnt and used (Zhang, 2000). It requires student writers to clearly, coherently, and concisely expound on an idea for their readers in English. At that time (before my pursuit of the doctorate), to help my students acquire the skills to handle the exposition genre, I usually spent a lot of time responding to their expository writing. As my students had great trouble formulating and developing arguments, I wrote many comments on the following expository argumentation-related (EA-related) problems exhibited in their work: unsupported ideas, lack of/inappropriate topic sentences, incoherent and illogical argumentation, and the traditional four-step (i.e., beginning, developing, turning, and integration) Chinese way of writing (Chen, 2002). Concerning the difficult EA issues, I felt students need individualized, tailor-made guidance and instruction/feedback from teachers. Without it or only with computer feedback which by far still "cannot evaluate the degree to which ideas are relevant, appropriate and well argued in an essay" (Hyland, 2010, p.178), it is difficult for them to realize what their problems are and clearly understand how to improve the argumentation quality of their expositions.

However, although I was eager to provide my students with EA feedback, my previous responding practice was bound up with doubts and questions. First, I felt uncertain about whether my EA feedback was well understood and well accepted by my students. Second, I was not clear about how my communication with students via EA feedback could be better established. To reduce my uncertainty and clear up my confusion, I consulted several journal articles about feedback. However, after reading them, I still felt puzzled. In fact, since the term *"feedback"* was vaguely defined or even undefined in most cases, for a long time, I did not realize that **error/corrective feedback** only addresses language and grammar errors and it does not address issues beyond surface errors. Meanwhile, as most studies view feedback merely as corrective information a teacher presented on student writing rather than two-way communication between the teacher and the student, the studies I previously read did not show me what I had expected and did not serve my needs and interests very well.

Overall, the doubts and questions that stemmed from my feedback practices triggered my decision to add new elements to the existing literature about non-error feedback. Taking my doubts and questions as prompts, I decided to pursue a study that

1) focuses on non-error EA feedback,
2) defines the term *"teacher written feedback"* at length,
3) presents a comprehensive understanding of teacher-student communication during non-error feedback, and
4) looks at the effectiveness of teacher-student communication via EA feedback specifically.

1.2.2 Theoretical Rationales: Sociocognitive Theory and Genre Pedagogy

Theoretically, my study this book reports was based on Atkinson's (2002, 2010a, 2010b, 2011, 2012, 2014) sociocognitive theory of learning and development, and the Systemic Functional Linguistics (SFL)-informed genre pedagogy. The theoretical rationales for my study are clarified below.

First, my study drew on Atkinson's sociocognitive theory of learning and development to understand teacher feedback. Similar to sociocultural theory, Atkinson's sociocognitive theory of learning and development emphasizes the role of ecosocial (combined ecological and social) interaction in cognitive development. With regards to the ecosocial interaction, sociocognitive theory does not limit it to the interaction between human beings alone; it acknowledges that it also occurs between humans and their non-human environments (including both the physical/ecological setting and social contexts, Atkinson, 2011). Furthermore, using the inseparability, adaptivity, and alignment principles, sociocognitive theory offers an explanation about what happens when humans, and humans and their ecosocial environment interact and how human cognition develops in the interactions. This theoretical position is particularly useful for understanding teacher feedback because it sheds light on ① how the teacher offers feedback, ② how the student attends to teacher feedback, ③ how the teacher, the student, the feedback itself (as the text-level context), and the environments/contexts interact with each other during the feedback process, and ④ how student learning and development occur during the feedback process. In Chapter 2, what teacher feedback means is fully defined based on Atkinson's sociocognitive theory of learning and development.

Moreover, my study drew on Atkinson's sociocognitive theory of learning and development to raise RQs. As mentioned above, Atkinson's sociocognitive theory gives centrality to the cognitive and the social and their inseparability. Informed by this theory, the three RQs investigated teacher-student communication via feedback (ecosocial interaction), teachers'/students' decision-making thought processes during feedback interactions (cognitive processing), and the helpfulness of the feedback process for student development (cognitive development). That is to say, the three RQs investigated in this book were theoretically well supported because they were consistent with Atkinson's sociocognitive theory of learning and development that places emphasis on interaction and cognition.

Second, the SFL-informed genre pedagogy provided a theoretical rationale for studying feedback and EA feedback. This is because it acknowledges that both feedback and EA feedback occupy an important place in teaching and learning, which, as a result, points to the necessity to study feedback and EA feedback. Briefly, the SFL-informed genre pedagogy, welcomed by teachers in various countries (Hyland, 2007), emphasizes the importance of teachers' "intervention" towards students' awareness of target genres and the development of their genre knowledge (Hyland, 2007). The implication derives from this is that teacher feedback is important, since it is a type of teacher intervention which offers teachers and students good opportunities to explore various genre-related issues together and helps students develop their genre knowledge and ability. Moreover, SFL-informed genre pedagogy particularly emphasizes the importance of EA feedback. According to genre theorists (e.g., Hyland, 2007), L2 students are unfamiliar with how to generalize, organize, and argue for ideas when writing expositions or arguments. As SFL-informed genre pedagogy prioritizes student needs (Hyland, 2007), it certainly encourages L2 teachers' intervention/feedback surrounding the argumentation-related issues in students' expository or argumentative writing. Clearly, the importance genre pedagogy attaches to teacher feedback and EA feedback provides a powerful theoretical justification for my study reported in this book.

1.2.3 Fivefold Empirical Rationales

Apart from the paucity of research on non-error feedback, the empirical rationale behind my study is fivefold.

First, my study followed a new research trend. Over the past 40 years, ① student perspectives on teacher feedback, ② the feedback itself, ③ teacher cognition, and ④ the feedback-and-revision process have become the important trends in feedback research. However, Hyland and Hyland (2006a) launched a new, important line of research by investigating the negotiation process during which teachers construct feedback and students interpret that feedback (i.e., the **feedback-and-interpretation** process). One important reason why this process deserves attention is because, when the writing is returned to the students with comments, it is impossible for them to move on to revision without processing or interpreting teacher feedback first. Thus, investigating the feedback-and-interpretation process can lead to a better understanding of the feedback-and-revision dynamic. My study, following Hyland and

Hyland's lead, investigated **the feedback-and-interpretation process**. Due to the importance of this process, it is apparently necessary to expand the repertoire of this line of research.

Second, my study about teacher-student communication via EA feedback and its helpfulness echoed Knoblauch and Brannon's (1981) and Goldstein's (2016) suggestion to study "the larger conversation between teacher and student" (Knoblauch & Brannon, 1981, p.1). So far, the research area concerning teacher feedback on L2 writing is still an emerging field. For this reason, it is important for researchers to holistically study it and devote attention to the feedback-and-response process. By holistically looking at the feedback process and its helpfulness, a study, like the one this book reports, ensures that teacher feedback can be better understood and researching into it is worthwhile.

Third, my study provided evidence from the Chinese EFL educational context. Currently, feedback research, such as Hyland and Hyland's (2006a) study, is mainly focused on ESL students' academic expository writing and on the United States (Goldstein, 2016). As such, my study, situated in **the Chinese EFL setting** and focusing on **expository writing**, could complement the findings mainly obtained in the ESL expository context.

Fourth, my study answered Goldstein's (2016) call to conduct in-depth investigations. According to Goldstein (2016), many important questions related to teacher feedback still have not been thoroughly addressed within any one particular context or across contexts. These questions include what teachers choose to comment on and why they decide to do so, and how and why students make decisions regarding the use of teacher feedback (Goldstein, 2016). My study examined how teachers decide on their feedback foci and feedback delivery approaches when constructing EA feedback. Also, it investigated how students make decisions regarding their acceptance and incorporation of EA feedback. Devoting attention to the in-depth "how" questions about decision-making can contribute greatly to a deeper understanding of teacher feedback.

Finally, but also importantly, my study echoed Ferris' (2001) call that feedback researchers need to launch precise investigations. For example, my study investigated teachers' decision-making thought processes when they construct EA feedback (RQ1). To be precise in the ways that feedback research is conducted, my study pinned down the behaviors involved in the teacher's feedback-providing process. According to Huot (2002), teachers' provision of feedback includes two essential procedures: reading a student's text and adding comments to it. Building on an awareness of these two procedures, my study chose to explore the decision-making process the teacher is involved in **when he/she is adding/constructing comments to students' texts**. The major reason for making this choice was that teachers may still need to read students' text while adding notes to it and thus the process of adding notes to students' texts may be more cognitively complicated. That is to say, at the comments-adding/constructing procedure, it is possible that richer data can be generated; and hence, the study is worth the effort.

1.3   Overview of Research Methodology

My study used a case study approach to conducting research. There are two main reasons why this approach was best suited to my study. Firstly, according to Yin (2014), the case study approach offers rich possibilities for a holistic, in-depth, and longitudinal investigation of a single individual or entity (or a few individuals or entities). As mentioned above, my study aimed to present a comprehensive picture of the feedback-and-interpretation process through an in-depth study. Thus, there was a good fit between the methodology and the aim of my study. Secondly, the case study approach is most suitable for answering the RQs addressed in my study. According to Schramm, the case study approach can "illuminate a decision or set of decisions: why they were taken, how they were implemented, and with what result" (as cited in Yin, 2014, p.12). As introduced in Section 1.2, teachers'/students' decision-making thought processes were thoroughly investigated in my study. In this sense, the case study approach was tailor-made for my study.

Aligned to the case study approach that supports longitudinal investigation, my study lasted one semester (18 weeks). According to case study methodologists, when conducting a longitudinal case study, there is an opportunity "to use many different sources of evidence" (Yin, 2009, p.114), such as "interview data, narrative accounts, classroom observations, verbal reports, and written documents" (McKay, 2006, p.71). My study collected document data (commented student writing and students' notes), think-aloud data (the teacher/student participant's verbal report about what they were thinking while the teacher was writing feedback and the student was interpreting teacher feedback), and data from interviews (background interview, retrospective interview, ongoing interview, and final interview) to ensure data richness. The data obtained from different sources were analysed qualitatively and quantitatively.

1.4 Significance of the Study

My study this book reports contributed to the literature on L2 feedback and writing in several ways.

Theoretically, my study advanced our understanding of teacher feedback by providing a sociocognitive explanation about ① how the teacher offers feedback, ② how the student attends to teacher feedback, ③ how the teacher, the student, the feedback itself (as the text-level context), and the context interact with each other during the feedback process, and ④ how student learning and development occur during the feedback process. Meanwhile, my study, from the perspective of teacher feedback, offered a clearer view of the role teachers and students play in classrooms that adopt a genre-based approach. It enriched our understanding of genre pedagogy as well.

Empirically, the empirical rationales behind my study indicated that my study was significant in its expansion of the current limited research base, its extension of the line of research into the feedback-and-interpretation process, its depth of investigation, and its purposeful choice of research foci. Moreover, it provided a point of departure for future inquiry since it highlighted that a variety of basic feedback issues need researchers' further attention and efforts. For example, teachers'/students' decision-making thought process is a topic of inquiry that deserves further empirical substantiation. An investigation into it can expose the cognitive, affective, social and behavioral domains of teacher feedback and may uncover more of its complexity. Furthermore, based on my study, researchers can continue to conduct studies in various contexts.

Practically, given that the existing studies on feedback are mainly conducted in the ESL academic writing class settings and most findings are not readily applicable to EFL undergraduate learners, my research widened the scope of data by investigating teachers and students from the EFL writing context and offered pedagogical implications for EFL teachers working in China or in educational settings similar to China. My study could assist EFL teachers in gaining a deeper insight into teacher feedback and developing a sound understanding of their feedback beliefs and practices.

1.5 Organization of the Book

This book consists of seven chapters. This chapter has introduced the research problems, research rationales, research methodology, and the significance of my study. Chapter 2 examines the literature related to my study and provides further explanation of the theoretical and conceptual frameworks my study built upon. It mainly argues that it is necessary to extend the EA feedback research base by investigating the feedback-and-interpretation process and explains the reasons behind the choices of research foci (e.g., teacher/ student decision-making). Chapter 3 discusses the research methodology. It introduces and justifies the case study research design of my study and provides information related to participants, research contexts, research instruments, data-collecting process, and data analysis. Chapters 4 to 6 present research findings on RQ1 (Chapter 4), RQ2 (Chapter 5), and RQ3 (Chapter 6). This book ends with Chapter 7, which reviews the main findings of my study, provides an empirical and theoretical discussion of the results, presents its contributions to existing knowledge, provides some pedagogical recommendations, acknowledges the limitations, and offers suggestions for further research.

Chapter 2 Issues in Teacher Feedback

2.0 Introduction

This chapter provides the comprehensive, theoretical, and empirical contexts within which my RQs arose. The main body of this chapter reviews the non-research literature (2.1), theoretical perspectives (2.2), and empirical research literature (2.3) related to L2 teachers' written feedback in turn. It justifies why my study focused on non-error EA issues and why it investigated the feedback-and-interpretation process and its helpfulness for student development in the Chinese EFL expository writing context. At the end of this chapter, how the three RQs addressed in my study were generated is explained (2.4).

2.1 Development of Teacher Feedback: Questions

This section chronologically reviews the seminal non-research works published in the field of L2 writing during the period from the 1980s, when the quest to understand teacher feedback started, through to the present day. This chronological review lays out a comprehensive background for my study. It enables four issues surrounding teacher feedback to emerge:

Chapter 2 Issues in Teacher Feedback

1) the importance of non-error feedback,

2) L2 students' need for argumentation-related feedback,

3) the conceptualization/theorization of teacher written feedback, and

4) the necessity for conducting feedback research in the EFL contexts.

The emergence of these issues justifies

1) why my study focused on non-error EA feedback,

2) why my study developed a theoretical consideration of teacher feedback, and

3) why my study was conducted in the EFL contexts.

The 1980s: The Origins of Non-error Feedback in the L2 Writing Contexts

In the 1980s, as L2 writing as an area of inquiry was still in its early stage, there were relatively few studies and publications on teacher feedback (Leki, Cumming, & Silva, 2008). The frequently cited book *Composing in a Second Language,* edited by McKay (1984), indicates the following four issues related to L2 teachers' feedback during the period from 1980 to 1989.

First, in this book for L2 writing teachers, one third of it is devoted to teacher feedback, among which two articles pertain to L1 and L2 teachers' error feedback and one article pertains to L1 teachers' feedback on various issues of student writing. As indicated by the fact that one third of the volume is dedicated to teacher feedback, teacher feedback had already been considered as an important issue in the L2 writing contexts in the 1980s. Second, terminological confusion existed at that time. This implication is drawn out because the three articles McKay (1984) selected for her book is organized in a section titled *"Evaluating"*. As the section title *"Evaluating"* suggests, McKay used "teacher feedback" and "teacher evaluation" synonymously. According to Reid (1993), these two terms must be distinguished, since teacher response was not always evaluative. Third, considering this book contains two articles about error feedback and one article about teacher feedback on various issues, it can be said that McKay distinguished error correction from teacher feedback but gave more attention to error correction. Fourth, works published on L2 teachers' non-error feedback in the 1980s seems to be sparse. This generalization is made because a research article about L1 teachers' non-error feedback was selected for this book about L2 writing. In fact, in the 1980s, as research on L2 writing was still rather limited, L2 writing researchers and teachers generally took L1 research as their researching and responding guides (Ferris, 2003).

The 1990s: Recognition of the Differences Between L1 and L2 Students

A number of important books related to L2 writing were published in the 1990s (e.g., Kroll, 1990; Leki, 1992; Reid, 1993; Ferris & Hedgcock, 1998). Tracking the major publications on L2 writing that appeared from 1990 to 1999 reveals the following main trends and issues related to teacher feedback in this decade.

First, during the 1990s, teacher feedback continued to be an important topic. The contents of the major L2 writing literature published in this decade point to this conclusion. For example, the frequently-cited collection *Second language writing: Research insights for the classroom* edited by Kroll (1990) includes three articles about teacher feedback (i.e., Cohen & Cavalcanti, 1990; Fathman & Whalley, 1990; Leki, 1990). In Ferris and Hedgcock's (1998, reprinted in 2005 and 2014) book, the authors reinforced the importance of teacher feedback by stating: "Teacher response to student writing is important at all levels and in all instructional contexts" (p.147).

Second, as in the 1980s, error feedback in the 1990s received greater amount of attention. In these ten years, error feedback was usually analyzed and discussed in a separate chapter of a book, instead of being made part of a chapter (e.g., Leki, 1992; Ferris & Hedgcock, 1998). According to Ferris and Hedgcock (1998), there had already been extensive examination of error correction in the field of English-as-a-second-language (ESL) writing, but little discussion on feedback beyond error correction had taken place from the 1980s to the late 1990s.

Moreover, during the 1990s, terminology was still problematic. On the one hand, L2 writing authors either did not define what feedback was in their books (e.g., Leki, 1992; Ferris & Hedgcock, 1998); or they just followed their L1 peers (e.g., Reid, 1993), defining it simply as "any input from reader to writer that provides information for revision" (Keh, 1990, p.294). On the other hand, some publications began to paint a complex picture of feedback. According to the suggestions made by Ferris and Hedgcock (1998), Leki (1992), and Reid (1993), feedback should be understood in combination with classroom contexts, teacher roles, students' writing intentions, feedback purposes, course goals, and grading procedures, to name a few. Ferris and Hedgcock (1998) also pointed out that teacher feedback was a form of interpersonal communication.

Most importantly, in the 1990s, a clear recognition of the differences between L1 and L2/ESL student writers began to emerge. According to Silva (1993), L2 students differed from L1 students in that they had different organizational preferences and used different approaches to manage argumentations, to create connection, to cite, and to attract readers. Leki (1992) particularly stressed the necessity to consider student differences when discussing teacher feedback. She pointed out that, because of the differences between L1 and L2 students, ESL teachers needed to be more open-minded and flexible when responding to L2 students' expository and argumentative writing.

The 2000s: More Attention to Non-error Feedback and Deeper Thinking on It

In the 2000s, there was a remarkable growth in publications about L2 writing (e.g., Casanave, 2004; Kroll, 2003; Hyland, 2002, 2003, 2004; Leki, Cumming, & Silva, 2008; Silva & Matsuda, 2001; Williams, 2005). Meanwhile, books focusing exclusively on teacher feedback appeared during this 10-year period (e.g., Ferris, 2003; Goldstein, 2005; Hyland & Hyland, 2006b). A review of the fast-growing number of literature about L2 writing and teacher feedback indicates that, in this decade, L2 scholars began to devote more attention to non-error feedback. For instance, most chapters of Ferris' (2003) work either delve deeply into or at least touch upon the issue of content and organization feedback. Goldstein (2005) published a book devoted exclusively to feedback on content and organization. The book edited by Hyland and Hyland (2006b) also focuses on non-error feedback, which includes only one article on error feedback. However, in their books, Ferris (2003) preferred using the term "teacher response/feedback" while Goldstein favored the words "teacher written commentary" to refer to non-error feedback. This indicates that the terminology still needed clarification in this decade.

However, Goldstein's (2005) and Hyland and Hyland's (2006b) works both moved the understanding of feedback to a deeper level. Goldstein (2005) did not simply look at the feedback itself, but approached it from a complex, contextualized, social perspective. According to Goldstein, teacher feedback should be conceptualized as a non-linear feedback-and-revision process in which the teacher factors, the student factors, and the contextual factors interact with each other in a complex way. Hyland and Hyland (2006b) offered a similar perspective of feedback in their work believing it should be viewed in a contextualized way and that every act of feedback involved a complex interaction among the teacher, the student, the contexts, and the feedback itself.

From 2010 to Present: Theorization and More Concerns with EFL Contexts
Since 2010, the number of publications on L2 writing and teacher feedback has increased dramatically (e.g., Ahmed, Troudi, & Riley, 2020; Andrade & Evans, 2013; Bitchener & Ferris, 2012; Bitchener & Storch, 2016; Ferris, 2013; Lee, 2017; Manchón, 2011, 2012; Manchón & Matsuda, 2016; Polio, 2017; Silvia & Matsuda, 2010). These works share the following similarities and differences with the works published in the previous three decades.

In a similar fashion, the popularity of teacher feedback has not changed in the 2000s. Although many of the recent publications (e.g., Ferris & Hedgcock, 2014; Lee, 2017; Polio, 2017) are interested in other sources or types of feedback as well (e.g., peer response, teacher-student conference), the written mode of teacher feedback remains central in the major literature on L2 writing and feedback. According to Ferris and Hedgcock (2014), the importance of teacher written feedback, as "a critical, non-negotiable aspect of writing instruction" (p.237), remains constant in the field of L2 writing over time.

Another similar conclusion that can be arrived at is concerned with the authors' or editors' increasing attention on non-error feedback. The handbook co-edited by Manchón and Matsuda (2016) about L2 and foreign language writing treats error and non-error feedback equally by addressing these two issues respectively in two chapters. Lee (2017) also pointed out some attention had been shifted away from language feedback to content and organization feedback with the introduction of process pedagogy in L2 writing contexts. Furthermore, since 2010, there has been a development of the L2 writing theories. The learning-to-write (LW) perspective Manchón (2011) created for L2 writing establishes a theoretical foundation for emphasizing non-error feedback. According to Manchón, apart from language learning, L2 writing also serves the purpose of learning-to-write (i.e., learning to master writing skills and competence in dealing with issues beyond the level of language). So, from the perspective of LW, teacher feedback on non-error feedback will help writing students achieve the goals of learning to write and building writing abilities.

As in previous decades, the definitions of teacher feedback offered in the most recent books are still problematic. It is either treated as a simple term, or considered as a complicated construct. For example, Andrade and Evans (2013) continued to follow Keh (1990) and defined it as "any input from reader to writer that provides information to revision" (p.294). In contrast, Lee (2014, 2017) developed a much deeper theoretical view of feedback. By drawing on sociocultural theory (mediated learning experience and activity theory), Lee conceptualized feedback as a mediating activity system which emphasized its components such as contextual factors, roles of teachers and student writers, and feedback purposes.

Even with these similarities, there exists a notable difference between the prior and latest publications. Recently, L2 writing specialists have begun to consider the distinctiveness of the EFL writing and responding contexts and give more attention to feedback on EFL students' writing (Lee, 2016). As a simple example, in 2016, the *Handbook of second and foreign language writing* edited by Manchón and Matsuda was published. As the book title suggests, in recent years, (E)SL and (E)FL writing are valued equally. Certainly, compared with the discussion and investigation related to the ESL contexts, more literature on the EFL contexts is still needed.

Chapter 2 Issues in Teacher Feedback

Summary of Section 2.1: About the Non-research Literature Review
From the body of L2 writing and feedback literature that has been reviewed in this section, we can make the following generalizations:

1) L2 teachers' error feedback and non-error feedback are both important, but scholars' attention to non-error feedback is still insufficient (see the above discussion of each decade);
2) Based on L1 and L2 writers' differences, argumentation-related feedback deserves attention since it matches L2 writers' uniqueness (see the above discussion of the 1990s);
3) The interests and needs of teachers working in EFL contexts need to be served (see the above discussion of the 2000s); and
4) It is time to offer a definition of what is meant by "*teacher written feedback*" (see the above discussion of each decade).

In short, a review of the non-research literature justifies the necessity for conducting feedback studies, like the one I did, which ① focus on non-error, argumentation-related issues, ② occur in the EFL writing context, and ③ give a sophisticated definition of what is meant by "teacher written feedback". To better define what teacher written feedback means, the theoretical perspectives related to it are to be reviewed in the section that follows (Section 2.2)

2.2 Theoretical Perspectives on Teacher Feedback and Its Importance

Section 2.2 takes up the theoretical issues and reviews the theoretical perspectives on teacher feedback. As it is not possible to conduct a study about teacher feedback without examining what it is and pointing out its importance, this section reviews ① perspectives on teacher feedback

23

(Section 2.2.1) and ② theories related to the importance of teacher feedback respectively (Section 2.2.2).

Specifically, in Section 2.2.1, six perspectives on teacher feedback are reviewed and discussed, including

1) a product-oriented textual perspective,
2) a contextualized perspective,
3) a social-oriented perspective,
4) a sociocultural perspective (teacher feedback as scaffolding),
5) an activity theory perspective, and
6) a sociocognitive perspective.

This section argues, by using Atkinson's sociocognitive theory of learning and development to view teacher feedback, we can provide a fuller, more insightful account of its basic elements (including teachers, students, contexts, student writing, teacher feedback, and student learning and development) and their interactions.

As mentioned in the Introduction Chapter, Manchón (2011) distinguished two perspectives on L2 writing: learning-to-write (LW) dimension and writing-to-learn-language/content (WL) dimension. From the LW perspective, non-error feedback is considered theoretically important and, hence, it is worthy of investigation. Section 2.2.2 further justifies the importance of teacher feedback and EA feedback from the perspective of pedagogical development. It begins from a product-oriented pedagogy, then moves to process-oriented and Systemic Functional Linguistics (SFL)-informed genre pedagogy. Section 2.2.2 reveals that, with the development of writing pedagogies, there is a recognition of the importance of non-error feedback and argumentation-related feedback. This review consolidates the importance of conducting research on non-error feedback in general and argumentation-related feedback in particular.

2.2.1 A Review of Perspectives on Teacher Feedback

As mentioned above, six perspectives on teacher feedback are to be reviewed and discussed in this section. It argues that teacher feedback can be better understood when grounded in Atkinson's (2002, 2010a, 2010b, 2011, 2012, 2014) sociocognitive theory of learning and development.

2.2.1.1 Teacher Written Feedback: The Product-Oriented, Textual Perspective

Although teacher feedback has been a subject of considerable interest to researchers and teachers for several decades, few studies have conducted an explicit and thorough conceptual analysis of what is meant by it (Hattie & Timperley, 2007). As shown in Section 2.1, in the field of L2 writing, the most often-quoted definition of teacher feedback is made by English L1 scholar Keh (1990), who defined it from a product-oriented perspective and considered it as "any input from reader to writer that provides information for revision" (p.294). Furthermore, as mentioned in the Introduction Chapter, due to researchers' interest in error feedback, teacher response to errors is often referred to as teacher feedback. Generally, these typical definitions that have gained acceptance mainly focus on the feedback outcome and conceptualize its textual aspects.

Undoubtedly, to clarify what teacher feedback is, it is necessary to look at the feedback itself and conceptualize its textual properties. However, comparing with taking a narrow view of teacher feedback as error correction, it seems much more adequate to define teacher feedback from a broad perspective and consider that it too addresses the content of student writing, the way in which ideas in writing are organized, the appropriateness of words and phrases, and so on (van Beuningen, 2010). After all, teachers may comment both on and beyond errors when providing feedback. Fiona Hyland (1998) supports the idea that it is more appropriate to broadly define feedback, stating:

> …discussion with the students… revealed that they considered all interventions on their text as feedback and did not differentiate them when using feedback to revise their essays. The teacher protocols also revealed that teachers dealt with both meaning and grammar related issues at the same time, when responding to the student. (p.261)

Although it seems fair to consider that teacher feedback covers both error and non-error responses, conceptualizing teacher feedback only by what issues it focuses on is still inadequate. This is because, apart from feedback foci, teacher feedback has other characteristics. According to Goldstein (2005), teacher feedback can be identified with various features, including "tones (praise, criticism, neutral tone), directness (direct, hedged), function (asking for information, providing information, providing instruction, asking for revision, etc.), linguistic form (question, statement, imperative, etc.), and text specificity (text specific, not-text specific)" (p.138).

However, as thinking about teacher feedback evolves, scholars (e.g., Carless, Salter, Yang, & Lam, 2011) have suggested that conceptualizing teacher feedback by only considering its textual features is not sufficient. This is because this product-oriented way of seeing teacher feedback "provides only a brief glimpse" (Ferris, 2003, p.3) of it and it is "contextually disembodied" (Hyland & Hyland, 2006a, p.212). Eddgington (2005) also pointed out responding to student writing is not only a textual act, but also a contextual act; and teachers' provision of feedback is influenced by classroom experiences, their relationships with students and other contextual factors. Since the early 1990s, scholars have discussed teacher feedback from a contextualized perspective, which is to be reviewed in the following sub-section.

2.2.1.2 Teacher Written Feedback: The Contextualized Perspective

Since the early 1990s, scholars have argued that teacher feedback does not operate in a vacuum, but within complex contexts. According to Leki (1992), teacher feedback should be looked at in combination with classroom settings, course goals, and grading procedures. In Reid's (1994) view, without information like teacher-student communication in class, it is inappropriate to label teacher feedback simply as appropriation. Conrad and Goldstein (1999) situated their discussion of teacher feedback within a wider contextualized perspective. They emphasized that examinations of the relationship between teacher comments and student revisions must take into account the contexts within which the comments and revisions take place.

In more recent years, scholars further advanced this contextualized perspective on teacher feedback and began to think about it more systematically. Goldstein (2005) distinguished four levels of contexts (classroom, institution, program, and sociopolitical forces) and claimed that those layered contexts must be considered when a teacher decides how best to provide feedback. Hyland and Hyland (2006b) defined macro-and micro-levels of contexts, which cover the wider sociocultural context, the institutional context, the social/interpersonal context, and the immediate textual context (i.e., the feedback itself). Apart from the classroom context and institutional context, Ferris (2003) and Goldstein (2006) also highlighted the influence of writing contexts (e.g., genre and text type of writing tasks) on the provision and use of teacher feedback.

Generally, scholars have provided different lists of influencing contextual factors. It seems that they are structured and systematically operate at the macro level (e.g., sociocultural context), the meso level (e.g., school and institutional context), and the micro level (e.g., classroom context; textual context; writing context). Furthermore, Goldstein (2006) pointed out it is the interaction between these layered contextual factors that shapes teacher comments and student revisions. According to Goldstein, the values of the institutions within which teachers and students teach and learn are inevitably transmitted to the program and classroom where writing is taught, and then it continues to be transmitted to the students. For example, in a school where there is support for provision of content and rhetoric feedback, teachers may provide more feedback on content and rhetorical issues; and then teachers' content and rhetoric feedback becomes the pathway along which the values of the school are transmitted to the students.

Furthermore, Goldstein (2006) acknowledged the dynamic nature of these contextual factors. She claimed that it is necessary to identify and distinguish contextual factors that "are quite open to modification or change" and contextual factors that "are largely impervious to any modification or change" (p.15). For example, Goldstein considered that the institution and programs' attitudes toward student populations are usually not readily modified and they may influence the programs such as the class size or the exit requirements.

Tracing the development of this contextualized view of teacher feedback, we can see that the view of teacher feedback has begun to manifest a certain degree of maturity. To some extent, it can explain how teachers provide feedback (by taking contextual factors into account). As seen in the above example, when the school supports teachers' provision of content and rhetoric feedback, it is possible that teachers may change their preference for providing error feedback and mainly give content and rhetoric feedback. However, dwelling on this contextualized view of teacher feedback is still not sufficient. This is because Goldstein (2001) points out that the interactive and social dimensions of teacher feedback should not be ignored either.

2.2.1.3 Teacher Written Feedback: The Social-Oriented Perspective

Since the late 1990s, there has been a growing number of feedback researchers (e.g., Ferris, 2003; Goldstein, 2001, 2004, 2005, 2006; Lee & Schallert, 2008a, 2008b) who either suggest taking or have already taken a social-oriented view on teacher feedback in their book or research. Ferris and Hedgcock (1998, 2005, 2014) argued that "when responding to a student's text (whether orally or in writing), it is helpful to think of teacher feedback as the continuation of a dialogue between reader and writer" (1998, p.132). Goldstein (2001), Hyland and Hyland (2006b), and Lee (2014, 2016, 2017) similarly pointed out that the traditional, simple (product-oriented) understanding of teacher feedback ignored a complex, non-linear, interactive process. That is to say, to approach teacher feedback, it is necessary to consider it as a system that consists of both the feedback process and the feedback product and to include in its definition a conceptualization of a complex, dynamic interactive process.

In general, this social-oriented, complex trend of looking at teacher feedback adds depth to the understanding of it. To some extent, it reflects the increasing influence of the sociocultural theory of learning and development on L2 writing. In the following sub-sections, how teacher feedback is viewed within the sociocultural frameworks is reviewed.

2.2.1.4 Teacher Written Feedback: The Sociocultural Perspective

The sociocultural theory of learning and development is a theory of mind first developed by Lev Vygotsky, a Russian child psychologist in the 1920s.

Basically, this theory views "learning as a mediated process in which the individual develops as they interact with the environment" (Loewen & Reinders, 2011, p.157). According to Villamil and Guerrero (2006), what is central to this theory is that "higher forms of thinking and the ability to perform certain complex skills originate in and are shaped by social interaction" (p.24). Under sociocultural theory, social interaction does not mean that the learner merely benefits from processing the information exchanged from others alone; it emphasizes that both humans and artefacts participate in the social interaction or "dialogue", and the socially constructed "dialogue" plays a central role in all cognitive development (Villamil & Guerrero, 2006).

Concerning sociocultural theory, there are several fundamental concepts. Among these concepts, scaffolding has been used to conceptualize teacher feedback (e.g., Freedman, 1987). Basically, scaffolding is defined as "…a process that enables a child or novice to solve a problem, carry out a task, or achieve a goal which would be beyond his unassisted efforts" (Wood, Bruner, & Ross, 1976, p.90). In the L1 writing context, based on this sociocultural concept, Freedman (1987) defined teacher response to student writing as social and collaborative scaffolding during which teachers and students work together with the aim of helping the student writers develop self-regulation.

In L2 writing contexts, there is still a lack of consensus on the meaning of scaffolding (Weissberg, 2006). Nevertheless, it is generally agreed that it includes the following three characteristics: ① one participant with greater expertise, ② a primary objective to make the novice participant self-sufficient, ③ social interaction founded on the novice participant's Zone of Proximal Development ("ZPD", the distance between what the novice participant is independently able to do currently and what he is able to do potentially with help).

According to Hyland and Hyland (2006b), in the genre-based L2 writing classroom, teacher feedback is a type of scaffolded instruction. It unfolds between an expert teacher and a novice student writer and aims to help the student to be able to solve problems in writing on his own and achieve self-regulation. Based on the above-mentioned characteristics of sociocultural scaffolding, it can be seen that it puts an emphasis on the teachers' dynamic provision of support, which needs to be based on the novice's ZPD. By implication, this approach of viewing teacher feedback as sociocultural scaffolding is fairly explanatory in terms of how the teacher provides feedback (based on the student's ZPD). The problem is, to some extent, it is not sufficiently powerful to explain how students respond to teacher feedback.

2.2.1.5 Teacher Written Feedback: From the Perspective of Activity Theory

In L2 writing contexts, Lee (2014, 2017) used activity theory (a subbranch of sociocultural theory) to offer a theoretical explanation for teacher feedback. So far, three generations of activity theories have emerged (Vygotsky's first-generation, Leont'ev's second-generation, and Engeström's third generation). Developing the work of Vygotsky (who views knowledge as sociohistorically mediated), Leont'ev (1978) considered all human activities to be embedded in socio-historical-cultural settings and they contain three levels: "the motives which elicit the activity, the actions brought about by goals to achieve the action, and the conditions (or operations) under which the activity is carried out [through appropriate mediational means]" (Wigglesworth & Storch, 2012, p.72). Engeström (1987) further expanded Leont'ev's (1978) three levels of activities and developed a model for activity theory. He argued that a human activity, as a system, is comprised of "subject" (e.g., teachers or students), "object" (the target of activities; e.g., student self-regulation), "mediating artifacts" (i.e., mediational tools or means; e.g., teacher feedback), "rules" (i.e., "conditions" in Leont'ev's term; e.g., product/process-oriented writing as a "rule"), "community" (i.e., "conditions" in Leont'ev's term; e.g., teachers, students, principal, parents, etc.), and "division of labor" (i.e., "conditions" in Leont'ev's term; e.g., teacher and student responsibility as feedback providers and receivers). Like Leont'ev, Engeström also assigned agency to the activity "subjects" (e.g., teachers and students), and highlighted the motivation/ goal-driven and situated nature of human activities (i.e., "conditions" in Engeström's term). Leont'ev's and Engeström's emphasis on subjects' agency and situated nature of human activities has implications for a good understanding of teacher feedback.

First, according to theorists' emphasis on subjects' agency, the "subject" of any social activity is agentic. By implication, when giving feedback and forging a social interaction with students, teachers are the "subjects" who have agency. In other words, they are the agentic feedback providers who have wills and capacities to act independently and make their own decisions (Gao, 2010). In fact, researchers have found that, when providing feedback, L2 writing teachers keep enacting their agency. They tailor their feedback activities according to who is receiving the feedback, what text the feedback is provided for, and in which context feedback is provided (Hyland & Hyland, 2006a; Cohen & Cavalcanti, 1990; Hyland, 1998; Ferris, et al., 1997).

As for the students, within the framework of activity theory, they are agentic learners when using mediational tools (or mediating artifacts; e.g., teacher feedback) and transforming themselves from a lower form of thinking (elementary perception, involuntary attention, natural memory) to a higher form of thinking (voluntary attention, logical reasoning, planning, problem solving, and monitoring of mental processes). As agentic learners, activity theorists consider they have the will and the capacity "to establish goals, set up conditions, and choose the means that best suit their motives or needs in learning" (Villamil & Guerrero, 2006, p.26). By implication, students, as subjects who have different capacities, motives, beliefs, needs, and learning goals, may view, interpret, and attend to teacher feedback differently and take an active role in the interactive response.

Second, Engeström's (1987) emphasis on the situated nature of human activities allows us to see that teacher feedback, as a social activity, is embedded in contexts and it is inherently dynamic. As mentioned above, activity theory emphasizes that all human activities are rooted in socio-historical-cultural settings. An implication of this for teacher feedback is that, when providing/dealing with feedback, teachers/students may be greatly influenced by the sociocultural and historical contexts they are rooted in. In addition, one of the focal points of activity theory is its "rules" (e.g., product/ process-oriented writing as a "rule"). From it, the following implication arises. That is, the rules and values of the institutions that teachers and students belong to may intrude into classrooms, which then may considerably influence the meanings teachers and students attach to the written feedback they give/receive, and the expectations they have about teacher feedback. This may then influence teachers' provision of feedback and students' response to feedback.

By comparison, looking at teacher feedback from the perspective of activity theory offers more useful explanations of it. It better explains how teachers provide feedback, how students deal with feedback, and how teachers' provision of feedback and students' response to feedback are influenced by the contexts they are rooted and situated in. However, in comparison with the sociocognitive perspective of teacher feedback to be presented in the following sub-section, it seems that activity theory-informed teacher feedback still cannot adequately explain the role of the teacher in providing feedback, the role of the student in responding to teacher feedback, how the student learns, the nature of teacher feedback itself, and the interaction among these elements. Sub-section 2.2.1.6 explains how teacher feedback is informed by the principles of Atkinson's sociocognitive theory.

2.2.1.6 Teacher Written Feedback: From the Perspective of Sociocognitive Theory

Most recently, with Atkinson's (2002, 2010a, 2010b, 2011, 2012, 2014) adequate elucidation of the sociocognitive theory of learning and development, this theory has had a wider influence. It has been applied to second language acquisition (e.g., Atkinson, 2011) and studies on L2 writing and error feedback (e.g., Ng & Cheung, 2018; Nishino & Atkinson, 2015; Han, 2016). In fact, it can lend itself to the conceptualization of teacher feedback as well.

Generally speaking, the sociocognitive theory of learning and development is in line with the sociocultural theory of learning and development. They both give centrality to cognition and social interaction. However, different from sociocultural theory that emphasizes the contribution of social interaction to cognitive development, sociocognitive theory emphasizes the inseparability of cognition and the ecosocial interaction that occurs between humans or that occurs between humans and their non-human environments (Atkinson, 2011).

Specifically, to understand the cognition dimension of the sociocognitive theory and its inseparability with environment, Atkinson (2011) offered the following reasoning:

> Like all organisms, human beings are ecological organisms—they depend on their environment to survive. For this same reason, humans are adaptive organisms—they survive by continuously and dynamically adapting to their environment. Cognition plays a central role in this endeavour by promoting intelligent, adaptive action-in-the-world, and to do so it must be intimately aligned with its environment. Put differently, cognition is a node in an ecological network comprising mind-body-world—it is part of a *relationship* (italics in original). (p.143)

In this passage, Atkinson attempted to justify at least three points of view. First, from the ecological perspective, cognition should be brought to the centre stage due to its role in the survival and prosperity of human beings. Second, to survive and prosper, cognition functions through its continuous and dynamic adaptation to the environment and it develops when its alignment with the environment occurs. Third, cognition does not stand alone; it is part of its body (e.g., bodily states, bodily orientation, and emotions, Atkinson, 2011) and the environment (including both the physical setting and social contexts, Atkinson, 2011).

Apart from cognition, Atkinson (2011, 2014) also believed that ecosocial interaction, inseparable from cognition, lies at the heart of sociocognitive approach. He pointed out ecosocial interaction, which involves interaction between human beings and interaction between human beings and non-human environments, underlies and supports learning and cognitive development. According to Atkinson (2014), when individuals interact with one another and/or they interact with the environment, the interactants become intercognizers. This is because the interactants/intercognizers, from moment to moment, are effecting and maintaining coordinated ecosocial interaction according to "who we [they] are talking to, the conventional formality of the situation, the physical setting and its affordances, the topic, and the interlocutors' background knowledge, emotional states, and linguistic competence" (Nishino & Atkinson, 2015, p.38). Simply put, the sociocognitive approach views ecosocial interaction and its result (cognitive development) as a moment-to-moment alignment process that builds upon the adaptations the interactants/ intercognizers continuously make according to human factors (e.g., "who we are talking to") and contextual factors (e.g., "the conventional formality of the situation").

As to the inseparability of cognition and ecosocial interaction, Atkinson (2011) has ever used one example to explain their integration. In his example, Atkinson said, when driving to work, he just needed to "turn right at the apartment entrance, left at Walmart, bear right onto Northwestern, and then the campus appeared straight ahead" (p.145). In Atkinson's opinion, as the roads thought for the driver and the cognition needed for driving was quite modest, the line between cognition and the supporting environment often dissolves and they are sometimes functionally integrated. Atkinson (2011) also used empirical evidence to argue that the body is intimately involved in cognition. He said that researchers have already proved with experiments that "bodily states, bodily orientation, and emotions affect are affected by cognitive processes, and cognitive development depends on embodied action" (Atkinson, 2011, p.145).

In brief, Atkinson claimed that his sociocognitive theory of learning and development, which is fundamentally cognitive and interactive, rests on the following three principles:

1) **The inseparability principle**

It holds that "... what *goes on between* [ecosocial interaction] and *what goes in* [cognition] cannot properly be separated" and "... [the interactants'/intercognizers'] thinking, feeling, doing, and learning are all parts of ecological circuit" (Atkinson, Churchill, Nishino, & Okada, 2007, p.169). In simple words, the interactants'/intercognizers' mind, body, and world function inseparably and they work as a "mindbodyworld" ecology in producing ecosocial interactions and reaching cognitive development (Nishino & Atkinson, 2015).

2) **The adaptivity principle**

In the course of ecosocial interaction, the interactants/intercognizers mutually, continuously, and dynamically adapt, adjust, and align their behaviour, and they also flexibly adapt their behaviours to the ever-changing physical and social environments. Furthermore, according to Atkinson (2010a), the ever-changing environment is highly structured for cognitive activity, which may be natural environment, or human environment, or cultural environment.

3) **The alignment principle**

Human beings survive and prosper primarily by aligning with human and non-human others, and alignment underlies all forms of ecosocial actions and interactions (Nishino & Atkinson, 2015).

As sociocognitive interaction is not limited to a face-to-face version and it is considered to concern "a wide range of social activities of more mediated types" (Atkinson, 2014, p.474), it appears that it can be safely assumed that sociocognitive theory can be extended to understanding and conceptualizing teacher feedback. Informed by sociocognitive theory, teacher written feedback can be defined as an ecosocial interaction. It involves teacher-student interaction (social interaction) and ecosocial interaction between the teacher/student and non-human environments (e.g., the interaction between students and teacher feedback as the text-level context), which both mediate student learning and development.

More specifically, from the perspective of the inseparability principle, during the feedback process (i.e., ecosocial interaction), the teacher and the student, both work as a "mindbodyworld" (Atkinson, 2014) ecology. In other words, the teacher's/student's thinking, feelings, actions and the world which the teacher/student is situated in and is shaped by function inseparably when the teacher provides feedback and the student responds to teacher feedback. From the perspective of the adaptivity principle, to enable the occurrence of alignment during the feedback process, the teacher and the student mutually adapt to each other. Meanwhile, the teacher as feedback provider and the student as feedback recipient also keep adjusting their behaviours to the structured and ever-changing environments. For example, as mentioned in Sub-section 2.2.1.5, researchers (e.g., Goldstein, 2006) have found that teachers often take the different contextual factors into consideration to tailor their feedback activities. What is more, from the perspective of the alignment principle that alignment underlies all forms of ecosocial actions and interactions, the achievement of a higher level of interactional alignment during the feedback process is at the core of teacher feedback.

In comparison with equating teacher feedback as sociocultural "scaffolding" and using activity theory to look at teacher feedback, viewing teacher feedback from the sociocognitive perspective better explains what it means. By drawing on the three sociocognitive principles to inform teacher feedback, its basic elements can be addressed as follows:

1) its essence

complex, dynamic ecosocial interaction which includes teacher-student interaction and the teacher's/student's interaction with structured, ever-changing contexts (e.g., student writing, teacher feedback);

2) the teacher

the feedback provider working as a "mindbodyworld" ecology;

3) the student

the feedback recipient working as a "mindbodyworld" ecology;

4) the contexts

the structured, ever-changing ecosocial environments, or in other word, the "world" in "mindbodyworld";

5) student writing: the text-level context the student constructs;

6) the feedback itself

the text-level context the teacher constructs; and

7) occurrence of learning and development

the occurrence of alignment during the feedback process (ecosocial interaction).

2.2.2 A Review of Writing Pedagogies: Importance of Teacher Feedback and Argumentation-Related Feedback

As introduced at the beginning of Section 2.2, following the review of perspectives on teacher feedback is a review of writing pedagogies. It shows the tendency towards a recognition of the importance of argumentation-related feedback, which provides a theoretical justification for my study.

Product-Oriented Pedagogy: Importance of Error Feedback

According to Silva (1990), when L2 writing studies began in the U.S. academic setting in 1945, learning to write in a second language was "essentially as reinforcement for oral habits" (p.12) and the writing text of L2 students was nothing but "a collection of sentence patterns and vocabulary items" (p.13). Under such circumstances, the L2 writer became "simply a manipulator of previously learned language structures" (p.12) and L2 writing teachers mainly played the role of editors and proof-readers who were primarily concerned with formal linguistic features.

In the mid-sixties, L2/ESL writing drew on the basic principles of "current-traditional rhetoric" from L1 composition instruction and particularly noted the differences between L1 and L2 rhetoric. According to Kaplan, rhetoric was "the method of organizing syntactic into larger patterns" (1967, p.15) and ESL writers usually "employ a rhetoric and a sequence of thought which violate the expectations of the native reader" (1966, p.4). Seen from the perspective of the L2 version of "current-traditional rhetoric", learning to write involved becoming skilled in identifying, internalizing, and executing these unfamiliar rhetoric- and cultural-specific patterns. However, as writing teaching and learning were still considered as a matter of assisting learners to remember and execute rhetorical patterns (Kaplan, 1967), this mechanical way of teaching rhetorical patterns did not provide much support for the importance of teacher feedback on rhetorical issues, although it seemed rather necessary. Today, this approach still exists, but it is not in vogue.

Process-Oriented Pedagogy: Importance of Non-error Feedback
The importance of feedback in general and non-error feedback specifically is acknowledged with the appearance of process-oriented approaches to writing instruction (Hyland & Hyland, 2006b). At the early stage, in the process-oriented classroom, writing was considered as a process that allowed the individual writer to experiment with language, to discover his own original

and authentic voice, and to write his personal experience. Seeing writing in this self-exploratory way, teachers usually needed to provide student writers with positive and cooperative environments to think actively through pre-writing tasks, to freely write as many words as possible, to talk with peers and teachers, and to revise. This orientation to writing as an expressive process directed both teachers and student writers' attention to content before grammatical form. According to Hyland (2003), this orientation required teachers to respond to the idea the students produce and not to dwell on formal errors.

In the 1980s, the cognitive process-oriented theory of writing gradually replaced the above-mentioned expressive process-oriented theory of writing. In the cognitive process-oriented writing classroom, feedback sessions were taken as one of the hallmarks of the process. During the writing process, teachers use feedback, which chiefly addresses global issues of organization and content on the early draft, and local issues like grammar, word choice, and mechanic at a later stage of the writing process to assist students in rethinking and improving their work before it is finalized. Therefore, in this context, non-error feedback is considered crucial for helping learners to move through the stages of the writing process, which involve discovering meaning, growing control over composing skills, and developing language and writing abilities.

SFL-Informed Genre Pedagogy: Importance of Non-error Feedback and Argumentation-Related Feedback

In genre-based pedagogical context, learning and writing are both considered as social activities. As such, the emergence of genre writing pedagogies signifies an important paradigm shift in teaching (from the behavioral and cognitive conceptions that underlie product-and process-oriented pedagogies to the social perspective of writing instruction that underlies genre pedagogy,

Hyland, 2004; Hyon, 1996). Nowadays, the Systemic Functional Linguistics (SFL) school and English for Specific Purposes (ESP) school of genre have become "the two most influential orientations in L2 classrooms worldwide" (Hyland, 2007, p.153). These two schools of genre pedagogies both acknowledge the importance of teacher feedback in general and EA feedback in particular. However, as my study is less relevant to ESP school of genre pedagogy, a school of genre pedagogy which is usually oriented to advanced essays and research reports, or to business and other workplace genres, the following review concentrates on SFL-informed genre pedagogy.

SFL-based genre pedagogy usually starts by identifying the important genres. For school students to learn and compose texts, *narrative*, *descriptive*, *expository*, and *argumentative* genres are often identified in teaching and examinations (Allison, 1999). To teach how to write these genres, according to Hyland (2007), L2 genre teachers need to prepare opportunities for the students to **engage in**, **explore**, **explain**, **extend**, and **evaluate their learning**, and implement the following activities: **planning learning, sequencing learning, supporting learning**, and **assessing learning**.

When L2 teachers are **planning learning**, according to Hyland (2007), the key role they play is identifying students' immediate needs and doing needs analysis to obtain ideas about what students already know, what they are able to do, and what they are interested in and expect. **Sequencing learning** is another key element of genre pedagogy. SFL-informed genre pedagogy makes expositions and persuasions central to L2 teachers' classroom instruction because of writers' particular difficulty in dealing with argumentation. According to Connors and Glenn (1987), L2 students are usually familiar with the narrative genre but have trouble in generalizing, organizing, and arguing for ideas when writing expositions or persuasions. Hyland (2007) also claimed that "exposition" and "explanation" are more difficult for learners to write than "recounts" (story-writing about what has happened, Martin, 1989) and "procedures" (a close type to narrative which is built up around a sequence of events, Martin, 1989).

As far as **supporting learning** is concerned, in the genre-based classrooms, L2 genre teachers' scaffolding is particularly considered important. As mentioned above, genre pedagogy considers writing and learning to write as social activities. As such, it emphasizes assisting the students through teacher-supported scaffolding and teacher-student interaction. According to Hyland (2003), L2 genre teachers need to explicitly assist the student to understand how texts in target genres are structured and why they are written the ways they are. Furthermore, Hyland (2007) suggested that teacher scaffolding take various forms depending on students' genre knowledge and abilities, genres of the writing task, writing purpose, and even student individuality (e.g., modelling of texts, discussion of texts, explicit instruction). Hyland's suggestion about providing individualized, teacher-supported scaffolding definitely makes teacher feedback, a type of scaffolding support that offers a kind of individualized attention, become central to SFL-informed genre pedagogy.

Concerning **the assessment of learning**, the importance of genre teachers' feedback is once again recognized. It achieves its centrality because genre pedagogies encourage using ongoing teacher feedback (rather than achievement assessment) to establish a writing environment (rather than a grading environment) so that students can gain greater motivation and confidence to write (Hyland, 2007). In fact, genre teachers, who explicitly organize their class around genres, are in a better position to identify student problems, provide informed feedback on student writing, and offer feedback with greater confidence that students will recognize and use their suggestions (Hyland, 2007). As they are able to take control of the degree of teacher intervention, usually their feedback support is gradually removed with the increase of student independence and confidence in using a particular genre.

In brief, as genre-related feedback connects the teacher and the student for an interaction on an individual level and creates a supportive teaching environment, it achieves its centrality in the genre-oriented writing classroom. In actuality, more value of genre-related feedback can be seen in the EFL writing environments. This is because in the EFL environments students are likely to be more strongly influenced by the rhetorical patterns of their home culture and may face greater challenges when learning new genres (Edlund, 2003, p.371).

To sum up, with the development of writing pedagogies, teacher feedback plays a more important role in the writing classrooms. Moreover, as producing English exposition and argumentation is an issue for L2 students, argumentation-related issues in L2 students' expository/argumentative writing has been placed at the center stage for L2 teachers when they offer scaffolding feedback. That is to say, from a theoretical perspective, carrying out studies on ESL and EFL teachers' EA feedback is highly worthwhile. In fact, EFL teachers' non-error EA feedback is worthy of in-depth investigation from an empirical perspective as well. In the following section, the justification for empirically researching into it is provided through a review of the previous studies about L2 teachers' non-error feedback.

2.3   Research on Teacher Feedback

In this section, an overview of the previous empirical studies about L2 teachers' feedback is offered. All the studies reviewed in this section took a broad view of teacher feedback. They focused on non-error feedback and often touched upon teachers' error feedback as well. According to Goldstein (2016), these studies can be categorized into four strands:

1) student perspectives on teacher feedback (e.g., student evaluation of it),
2) the feedback itself (e.g., feedback foci and delivery approaches),
3) teacher cognition (i.e., the teacher's feedback beliefs and practices), and
4) the feedback-and-response process (i.e., feedback-and-revision process).

Certainly, there are overlaps across these four strands of research. For example, before studying students' reactions to teacher feedback, researchers often first investigate the teacher feedback itself so as to contextualize their studies (e.g., Lee, 2008b). Thus, there is some overlap between the first and second strands of research. The third and fourth strands of research overlap with the second strand of research too. For example, when studying teacher cognition and investigating the teacher's belief-practice (mis)matches, Wang (2011) examined the feedback itself to understand the teacher's feedback practice. To understand the feedback-and-interpretation process, Hyland and Hyland (2006a) investigated the key elements of the teacher feedback itself (feedback foci and delivery approaches). Taking the research overlaps into consideration, the following literature review critically discusses and evaluates each of these four research strands. It argues that the three RQs raised at the end of this section are worthy of study.

2.3.1 Research Strand 1: Studies About Student Perspectives on Teacher Feedback

This strand of research, which has generated great research interest (Casanave, 2004; Ferris, 2003; Goldstein, 2001, 2016), mainly investigates the following issues:

- **students' expectations, preferences, evaluation, and reactions regarding teacher feedback** (Best, Jones-Katz, Smolarek, Stolzenburg, & Williamson, 2015; Brice, 1995; Cohen, 1987; Cohen & Cavalcanti, 1990; Diab, 2005a, 2005b; Elwood & Bode, 2014; Enginarlar, 1993; Ferris, 1995; Hedgcock & Lefkowitz, 1994, 1996; Radecki & Swales, 1988; Lee, 2008b; Li, 2016; Mahfoodh, 2017; Mahfoodh & Pandian, 2011; Mustafa, 2012; Saito, 1994; Seker & Dincer, 2014; Song, Lee, & Leong, 2017; Treglia, 2008; Zacharias, 2007),
- **students' views about their reading, understanding, processing, and use of teacher feedback, and the way students actually process and use teacher feedback** (Brice, 1995; Chapin & Terdal, 1990; Cohen, 1987; Cohen & Cavalcanti, 1990; Ferris, 1995; Kumar, 2012; Kumar, Kumar, & Feryok, 2009; Kumar & Kumar, 2009; Lee, 2008b; Radecki & Swales, 1988; Saito, 1994; Yu, Zhang, & Liu, 2022; Zacharias, 2007),
- **the (mis)matches between students' perceptions of teacher feedback and teachers' perceptions/assessment of their own feedback practices** (Cohen & Cavalcanti, 1990; Diab, 2005b; Montgomery & Baker, 2007), and
- **the factors that influence student perspectives on teacher feedback** (e.g., Lee, 2008b; Mahfoodh & Pandian, 2011; Zacharias, 2007).

A comprehensive review of this large body of studies points to the following conclusions:

1) students' positive attitude to teacher feedback,

2) uniqueness of studies from the perspective of methodology,

3) lack of in-depth studies,

4) imprecise findings,

5) inconsistent findings related to student difficulty in understanding

teacher feedback,

6) a scarcity of a type of "student perspectives" study, and

7) a growing expansion of the scope of inquiry.

In the following, these conclusions are discussed in turn.

Students' Positive Attitude to Teacher Written Feedback

Generally speaking, students favored teacher feedback. They reported that they expected to receive feedback from teachers, welcomed it, took it seriously, and felt it was helpful (e.g., Brice, 1995; Clements, 2008; Diab, 2005b; Enginarlar, 1993; Ferris, 1995; Hedgcock & Lefkowitz, 1994; Lee, 2008b; Li, 2016; Seker & Dincer, 2014; Yang, 2013; Zacharias, 2007). In Lee's (2008b) words, regardless of students' proficiency levels, "there seemed a tendency for students to wish for 'more [feedback]' from the teacher (p.151).

Also, it was found that students read most, or even all of teacher comments (Brice, 1995; Chapin & Terdal, 1990; Cohen, 1987; Ferris, 1995; Radecki & Swales, 1988). According to Radecki and Swales' (1988) study of students' attitudes towards their use of teacher feedback, only 13% of students were feedback resistors. In contrast, 46% were receptors and 41% were semi-resistors (receptors, semi-resistors, and resistors: three types of students categorized by the researchers according to student attitudes towards their use of teacher feedback). Cohen (1987) further reported that students extensively attended to teacher comments on grammar and mechanics, vocabulary, organization, and content.

Uniqueness of Studies from the Perspective of Methodology

In fact, each "student perspectives" study seems to be a unique one when the research methodology is considered. This conclusion was drawn on the basis of the following evidence. First, in these studies, the student participants came from heterogeneous backgrounds in terms of their first language (e.g., English L1, ESL, EFL, FL), learning experience, learning and teaching contexts (e.g., university, institute, community college, or secondary schools), and the levels of the courses they were in (e.g., academic or non-academic courses for undergraduates, graduates, and English and non-English majors). Second, terms in these studies were often used in different ways. For example, Zacharias (2007) and Treglia (2008) both investigated students' "affective reactions" to teacher feedback. However, Zacharias looked at students' perceptions of the impact of teacher feedback on their feelings (e.g., "helpless" "disappointed", "sad", or "discouraged"), while Treglia (2008) examined student perceptions of what types of teacher feedback they preferred (e.g., students' preference for mitigated commentary). Given the uniqueness of studies, it seems it is still not easy to generalize the findings of the existing body of work.

Lack of In-depth Studies

Generally, "student perspectives" studies still have not provided an in-depth look at student perspectives. One of the reasons that restricts the depth of this strand of research is that the scope of most studies is still broad. Researchers often just studied students' perspectives on teacher feedback on content, organization, vocabulary, grammar, and mechanics but did not go beyond that. For example, Lee's (2008b) interviews just showed 11% of highly proficient students said they had no difficulty in understanding teacher feedback. As students' attitudes towards the various types of content feedback and/or organization feedback have seldom received further examination, this strand of work must continue to increase its depth by narrowing its scope.

Imprecise Findings

Sometimes the findings related to "student perspectives" studies were reported imprecisely. For instance, concerning the studies that touched upon students' views about how they handled feedback (e.g., making a mental note, writing down points, identifying points to be explained, asking for teacher explanation, referring back to previous compositions, consulting a grammar book, and rewriting), researchers' (e.g., Cohen, 1987; Cohen & Cavalcanti, 1990) finding reports were often general and vague. For example, there were findings reported as follows: **some** intermediate proficiency level students **sometimes** just made a mental note of teacher written feedback; or "poor" writers (self-rated), rather than high proficiency level students, **frequently** consulted other sources (not teachers) to solve their problems. These results indicated that students' writing ability might influence how the students handled teacher feedback, but they were still too general and a little vague. More importantly, they did not contain information about how students handle teachers' error and non-error feedback respectively.

Inconsistent Findings Regarding Difficulty in Understanding Teacher Feedback

In feedback studies (Brice, 1995; Chapin & Terdal, 1990; Ferris, 1995; Zacharias, 2007), students' perceptions of their understanding of teacher feedback were often found to be inconsistent. In fact, the available findings about students' understanding of teacher feedback are diverse. Students either largely agreed that they never had any problems understanding teacher comments (e.g., Ferris, 1995), or reported that they had difficulty in understanding teacher feedback (e.g., Nazif, Biswas, & Hilbig, 2004; Zacharias, 2007), or acknowledged that they did not always understand teacher comments although they could make revisions appropriately (e.g., Chapin & Terdal, 1990), or claimed that they could understand teacher feedback but did not always agree with it (e.g., Ferris, 1995).

Several studies attempted to correlate students' competence in writing/ language and their understanding of a particular type of teacher feedback, which further hinders the emergence of consistent findings. For example, in Brice's (1995) study, one of the three participants (self-rated **intermediate-level** ESL writer from Asia) mentioned she had difficulty in understanding her teacher's implicit feedback on content. In Cohen's (1991) study, **high- and low-performing** EFL students seemed to have greater difficulty understanding teacher feedback on supporting evidence than the intermediate student. In general, it seems that student ability is a variable which may influence the findings of research into students' understanding of teacher feedback, but previous work reported different findings about the influence of this variable.

A Scarcity of a Type of "Student Perspectives" Studies
However, research literature about "student perspectives" is still scant. This is because, as mentioned above, in-depth investigations into student perspectives are still needed. Moreover, studies about how students actually process teacher feedback are rare. A review of the literature shows that the earliest "student perspectives" study, titled *"Student processing of feedback on their compositions"*, is a study about how students process teacher feedback (Cohen, 1987). In his study, Cohen surveyed ESL, L1, and FL college students' opinions about how they "processed" teacher feedback by utilizing a 12-item questionnaire. The survey showed most of the students, whatever their L1 was, said that they wanted teacher feedback on different areas of their writing (e.g., content feedback, organization feedback, grammar feedback, etc.). Also, the students noted that "making a mental note" was the chief strategy they employed to attend to teacher feedback while "rewriting papers" was more popular among students who rated themselves as poor writers. However, in this "processing" study, Cohen's student participants did not really undergo feedback-processing processes. As mentioned above, they were only asked to

respond to a questionnaire, instead of reporting what they were doing at the moment they were processing teacher feedback.

Different from Cohen (1987), Brice (1995) asked her participants to do think-alouds and the students did engage in feedback-processing processes. In Brice's study, three types of students were reported. They either spent a great deal of time and effort explaining and justifying their work, or carried out various cognitive operations (e.g., describing teacher comments, explaining their understanding of teacher comments, and responding to teacher comments), or frequently just read teacher feedback. In her study, Brice placed her findings into six broad categories. That is, the students' understanding of and agreement with teacher feedback on "content" "organization" "grammar" "vocabulary" "conventions", and "the student writers". Brice found that only the student who often just read teacher feedback expressed a lack of understanding of implicit content feedback while the other two had no difficulty in understanding content feedback. In addition, although Brice did not further categorize content and organization feedback, the examples she provided in her report showed that one student could not agree with the teacher's feedback on supporting evidence.

Kumar (2012) and her colleagues (Kumar & Kumar, 2009; Kumar, Kumar, & Feryok, 2009) also used think-alouds to study students' processing of feedback on their work. In these studies, the researchers reported that their student participants' acceptance and use of teacher feedback resulted from their recursive thought process, which included their interpretation and evaluation of teacher feedback, their consideration of and reflection on the issues that were highlighted in teacher feedback, and their justification and explanation of their own work. Unlike Brice who correlated the students' thought process and feedback types (e.g., content and organization feedback),

Kumar and her colleagues devoted most of their attention to uncovering the recursion of the students' cognitive thought process and did not highlight its connection to feedback types or other feedback variables. In this sense, the depth sought in Kumar and her colleagues' studies is still somewhat lacking.

Devoting attention to what students undergo when they are attending to teacher feedback is highly worthwhile. It reflects researchers have begun to target the cognitive aspect of teacher feedback and attempt to advance the study of "student perspectives". Obviously, research into it remains limited. Students' understanding of, agreement with, and acceptance of teacher feedback need to be better understood.

Expanded Scope of Inquiry

In early studies, researchers usually just looked at the link between student reactions and the teacher feedback itself. For example, in an early study, it was reported students perceived teacher feedback that gave attention to linguistic errors, provided guidance on compositional skills, and included overall evaluative comments on content and quality of writing to be effective (Enginarlar, 1993). However, since the 2000s, "student perspectives" studies are becoming increasingly contextualized. Researchers have recognized that student perspectives are closely bound up with specific contexts and are greatly influenced by the contexts, both micro and macro.

Currently, an array of personal and contextual factors that may influence student perspectives on teacher feedback have been uncovered. The influential factors that had been identified include: student language proficiency/writing abilities (e.g., Cohen, 1987; Cohen & Cavalcanti, 1990; Lee, 2008b), student motivation (e.g., Lee, 2008b), power distribution between student and teacher (e.g., Zacharias, 2007), students' past experiences (Mahfoodh & Pandian, 2011), students' acceptance of their teacher to control their written text (Mahfoodh & Pandian, 2011), grades (Best, Jones-Katz, Smolarek, Stolzenburg, & Willimamson, 2015), instructional contexts (e.g., Hedgcock & Lefkowitz, 1994, 1996; Lee, 2008b), and sociocultural contexts (e.g., Treglia, 2008; Zacharias, 2007).

Kumar, Kumar and Feryok's (2009) study further complicated the issue about what factors may influence students' perceptions of and reactions to teacher feedback. They found that culture did not play a strong role in students' responses to teacher feedback and claimed that sometimes students' responses to teacher feedback might be mainly influenced by a variety of other personal and contextual factors (e.g., language proficiency, level of study, relationship with the teacher, and instructional context). Generally, it is reassuring to observe that the breadth of recent "student perspectives" scholarship is improving; but in-depth investigations are still needed so that the complexity of findings can be explained.

"Student Perspectives" Studies: A Summary
A review of "student perspectives" studies suggests that, for this line of research, problems still exist regarding terms, methodology, depth of studies, consistency of findings, and underexplored issues. To advance "student perspectives" studies and move the discussion of "student perspectives" forward faster, researchers need to consider addressing these issues in their studies.

2.3.2 Research Strand 2: Studies About the Feedback Itself

On the whole, "the feedback itself" studies mainly investigate teachers' feedback foci and feedback delivery approaches and their influence on students' use of teacher feedback (e.g., Hyland, 1998; Lee, 2008a; Ferris,

Pezone, Tade, & Tinti, 1997; Yu, 2021). A review of this strand of studies leads to a number of generalizations. They include:

1) a negative conclusion about teacher feedback,
2) uniqueness of studies in terms of methodology/terminology,
3) lack of in-depth studies related to feedback focus,
4) two research traditions,
5) inconsistent findings related to feedback foci and the influence of teacher feedback,
6) a scarcity of a type of "the feedback itself" studies, and
7) a growing expansion of the scope of inquiry.

This sub-section focuses on these generalizations.

A Negative Conclusion About Teacher Feedback
It seems that the beginning of "the feedback itself" research can be traced back to the 1980s when researchers mainly reported its problems. According to Reid (1994), during the 1980s, it was difficult to go to a conference presentation without hearing about teachers' appropriation of students' writing via feedback. For a long time, the key words for characterizing teacher feedback were "appropriation" and "unclear and not text specific" (e.g., Zamel, 1985). As mentioned in Section 2.2, Reid (1994), as well as Silva (1988), considered that the strong viewpoint researchers like Zamel (1985) embraced overlooked the role of social contexts (e.g., teacher-student relationship and classroom context) and therefore their equation of teacher feedback with appropriation was exaggerated.

Nowadays, it seems that researchers continue reporting findings similar to Zamel's conclusion and pointed out that teacher feedback was unclear and not text specific (e.g., Ferris, Liu, & Rabie, 2011). That is to say, the problems with teacher feedback may continue to be discussed by researchers. However, Reid's and Silva's argument implies that, when researchers' thinking about teacher feedback is mature sufficiently, it is possible that teacher feedback is to be seen in a more positive light.

Uniqueness of Studies in Terms of Methodology/Terminology

A review of literature shows a typical feature of the "the feedback itself" studies seems to be the uniqueness of each study. The following is the evidence that supports this claim. First, the studies are unique because different feedback foci existed in different studies, which included "content feedback" (e.g., Ashwell, 2000; Diab, 2005b; Fathman & Whalley, 1990), "content and organization feedback" (e.g., Lee, 2008a), "idea feedback" (content and organization feedback; e.g., Hyland & Hyland, 2006a), "text-level feedback" (content and rhetoric feedback; e.g., Goldstein, 2006), "discourse feedback" (e.g., Wang, 2011), "feedback on 'high-order concerns'" (content and organization feedback; e.g., Ferris, 2014), and "global corrective feedback" (content and organization feedback; e.g., Junqueira & Payant, 2015).

Second, these studies are unique because the same term was often defined differently. Take "content feedback" as an example. Ashwell (2000) used it as feedback on organization, paragraphing, cohesion, and relevance. Diab (2005b) defined it more broadly as feedback on development, thesis statement, consistency, organization, and content/ideas. Fathman and Whalley (1990) did not define it in their study. The examples they used in their paper indicated that it referred to feedback on genre, supporting evidence, cohesion, and paragraph development.

In fact, employing different terms creates not only uniqueness but also confusion. Here is an example. Junqueira and Payant (2015) used "global written corrective feedback" to refer to content and organization feedback. However, according to Bitchener and Storch (2016), "written corrective feedback" is generally understood as the feedback that is provided on linguistic errors rather than on content or organization. In this sense, future feedback studies need to address this terminological diversity and confusion, or at least exercise caution when generalizing findings.

Lack of In-depth Studies

Similar to "student perspectives" studies, "the feedback itself" studies also lack depth. This is also because most studies did not move beyond the boundary of content and/or organization feedback to further break it down into sub-categories (e.g., Brice, 1995; Lee, 2008a; Ferris, 2014; Junqueira & Payant, 2015). Moreover, even if the researchers further divided content and/or organization feedback, they often simply reported findings in the following simple, general way: "In addition to grammar and sentence-level feedback, the instructor responded to content-level issues such as structure and organization, development, logic and consistency, attention to audience, and focus or thesis statement" (Diab, 2005b, p.34). In Ashwell's (2000) paper, the researcher presented a more finely grained analysis of content feedback (in his word), including organization, paragraphing, cohesion, and relevance; but in his paper there was no findings related to these various types of content feedback. It seems that he just provided the sub-categories he created to explain how he analysed data.

Two Research Traditions

A review of "the feedback itself" literature reveals that at present there exist two main traditions of research. In the tradition of Ferris, by categorizing teacher feedback into statement, imperative, and question according to its pragmatic functions, researchers attempted to correlate these types of feedback and students' use of feedback/revision (e.g., Best, 2011; Conrad & Goldstein, 1999; Ferris, 1997; Nurmukhamedov & Kim, 2009; Sugita, 2006; Treglia, 2009). In the tradition of Hyland and Hyland, teacher feedback is grouped into praise, criticism, and suggestion according to its orientation; and researchers attempted to investigate students' response to and use of praise, criticism, and suggestion (e.g., Clements, 2008; Hyland, 1998; Hyland & Hyland, 2001, 2006; Treglia, 2009). Of course, it is important to note that this is not a strict division since some studies touched upon these two traditions (e.g., Treglia, 2009). Ferris also reported findings about the extent to which teachers provide positive feedback or suggestion and how students respond and use positive feedback (e.g., Ferris, 1995, 1997).

Inconsistent Findings

Currently, findings are still not consistent regarding

※ what teachers focus on,

※ how teachers deliver feedback,

※ what the influence of ① "positive feedback", ② "the hedges implied in feedback", and ③ "questions, statements, and imperatives" on students and their revision is, and

※ whether feedback delivery approaches influence students' revision.

These inconsistent findings are offered below.

a. What Teachers Focus on

According to Goldstein (2016), researchers have a continued focus on the issue of what concerns teachers mainly respond to. However, the findings available up to now just show the extent to which teacher feedback broadly focuses on and the results vary across studies. For example, Lee (2008a, 2008b) and Montgomery and Baker (2007) found that teachers gave some attention to content/ideas, but they rarely provided feedback on organization (e.g., development of ideas, paragraphing, and overall organization). Li (2016) reported 31% of an EFL teacher's feedback was on content and 14% of her feedback was on organization. Wang's (2011) and Ashwell's (2000) studies reported a high proportion of organization feedback, about 60% and 80% respectively. In these studies, when reporting findings about teachers' feedback foci, researchers (e.g., Lee, 2008a, 2008b) often connected them with the students' writing/language proficiency and which draft is submitted for commenting. By implication, the differences in findings across studies can be somewhat explained when teachers' feedback foci are contextualized.

b. How Teachers Deliver Feedback

Concerning the studies that followed Hyland and Hyland's tradition, the empirical evidence on L2 teachers' feedback delivery approaches does not paint a consistent picture. For example, Hyland and Hyland's (2001, 2006a) results indicated a similar amount of positive and negative feedback, but a different amount of suggestions. Treglia (2009) confirmed Hyland and Hyland's study in the sense that teachers provided a similar amount of positive feedback and criticism. Differently, Wang (2011) reported an extreme case: 96% of her teacher participant's feedback was negative, 11% of which were suggestions (a type of negative feedback according to the researcher). Although Best (2011), as a teacher researcher, also provided considerable negative feedback on the second draft of student writing, she often used mitigation to soften her criticism. However, Clements' (2008) case study teacher preferred to provide positive comments (e.g., offering forced positive feedback) and he became more positive with the passage of time; but he did not manage to provide suggestions.

c. What is the Influence of Questions, Statements, Imperatives on Students' Revision

The studies following Ferris' (1997) lead mainly looked at the relationship between questions, statements, and imperatives and students' use of them; but the findings across studies are inconsistent. Ferris (1997), by doing a textual analysis of teacher comments and student revision, found requests phrased as questions or statements (rather than imperatives) usually led to successful revisions. Not consistent with Ferris' finding, the findings Sugita (2006) and Nurmukhamedov and Kim (2009) obtained in the EFL and ESL contexts respectively similarly found that imperative comments were more effective for treating surface-level errors than for dealing with content issues, and imperatives produced more substantive and/or effective revisions compared to question or statement comments.

d. What is the Influence of Positive Feedback on Students and Students' Revisions

Findings about the influence of positive feedback on students and students' revisions are also mixed. Even within one study, the students' responses to positive feedback have been found to vary. For example, in Hyland and Hyland's (2001, 2006a) studies, the students either reported that it was useless, or they disregarded it, or it motivated them to attend to teacher feedback. However, Hyland (1998) found that the two students she focused her attention on in her study both felt that positive feedback could motivate them to deal with teacher feedback, but their proficiency levels were different (low and high intermediate levels respectively). Ferris also reported two opposite findings. In one study (Ferris, 1995), she found that students could particularly remember the teachers' positive comments on their ideas and organization, while in another study (Ferris, 1997) she reported that positive comments had little effect on revision.

e. What is the Influence of Hedges on Students' Revision

As for the influence of hedges, the results have not been consistent either.

One group of studies found that hedges had little effect on revision. Conrad and Goldstein (1999) reported that students could follow even very indirect and hedged suggestions in most cases. The students in Treglia's (2009) study said they could clearly understand the intent of them, and the revision linked with mitigated and unmitigated comments did not reveal a noticeable difference. In fact, there were also findings supporting that hedges produced substantive revisions (Sugita, 2006). The other group of studies reported the harmful influence of hedges since providing hedged comments "carries the very real potential for incomprehension and miscommunication" (Hyland & Hyland, 2001, p.185). However, Nurmukhamedov and Kim (2009) found that hedges lead to effective revisions when they used the text-analysis method to obtain findings; but when they used a stimulated recall interview to gain deeper insight into student revision, they found that some students felt hedged comments might cause confusion.

f. Whether Feedback Delivery Approaches Influence Students' Revision
Unlike researchers who reported there was a relationship between questions, statements, and imperatives and students' revisions, Conrad and Goldstein (1999) concluded that how teachers provided feedback on students' academic expository writing did not consistently affect revision. They found that students always failed to revise complicated problems concerning logic, argument, and development. Similar findings were reported in the work of Treglia (2009). Treglia's results showed that the way feedback was written did not appear to determine the success of revisions; students had problems following comments that required a great deal of decision-making, such as the one asking students to reconsider the logic of their writing.

A Scarcity of a Group of "the Feedback Itself" Study
Because Ferris, Pezone, Tade and Tinti (1997) conducted cross-time, cross-

writing assignment, and cross-student analyses of teacher commentary, it seems that they drew a fuller and clearer picture of teacher feedback. According to Ferris et al., teacher feedback varied due to factors such as the point in a semester at which the feedback is given, essay assignments, and student ability levels. Specifically, they found that there was a constant increase in positive comments and hedges over time and that it was the increased teacher sensitivity that caused this increase. Concerning the variation of feedback across students, Ferris et al. reported that "teachers take a more collegial, less directive stance when responding to stronger students, while focusing more on surface-level problems with weaker students" (p.175).

Thus far, it appears that scholarship on the cross-time, cross-writing assignment, and cross-student changes in teacher feedback is still limited. Apart from Ferris et al.'s study, Clements (2008) found that his teacher participant's comments became more positive during a course. Best (2011) found that she used less mitigation over a one-year time period. Moreover, it has been found that university ESL teachers varied their feedback focus on ESL and L1 students' writing (Ferris et al., 2011). Considering "variability in a teacher's feedback is commonplace" (Goldstein, 2016, p.415), what has been discovered is still too limited.

Expanded Scope of Inquiry

In recent years, feedback scholarship has expanded beyond focusing on the feedback presented on the pages of student writing to studying why teachers provide feedback in the way they do (Best, 2011; Ferris et al., 2011; Feuerherm, 2011–2012; Lee, 2008a). Methodologically, apart from text analysis, researchers used more methods (e.g., questionnaire, interview; Ferris et al., 2011; Lee, 2008a) and qualitative action research (Best, 2011; Feuerherm, 2011–2012) to collect data. It has been found that teachers' feedback practice was influenced by the following student-, teacher-, and context-related factors: student individuality, students' writing problems, students' reasons for writing, teacher knowledge of what students need and how to help them, teachers' beliefs in good writing and the purpose of English writing practice, teaching loads, lack of training or preparation for working with L2 students, teacher-student relationships, institutional constraints, examination culture in the EFL teaching and learning contexts, institutional appraisal of teacher performance, and expectations of parents and students (e.g., Ferris et al., 2011; Hyland & Hyland, 2001; Lee, 2008a).

Studies About the Feedback Itself: A Summary

As mentioned above, the expanded scope of inquiry related to "the feedback itself" studies indicates that researchers have begun to move away from looking at teacher commentary as something largely textual to looking at why teachers provide feedback in the way they do. In fact, nowadays, why teachers comment the way they do has begun to be investigated through the cognitive window. In the section that follows, the studies that adopt a cognitive perspective and are devoted to "teacher cognition" are reviewed.

2.3.3 Research Strand 3: Feedback Studies About Teacher Cognition

Feedback studies about teacher cognition only have a history of about 10 years (Goldstein, 2016). Generally, this line of limited research has mainly examined (mis)matches between teacher beliefs and practices in teacher feedback, and the findings available presently are not completely consistent.

Diab's (2005b) findings, obtained from an ESL teachers' feedback, think-alouds and teacher interview, indicated that her feedback practice corroborated her beliefs concerning the necessity to provide content-level feedback. However, according to Lee (2008a), some teachers believed that students had problems in content and organization; but responding to errors had taken up so much of their energy that they did not have time to comment on issues other than grammar and vocabulary.

Ferris (2014) conducted a study that was broad in terms of participant identities. Both L2 and L1 teachers were invited to participate in her study (129 survey respondents and 23 interview participants). As to the belief-practice matches, she reported both matches and mismatches. On the one hand, in her study, the teachers' beliefs regarding the importance of providing feedback on "higher-order concerns" (content and organization) and offering suggestions in end comments were confirmed by their responding behaviors. On the other hand, the teacher participants considered that they had the ability to apply their feedback beliefs to practices, but it turned out that they were not good at it in actual practice.

In Junqueira and Payant's (2015) single-case study, the researchers reported a novice teacher's belief-practice mismatch and match. As to the mismatch, the teacher believed in the importance of non-error feedback, but in practice, she provided a large amount of error feedback. As to the match, the teacher's philosophy that it was necessary to give explanation comments on content/ organization and her practice showed consistency. Furthermore, Junqueira and Payant (2015) found that the teacher's feedback practice was influenced by contextual factors, such as workload, time constraints, and lack of space to offer explanation.

In a Chinese university-level EFL expository writing context, Wang (2011) focused her attention on the teacher's beliefs and practices regarding providing discourse feedback (i.e., feedback on cohesion, meta-discourse, macro-structure, topical development, rhetorical function development and purpose, and audience and context of situation), and she mainly reported belief-practice consistencies. According to Wang, the teacher believed it was necessary to give most of her attention to discourse because it met student needs, and it had successfully helped the students before. Consistently, in practice, 60% of the teacher's feedback was devoted to discourse feedback. However, a table presented in Wang's paper indicated that there was a lack of belief-practice consistency in the teachers' beliefs and practices regarding how to provide feedback (e.g., providing negative or positive feedback). Wang provided the following reasons why there were mismatches between the teacher's beliefs and her "feedback strategies": the teacher's consideration into student expectations and motivation, a lack of feedback guidelines to follow, and a lack of self-confidence.

Min (2013), as a teacher researcher (teaching English majors' academic writing), reported that her beliefs and practices exhibited good matches both at the beginning of a semester and by the end of the semester even though her beliefs changed. Over the course of one semester, Min's feedback philosophy shifted from believing in the importance of providing explanation, suggestions, and specific feedback to realizing the importance of commenting as a probing and collaborative reader. To a large extent, her actual responding behaviors at the two points of a semester typically signified the stances she took. At the end of the semester, Min began to assume the role of a probing and collaborative reader and increased the amount of feedback that clarified student intentions.

Although the "teacher cognition" research is still limited, it answers the call of Borg (2003) to study language teaching in relation to teacher cognition. The emergence of this strand of research also suggests an increased maturity and complexity in researchers' understanding of teacher feedback. For example,

Min's (2013) study emphasized the dynamic nature and the fluidity of teacher feedback, pointing to the trend to understand it as a dynamic, contextualized concept. In the following section, a more complicated strand of research is reviewed.

2.3.4 Research Strand 4: Studies About the Feedback-and-Response Process

The significance of the fourth strand of "feedback process" research is that the researchers are no longer restricted to thinking about feedback as something simple and static. Nowadays, two types of "feedback process" studies have been launched. They are studies about the feedback-and-revision process (Clements, 2008; Conrad & Goldstein, 1999; Goldstein, 2006; Lee & Schallert, 2008a) and studies about the feedback-and-interpretation process (Hyland & Hyland, 2006a). Below, the complex, dynamic feedback-and-revision process is outlined first and then Hyland and Hyland's study about the feedback-and-interpretation process is reviewed.

The Feedback-and-Revision Process: Messiness and Dynamics

All the "feedback-and-revision process" studies reveal the "messiness" of teacher feedback. Building on Ferris' (1997) study, Conrad and Goldstein (1999) focused their attention on the connection between successful revision and the teacher's feedback in the form of questions, statements, imperatives, hedges, and requests. They found that there was no strong relationship between students' revisions and how teacher feedback is delivered; and they also identified the following factors that interactively played a role in the feedback-and-revision process: teacher/student beliefs, teacher consideration of student knowledge, students' interpretation of teachers' role as feedback provider, in-class instruction, and time pressure.

Goldstein's (2006) studies demonstrated two complex processes different from the above one. In one process, the following factors came together and influenced student revision: feedback clarity, student knowledge, motivation, time, course requirement, and classroom instruction. In the other process, grading policies, time pressure, and how the teacher and student constructed each other during the feedback process came together.

Lee and Schallert's (2008a) study revealed that, during the feedback-and-revision process, the teacher's provision of feedback was influenced by the teacher's motivation and confidence to provide feedback, the quality of the first draft and the students' use of feedback was influenced by the grade the teacher provided on the first draft, the student's attitude towards the teacher, student reactions to feedback on drafts and grade, and the substance and tones of teacher comments. Most importantly, both the teacher and the students were influenced by the trusting relationship between them.

In Clements's (2008) study, the researcher summarized the messy feedback-and-revision process the teacher and the students went through as a process influenced by a complex interaction of personal, professional, institutional, and pedagogical factors. Beyond this, Clements's study highlighted the dynamics of the feedback-and-revision process. The following evidence clearly points to this nature. As indicated in Section 2.3.2, in Clements' study, the teacher's feedback beliefs and practices underwent a process of change during the course. What is more, the teacher's feedback adapted in response to practical demands (e.g., short course), and his sense of individual students' personalities and needs.

The Feedback-and-Interpretation Process
Thus far, only Hyland and Hyland (2006a) have studied the feedback-and-

Chapter 2 Issues in Teacher Feedback

interpretation process. By focusing on the interpersonal dimension of teacher feedback, Hyland and Hyland took a preliminary look at the feedback constructing and interpreting process. They described how two ESL teachers, with establishing social harmony with their students in mind, focused on five main areas of students' academic writing (the ideas, language, academic conventions, the writing process, and global issues), and provided praise, criticism, suggestions, and unmitigated feedback. The study revealed how teachers' interpersonal concerns, teachers' "conceptualization" of the students (i.e., teachers' consideration of student strengths/weaknesses, student personality, student knowledge/problems/needs, students' possible response to teacher feedback, etc.), and contextual factors (e.g., institutional context in which the teacher worked, in-class instruction, etc.) mediated the teachers' construction of feedback. However, in their paper, Hyland and Hyland only briefly reported the students' "interpretation" of teacher feedback. To be exact, it was only the students' perceptions and evaluations regarding their teachers' positive feedback (e.g., good but not most needed, or insincere and worthless), criticism (e.g., demotivating), and mitigated comments (not understandable or partly understandable) were reported due to the space limitation of the book article.

2.3.5 Review of Empirical Literature: A Summary

A review of the literature demonstrates that, in each strand of feedback research, there are still questions that remain underexplored or unexplored. However, the strand of research that investigates the complex feedback-and-response process is likely to be an area that requires the significant efforts of researchers. The reasons for this position are twofold. The theoretical reason is that new research along this line will more directly help clarify the complexity and the dynamics of teacher feedback, which in turn affords a greater possibility to advance our understanding of teacher feedback.

Empirically, more in-depth and precise studies that address the complex, reciprocal, interacting processes of feedback are still needed (Goldstein, 2016).

2.4 Research Gaps and Emergent Issues

In Section 2.3.5, the great necessity to extend the feedback-and-response process was justified. I chose to follow Hyland and Hyland (2006a) to investigate it for two other reasons. First, when the writing is returned to the students with comments, it is impossible for them to move on to revision without processing or interpreting teacher feedback first. As such, investigating the feedback-and-interpretation process can lead to a better understanding of the feedback-and-revision process. The second reason was related to the research focus: non-error feedback. As argued in Section 2.1, feedback studies that go beyond surface-level errors are lacking and it is worthwhile investigating non-error feedback. As to non-error feedback, students may only read and cognitively process it, but do not or cannot actually act on it. Given revisions may only take place in students' minds as they interpret teacher feedback, the pressing need for studying the feedback-and-interpretation process (rather than the feedback-and-revision process) can be justified.

Despite the commonality, Hyland and Hyland's (2006a) study and my study had **three** key differences. **First**, instead of focusing on the interpersonal aspect of the feedback-and-interpretation process, my study looked at the teacher's and the student's cognitive decision-making during the feedback process (RQ1 and RQ2, as shown at the end of this section). My focus on teacher decision-making (RQ1) was chosen for two main reasons. Most importantly, there was a theoretical reason for looking at teacher, as well as student decision-making. That is, it was in line with the sociocultural and sociocognitive perspectives on teacher feedback, which both consider cognition as an issue of central importance. Also, according to Hyland and Hyland (2006a), teacher decision-making that underlies their feedback foci and feedback delivery approaches is a key issue. The other reason was that the available research on L2 teachers' decision-making is mainly related to classroom teaching (e.g., Nunan, 1993; Woods, 1996, 2006), test rater's evaluation of writing (e.g., Cumming, Kantor, & Powers, 2002), and peer review (e.g., Ma, 2010, 2012). Investigations of decision-making of teachers, who act as feedback providers, are still scant.

As to my focus on student decision-making (RQ2), it was identified mainly because Hyland and Hyland (2006a) considered it underexplored. My study aimed to overcome this weakness. More specifically, my study mainly addressed how students make decisions regarding their acceptance and incorporation of teacher feedback when they process it. Investigating what is taking place in students' minds when they decide to accept and incorporate teacher feedback will contribute to our understanding of students' readiness to use teacher feedback to make revision, which will in turn help the teacher provide the right kind of scaffolding. Moreover, as indicated in Section 2.3.1, findings related to students' understanding and acceptance of teacher feedback are still inconsistent and insufficient.

Here, it is important to note the following detail: I decided to focus on the teacher's decision-making process while they are adding comments to student texts. According to Huot (2002), the process of providing feedback includes two essential procedures: ① reading the student's text and ② adding comments to the student's text. The latter procedure has drawn my attention because, when adding comments to students' texts, teachers may re-read the texts. That is to say, it is possible that when teachers are adding/constructing comments to students' texts, what they undergo may be more cognitively complicated. By focusing on this more complicated thought processes, it is very possible that richer information and data can be gathered.

Second, unlike Hyland and Hyland (2006a), in my study, student interpretation (processing) and student perceptions of teacher feedback were clearly distinguished, and student perceptions of the helpfulness of teacher feedback were addressed in a separate research question (RQ3, as shown at the end of this section). There were two main reasons for my investigation of RQ3. A major reason was that, considering there was a great interest in student perspectives on teacher feedback in the past, my study continued to investigate students', as well as teachers' perceptions of the helpfulness of the feedback-and-interpretation process. Meanwhile, according to Goldstein (2005), whether L2 teachers' "text-level" (non-error) feedback can help students is a crucial question L2 teachers have.

Third, as can be seen in Section 2.3.4, Hyland and Hyland's (2006a) study focused on ESL students' academic expository writing. According to Goldstein (2016), looking at teacher feedback and student revision in EFL settings is a welcome direction. As such, I chose to add to this research line with an exploration of EFL students' expository writing. Considering feedback studies conducted in the Chinese EFL context is still scarce, my study focused on the Chinese EFL student population.

As mentioned in the Introduction Chapter, in the Chinese EFL setting, English expository writing is the genre that is most frequently learnt and used (Zhang, 2000). The following is the typical structure of expository writing that Chinese EFL students usually follow:

- **Introduction:** A good teacher needs to be understanding to all children.
- **Argument:**
  - He or she must be fair and reasonable.
  - The teacher must work at a sensible pace.
  - The teacher also needs to speak with a clear voice so the children can understand.
- **Conclusion:** That's what I think a good teacher should be like.

(Hyland, 2002, p.62)

In general, to master skills and competence in dealing with the expository, Chinese EFL students need to learn how to open and conclude expository writing and how to use techniques like details, specific instances, comparison/contrast, and cause and effect to set forth arguments and expound on ideas (Connors, 1985). Due to the obvious relevance of teacher feedback on these organization-related, argumentation issues to Chinese EFL students' learning of expository writing, my study chose to focus on **teacher feedback on various issues of expository argumentation** (EA) and how teacher feedback on EA is delivered.

In brief, from the review of literature and the above analysis, the following RQs were generated:

- **RQ1**: When constructing feedback, how does the Chinese EFL teacher decide what EA concerns to focus on and how to deliver EA feedback?
- **RQ2**: When processing the teacher's EA feedback, how does the Chinese EFL student decide the extent to which it is accepted and incorporated?
- **RQ3**: According to the student and the teacher, to what extent does the process of constructing and interpreting EA feedback help students improve, if it is considered effective?

2.5 Chapter Summary

This chapter has presented a review of the literature about teacher feedback and L2 writing over the past 40 years, covering a discussion of the seminal publications, conceptual thinking development, and typical empirical studies. This discussion has helped to identify the areas worthy of further exploration and highlighted a new direction for investigation. Based on the trends and gaps that have emerged from the literature, this chapter argues that: ① Studies on non-error focused feedback are scarce; ② It is necessary to define teacher written feedback as a complex, dynamic system from the sociocognitive perspective; ③ Theoretically, research into argumentation feedback is important and necessary; and ④ More studies are needed in the Chinese EFL context. More specifically, this review argues that it is worthwhile continuing Hyland and Hyland's (2006a) strand of research about the feedback-and-interpretation process and explains how the three RQs addressed in this study were generated. In fact, two research methods Hyland and Hyland used in their study, think-alouds and retrospective interviews, was used in my study as well. Further explanation as to why they were used in my study and more information about how my study was conducted is to be provided in the following methodology chapter.

Chapter 3   Research Design

3.0   Introduction

Methodologically, my study employed a case study approach to conducting research. This chapter is devoted to explaining this approach. It begins with the rationale for choosing a case study design (3.1). Then, a precise definition of what case study research means in my study is provided (3.2). After that, how the research site and cases were selected is described, along with how the data were collected, organized, analyzed, and evaluated (3.3). Finally, the chapter concludes with a summary of the main points addressed in this chapter (3.4).

3.1   Research Design: The Rationale

According to Hood (2009), the decision of whether to conduct case study research or not is based on careful consideration of "the object of the study, what the researcher wishes to learn about it, and what he hopes to do with the findings" (p.72). With reference to these three issues, the following illustrates the rationale for using a case study design in my study.

1) The Object of the Study

As detailed in previous chapters, my study aimed to understand the feedback-and-interpretation process. According to van Lier (2005), processes can be adequately researched in case study research. Duff (2008) also pointed out that researchers can focus on tracing processes that students/teachers participate in in a case study. As such, a case study research design is well suited to reaching the goal of my study.

2) What the Researcher Wishes to Learn About the Object

According to the focus of the RQs, my study sought to explore the decision-making thought processes that the teacher and the student (i.e., the cases) experience when they construct/interpret EA feedback. According to Schramm, case study research can "illuminate a decision or set of decisions: why they were taken, how they were implemented, and with what result" (as cited in Yin, 2014, p.12). In this way, this approach is tailor-made for my study.

3) What the Researcher Hopes to Achieve with the Findings

My study was conducted in the hope that it would extend the research base on the feedback-and-interpretation process. Considering little research has examined this process, my study was exploratory in nature. According to most case study experts (e.g., Creswell, 2013; Duff, 2008; Liamputtong, 2009; Yin, 2009), case study research can provide good answers to studies that explore anything that is little understood.

3.2 Research Design: Defining the Term "Case Study"

As it is impossible to conduct a case study without defining what it is, in what follows, a definition of what case study research refers to in my study is offered. According to Hood (2009), a simple definition of case study research is "elusive" (p.68). To clearly define it, a full description of it is offered in the next few pages. It is based on the definitions and descriptions provided by leading case study methodologists in applied linguistics (e.g., Casanave, 2010; Duff, 2008; Hood, 2009; Johnson, 1992; Mckay, 2006; Nunan, 1992; Nunan & Bailey, 2009; van Lier, 2005). In turn, the issues to be described and explained are:

- the "case" in my study (3.2.1),
- the purposes of my study as a case study (3.2.2),
- special defining features of my study as a case study (3.2.3), and
- the philosophical underpinnings of my study as case study research (3.2.4).

3.2.1 The "Case" in My Study

As the term *"case study"* suggests, at the heart of it is the "case". In the field of applied linguistics, case study methodologists generally talk about the "case" in two ways. For one, most methodologists consider the case as a bounded system, which is composed of an individual (or institution) and a site that includes the contextual features which can inform the relationship between the two (Hood, 2009). For another, case study theorists like Johnson (1992) have defined the case as a unit of analysis. Johnson pointed out that in L2 research, a case, or a unit of analysis, could be a teacher, a classroom, a school, an agency, an institution, or a community. My study brought the two definitions mentioned here together, suggesting that the "case" is a unit of analysis (often a real-life entity, such as an individual learner/teacher orseveral learners/teachers) around which there are boundaries in time, place, processes or context (Creswell, 2013).

As already mentioned in Section 3.1, my study was to understand the feedback-and-interpretation process. To achieve this aim, the teacher and the student who participated in the process were both needed to be studied.

That is to say, in my study, it was the teacher-student pair (i.e., the feedback provider and feedback recipient pair) that constituted a unit of analysis or a case. In Yin's (2004) words, this type of case study is an "embedded" case study. It contains a single unit of analysis as the main subject of study and its dyadic partners as the "subunits" (p.113) of analysis.

3.2.2 Purposes of My Study as a Case Study

According to Creswell (2013), to define case study research, it is necessary to clarify its intent. Methodologists in applied linguistics appear to have reached a consensus on the purposes of conducting case studies (e.g., Duff, 2008; Johnson, 1992; van Lier, 2005). They have agreed that the purpose is to provide insights into the complexity of a case or "an issue/problem using the case as a specific illustration" (Creswell, 2013, p.97). In Johnson's (1992) words, the purpose of case study research is "to understand the complexity and dynamic nature of the particular entity, and to discover systematic connections among experiences, behaviors, and relevant features of the context" (p.84). Duff (2008) further pointed out that Larsen-Freeman's (2012) complexity theory, which argues for an in-depth and holistic perspective to look for nonlinear interacting relations among variables/factors within a complex system (such as a case in applied linguistics), provides a philosophical base for the above-mentioned case study methodologists' common position.

Given the consensus among methodologists and their position's solid relation to Larsen-Freeman's (2012) complexity theory, my study shared the view that the purposes of case study research are to build a complex picture and gain a holistic, in-depth understanding of a case or an issue (usually language teaching/learning process, and language development process in applied linguistics) through exploring and explaining the complex dynamic interactions among variables/factors within the case or within the issue.

Furthermore, from the perspective of the purposes of case study research, Hood (2009) classified case study research as intrinsic case study research and instrumental case study research. The interest of the former type "lies purely in one particular **case** itself" (p.69) while the latter type seeks to study a case "with the goal of illuminating a particular issue, problem, or theory" (p.70). Apparently, my study was an instrumental case study. This is because the goal of my study was to illuminate the issue of the feedback process through studying the teacher-student dyad as a case.

3.2.3 Special Defining Features of My Study as a Case Study

According to Merriam (2009), the case study needs to be further defined by its particular features. Based on Duff's (2008) and other case study methodologists' intensive discussion of case studies, my study, as a case study, has the following defining features.

1) According to Duff (2008), the case in applied linguistics is usually an individual language learner/teacher, but sometimes more than one participant constitutes the cases. To produce more insights into the feedback-and-interpretation process, my study chose to study several cases (See Section 3.3 for more information).

2) Duff (2008) pointed out that contextualization is a key characteristic of a case study. That is to say, in a case study, to better understand the case study participants and answer RQs, it is necessary to carefully look at and keep in mind the boundedness of the case, or the context in which the case is situated or acts. My study described the schooling, teaching, course and personal contexts in which my study took place (See Section 3.3 for more information) and it also used background interviews to

capture contextual data particularly (See Chapters 4 and 5 for more information).

3) It is generally considered that case study research provides researchers with an opportunity to use various sources of data, such as "interview data, narrative accounts, classroom observations, verbal reports, and written documents" (McKay, 2006, p.71). My study used different sources of data and collected interview data, verbal reports, and written documents (See Section 3.3 for more information)

4) Case study research is also considered as research that can triangulate data collection. This multi-instrument/perspective approach, or triangulation, is useful to cross-check information and provide a more complete picture for each investigation in case studies. My study cross-checked information not only by triangulating methods and but also by conducting data analyses quantitatively and qualitatively.

5) Case study research is often longitudinal because the number of cases is always small (Duff, 2008; Johnson, 1992). My study was a longitudinal one and lasted a semester (18 weeks).

6) Yin (2015) classified case study research into three types: exploratory, descriptive, and explanatory case study research. Duff (2008) believed that an exploratory case study can open up new areas for future research; a descriptive case study can present a complete description of a phenomenon; and an explanatory case study can explain how events happen. As mentioned in Section 3.1, as little research has examined the feedback-and-interpretation process, my study was largely an exploratory case study.

3.2.4 The Philosophical Underpinning of My Study as a Case Study

Generally speaking, case study research is often undertaken and discussed as a form of interpretative qualitative research. However, most case study methodologists also agree that it is not exclusively concerned with qualitative methods and analysis (Casanave, 2010; Dörnyei, 2007; Duff, 2008; Hood, 2009; Nunan, 1992; van Lier, 2005). They argue that qualitative and quantitative data and analysis can both be included in case study research. My study followed the lead of these leading case study methodologists, considering case study research primarily as a form of qualitative and interpretative study. However, as it is compatible with both qualitative and quantitative data and analysis, it is not a purely qualitative study in nature.

As to the fact case study research does not fall cleanly within the domain of either a qualitative or quantitative study, methodologists generally believe what underlies it is not a worldview that contrasts (post)positivism and interpretivism/constructivism (i.e., objective or subjective construction of knowledge or social phenomena; Merriam & Tisdell, 2016) as a dichotomy. In their view, the stance case study research takes is that there is a continuum between (post)positivism and interpretivism/constructivism and the case study is situated somewhere on the continuum (Duff, 2008). In line with this philosophical viewpoint, my study considered that case study research, including the one I did, falls somewhere toward the middle of this continuum, but more on the interpretative side and less on the (post)positivist side.

In brief, by heavily drawing on the frequently cited works of case study methodologists and by explaining the most crucial issues that concern case study research (the notion of a case, its purposes, its special characteristics, and its philosophical underpinnings), what case study research meant in my study has been established. In the following section, how the case study was implemented is described.

3.3 Research Design: Key Issues

Based on the above-outlined understanding of my study, this section sets out

1) selection of the research site,
2) selection of cases,
3) research contexts (larger schooling context, teaching and course context, and personal context of the cases),
4) data-collection methods,
5) research instruments,
6) data-collection procedures,
7) data treatment,
8) the roles of the researcher,
9) research ethics, and
10) the issues of validity and reliability in my study.

3.3.1 Selection of Research Site

One well-reputed university in China (sitting around No. 50 according to the 2022 Shanghai Ranking, which evaluated 600 universities in China), with which I had already worked for many years was chosen as the research site for this study. According to Duff (2008), researchers can rely on their familiarity with the site and their "insider" status to ease the difficulty of "gaining entry to the research context and access to the case… for a longitudinal study" (p.117). My connection with this university and my familiarity with the course content, the instructors at this university, and students' proficiency levels and abilities are the main reasons why this university was selected as the research site. Below, it is referred to as KEY, a pseudonym used to protect the identity of the participants.

3.3.2 Case Selection and Sampling

As already mentioned, my study was an "embedded" case study and the teacher-student pairs constituted the cases, or the units of analysis. To select the unit of analysis, my study primarily followed Creswell's (2013) advice to choose accessible cases who are willing to take part in the study voluntarily. This is because case study research usually extends over a long period of time, and the potential cases' voluntary participation can reduce the possibility that "there is attrition [loss of participants] among the participants" (Dörnyei, 2007, p.152).

As for the selection of the main case, the teacher participant, it proceeded as follows. With a purpose of recruiting the teacher participant, I attended a workshop organized by KEY. During the lunch break, I gave the workshop participants a brief introduction of my study and invited them to participate in my study. To capture rich data, I informed them that teachers whose feedback beliefs and strategies were particularly related to non-error issues were needed. One teacher (simply referred to as Teacher T, she, or her in the following for identity protection), whose research interest is discourse analysis, responded to my invitation after the workshop and confirmed her willingness to participate in my research.

When selecting student participants, two main issues were considered: the number and the way to invite participants. Based on Creswell's (2013) suggestion that no more than four or five cases should be recruited, I chose to invite four student participants. They were approached during my visit to Teacher T's classrooms. With Teacher T's permission, I made a brief presentation of my study to the students at the end of her three lectures (same lecture content, different students) and asked for four student volunteers.

Students were also told that they could respond to my invitation via email or telephone call after class if they usually read teacher feedback very carefully and felt interested in my study.

Due to the time limit, the first four respondents to this invitation were invited into my study. However, one of the four withdrew from the study just before it was going to be completed because she was too busy to continue. Thus, in what follows, only three student participants' information is provided. To preserve their privacy and their right to anonymity, they are respectively referred to as Student A, Student B, and Student C in alphabetical order by their family names. In addition, to protect their anonymity, all of them, including Teacher T, have been referred to as "she" or "her".

As participants who are open to speak about their ideas are likely to provide better data, I asked Teacher T for an introduction to these students. Teacher T considered that they were all hard-working, but Student A was somewhat introverted. Then, I had a conversation with each of the students but felt our communication proceeded very well. Following our conversation, the students received the Information Sheet and Consent Form; and they were allowed two days for further consideration. At last, all of them chose to participate in my study and signed the Consent Form. Here it is necessary to note that, as for the students who contacted me afterwards, they were informed that I could not invite more than four participants, but they were free to ask me for help at any time when they had writing problems, and I could read their writing for them if they wanted me to.

3.3.3 Research Contexts

As explained in Section 3.2.3 (the section about defining features of case studies), contextualization is crucial to a case study, and it is necessary to provide a rich description of contextual factors that surround the case(s) being investigated (Mckay, 2006). To contextualize the study, this section gives an account of

- the schooling context,
- the course and teaching context, and
- the personal context (a brief introduction to the cases from my point of view; more information about personal contexts is to be provided in the following chapter, which was from data collected from the background interviews).

The Schooling Context

KEY University, though small in size, is a university with a good reputation in China. As gaining admission to KEY is rather competitive, students admitted to it generally have a high level of academic performance and comprehensive ability. KEY has two major campuses: the City Campus and the Suburban Campus, which respectively provide teaching, learning and living environments for PhD, master's students and undergraduates from different schools.

At KEY University, School of Foreign Studies (SFS) undertakes the task of helping non-English major students with their English listening, speaking, reading, and writing. Like most universities in China, SFS at KEY offers compulsory English courses to non-English majors under the guidance of the national syllabus issued by the Ministry of Education.

When my study was carried out, SFS allocated one and half years (three semesters) to teach a course series entitled *College English*, aiming to improve the students' English abilities in reading, writing, listening and speaking. In the fourth semester, to enhance students' motivation to learn English, SFS offered a variety of English courses for the students to select. They included *Academic English, Business English, American/British Society and Culture, English Debate and Speech, English Newspaper and Magazine Reading*, and so forth.

At KEY University, before the new first-year undergraduates start their university study, SFS usually requires them to take an English placement test. Based on the test scores, the newly-enrolled students are labelled as learners with English proficiency levels A (advanced), B (intermediate), and C (basic). They are then assigned to advanced-level, intermediate-level, and basic-level English classes (i.e., A-level, B-level, and C-level English classes). Generally, most newly-enrolled freshmen at KEY are placed into level B and they need to enroll in courses entitled *College English II, College English III,* and *College English IV* within a three-semester time period. Usually, Teacher T teaches the intermediate students.

The Course and Teaching Context

My study took place in the context of teaching and learning *College English (III)* course during a spring semester. It was the second semester of the first-year students. This course required the students to attend English classes covering reading and writing (once every week, two hours per week), listening (once every two weeks, two hours each time), and speaking (once every two weeks, two hours each time). The specific setting where I had access to the data of teacher feedback was Teacher T's reading and writing class.

During the semester when my study was conducted, Teacher T taught three classes of more than 120 first-year students (around 40 students in each class). Her lectures were mainly based on the textbook that was used for the course, *New Horizon College English: Reading and Writing (Book III)*. This textbook is one of a book set of six series (*New Horizon College English: Reading and Writing* from Book I to Book VI). It contains a total of 10 units with topics such as western society and culture, love, environmental protection, and so forth. Each unit contains two expository reading passages, techniques for reading and writing expository texts, and exercises about vocabulary, translation, reading and expository writing. According to the syllabus used by Teacher T and her colleagues who also taught B-level English class, five units must be covered in class and the other five units were assigned as outside-class units taught by students themselves. The selection of in-class units depended on which topic all teachers considered appealing to the students and particularly useful for them to improve their English.

Due to time constraints, Teacher T can usually only assign three writing tasks each semester. In the semester when my study was conducted, Teacher T, as usual, assigned three expository writing tasks to the students and asked them to practice the following argumentation techniques: ① making cause-effect analysis, ② providing examples as supportive evidence, and ③ using whatever method(s) the students learnt from the textbook. Making cause-effect analysis and providing examples to support argument are the writing techniques that the textbook series *New Horizon College English: Reading and Writing* repeatedly touch upon.

It is known that Chinese education is dominated by examinations, and examinations are always considered important by teachers and students (Qi, 2007). The final examination Teacher T's students needed to take was based on the above-mentioned textbooks and the lectures they attended throughout the semester. It was a comprehensive English test to assess students' improvement of all four skills (reading, writing, listening, and speaking). The writing section accounted for 15% of the score of the examination paper.

Speaking of examinations, it is also necessary to mention two standardized English tests in China, the College English Test Band 4 (CET-4) and Band 6 (CET-6) because they greatly influence English teaching and learning in many universities. In China, the National Education Ministry used to use these two tests to evaluate the teaching and learning of College English. Each test includes four main sections: writing, listening, reading, and translation. In the past, taking CET-4 was a requirement for students to obtain a bachelor's degree at most universities (including KEY). Although today this is no longer the case, students still consider CET-4 and CET-6 important and useful because many employers prefer hiring the applicants who have achieved high scores on these tests. These two tests are held nation-wide twice each year, one in late June and the other in late December. At KEY, nearly all non-English major students choose to sit the CET-4 and CET-6 tests.

Although the College English courses are not created to help students prepare for the CET-4 and CET-6, many English teachers in China give special attention to these tests. During classroom instruction, Teacher T also takes the CET-4 test into account. For example, when assigning writing tasks, Teacher T usually does not assign the writing topics provided in the textbook, but chooses the prompts used in previous CET-4 tests as the writing topics. In the semester Teacher T participated in my study, she assigned the following three CET 4/6 writing topics: ① "*the benefit of taking part in social practice activities*", ② "*the importance of reading literature*", and ③ "*reducing campus waste*" (See Appendix K for more information about Teacher T's writing assignments).

Finally, let me point out what the classroom instructions are generally like in China. In Confucian tradition, teachers are usually regarded as transmitters and authorities of knowledge and students are receivers of knowledge (Huang &

Shi, 2010). Under the influence of Confucian tradition, even today, teachers in China still lecture most of the time in class, and the teacher-student relationship is vertical or hierarchical, instead of horizontal or equal (Huang & Shi, 2010). Generally speaking, lectures that are mainly based on the textbooks are still the primary form of instruction in colleges and universities, and there is a lack of teacher-student interaction in the classroom.

Personal Context: A Brief Introduction to the Cases from My Point of View

Working as colleagues at KEY for about seven years, Teacher T and I knew each other well. In my eyes, she has developed a specialized domain of knowledge in both English and Chinese as a result of receiving a master's degree in English Language and Literature and a Doctoral degree in Chinese Language and Literature. According to student evaluations of teaching at the end of each semester, she is generally considered as an excellent and competent English teacher who takes her work very seriously. Apart from teaching, when I conducted my research, Teacher T also undertook a wide range of administrative duties such as coordinating the work of teachers, organizing staff meetings, establishing an agreed teaching syllabus, and so forth. Table 3.1 provides the basic information about Teacher T.

Table 3.1 Participant Profile: Teacher T

Ethnicity	Educational Background	Experience of Teaching	Number of Students	Course	Teaching Hours
Chinese	PhD in Chinese Language and Literature	7 years	More than 100	*College English III* (Integrated Reading and Writing)	12 hours/week

As mentioned above, the three students were first-year university students who had just begun their second-semester study at KEY when we met each other. Among the three students, my conversation with Student A before the study showed that she could communicate her ideas effectively and her thinking was insightful. The first impression Student B left on me was that she was confident, ambitious, and very cooperative. During the study, it was confirmed that she was this type of person. Student C was intelligent and had a nice personality. During our first conversation, I found sometimes that she could initiate a new topic to steer our conversation.

The three students varied from each other in terms of their study areas, and they happened to come from different English classes that were taught by Teacher T. Table 3.2 provides the basic information about the student participants.

Table 3.2   Participant Profile: The Students

Students	Ethnicity	Age	Year of Study	Major	Educational Background of English	English/Writing Proficiency
A, B, and C	Chinese	19	2nd semester, 1st year	non-English major	more than 10 years	intermediate

3.3.4 Data-Collection Methods

As explained in Section 3.2.3, case study researchers can use various methods that are appropriate for their research purposes and RQs to collect data. In my study, the methods that could provide the most relevant data were used to seek information. This section supplies detailed information about the methods my study used to address each RQ. Table 3.3 summarizes those methods.

Table 3.3 Research Methods

	RQs 1 & 2	RQ 3
Methods	Background Interview Think-Aloud Protocol Retrospective Interview Document Data Collection	Ongoing Interview Final Interview

RQ1: When constructing feedback, how does the Chinese EFL teacher decide what EA concerns to focus on and how to deliver EA feedback?

Clearly, RQ1 was to explore the decision-making thought processes the teacher experienced when she was constructing EA feedback on student writing. My study used think-alouds, retrospective interview, background interview, and document data collection to address RQ1. First, think-aloud protocols were used because, in L2 contexts, think-alouds is one of the few available means for finding out more about thought processes (McKay, 2009) and it is widely used in studies concerning decision-making (Bowles, 2010). However, the think-aloud method is often criticized because it is unnatural and obtrusive and may not be able to elicit all of the cognitive process (Kasper, 1998). Due to this criticism, retrospective interviews were conducted after each think-aloud task. The reason retrospective interviews were chosen to be used after think-alouds was because they can investigate the participants' decision making in L2 research (Nunan & Bailey, 2009), and "supplement any other research method" (Dörnyei, 2007, p.148). In their study, Hyland and Hyland (2006a) also used teacher think-aloud and retrospective interview to collect data.

As explained in Section 3.2.3, my study used background interviews to capture contextual data since in case study research background or contextual information is needed to be gathered. For RQ1, a background interview with Teacher T was conducted. Interviews were employed to collect background or contextual information because they are useful to "get large amount of data quickly" (Marshall & Rossman, 1999, p.108) and gain "privileged access to others' lives" (Cohen, Manion, & Morrison, as cited in Hyland, 2002, p.181).

Very importantly, my study collected student writing with Teacher T's comments (i.e., document data). Teacher comments were collected because of the necessity to find out what EA-related concerns Teacher T focused on and how she delivered EA feedback.

RQ2: When processing the teacher's EA feedback, how does the Chinese EFL student decide the extent to which it is accepted and incorporated?

The same methods used for RQ1 (think alouds, retrospective interviews, background interviews, and document data collection) were used to address RQ2. This is because RQ2 also aimed to gain a good understanding of the decision-making thought processes. For RQ2, two forms of document data were gathered: ① student writing and ② the notes the students wrote down when they were interpreting teacher feedback. However, the amount of student notes was not large. In fact, it was unexpected that the students took notes and provided this form of data, since they were only asked to cognitively interpret teacher feedback. As the three students all provided some notes, their notes were collected as a type of data to answer RQ2.

RQ3: According to the student and the teacher, to what extent does the process of constructing and interpreting EA feedback help the students improve, if it is considered effective?

RQ3 focused on Teacher T and the students' experiences during the feedback constructing/interpreting processes. Interviews were utilized for RQ3 due to the fact that they can provide in-depth insights into people's experiences and perceptions (Creswell, 2013; Richards, 2009). According to Yin (2009), case study can study the case at two or more different points in time. My study collected interview data at different times: ① ongoing interviews with Teacher T and the students (conducted after each retrospective interview) during the semester; ② final interviews with Teacher T and the students before my study was completed.

3.3.5 Research Instruments

According to Murray and Beglar (2009), research instruments are tools such as interview prompts, observation categories, and the like. The tools used in my study include interview prompts (background interview prompts, retrospective interview prompts, ongoing interview prompts, and final interview prompts) and a set of instructions for the think-aloud task. Below is a detailed description of all tools designed for my study and employed over the course of it. All the instruments used in my study were piloted. Due to my pilot study, I developed better instruments and accumulated experience of how to better use these instruments (e.g., sensitive to the hidden messages or special points put forward by the interviewee and asked them to make further explanation; mindful of whether the interviewee was on the right track).

Teacher/Student Background Interview Prompts

As explained in Sections 3.2.3 and 3.3.4, the purpose of conducting the background interviews with Teacher T and the students was to contextualize the study and seek information associated with what they brought to the classroom, such as Teacher T's specific schedule for the semester, the materials to be used in the classroom, and her feedback-providing beliefs and strategies. In the Literature Review Chapter, a number of teacher factors and student factors that might influence the feedback-and-response process had been identified, mainly including teachers'/students' experiences, beliefs, motivation, and confidence and the teacher-student trusting relationship. The questions raised for the background interviews were primarily related to these factors. Appendices A and B are the prompts that were used in the background interviews.

Teacher/Student Retrospective Interview Prompts

As noted in Section 3.3.4, retrospective data for RQ1 and RQ2 were collected for the recollections of the participants' thought processes when thinking aloud. Thus, one of the most important questions raised for the retrospective interviews was to ask the teacher/students to recall and verbalize what they were doing when thinking aloud. The other important questions were mainly used to elicit the participants' more explanations of how they decided to provide/accept each EA feedback. In addition, the participants were asked questions about their plans before providing/processing feedback. Appendices D and E contain the guided questions used in the retrospective interviews with Teacher T and the students.

Teacher/Student Ongoing Interview Prompts

During ongoing interviews, open-ended questions were asked to encourage the participants to talk about their ideas concerning the effect of the feedback interaction on the development of student ability to deal with EA-related writing issues and teacher feedback. Three questions guided the ongoing interviews and the interviewees were also asked to further explain their answer. As ongoing interviews were usually conducted immediately after retrospective interviews, Appendices D and E also contain the questions for the ongoing interviews.

Teacher/Student Final Interview Prompts

The final interviews of this study were also conducted to evaluate teacher-student communication and student development. To achieve these purposes, unstructured interviews were conducted to ensure the interviewees could feel at ease and express freely what they thought of the teacher-student interaction via EA feedback. In the final interviews, the participants were requested to make overall assessments (about student improvement as writers and feedback receivers after feedback), and separately assess the helpfulness of teacher feedback on various EA issues. In addition, to seek to find the underlying reasons, the participants were requested to further clarify their perceptions. Appendix F provides the prompts for the final interviews.

Think-Aloud Instruction Protocol

The think-aloud instructions designed for this study were based on Bowles (2010). Following Bowles, the instructions used in my study involved the following steps:

1) explaining what is meant by "thinking aloud", and its purpose;
2) specifying the language(s) participants are allowed to use to verbalize their thoughts;
3) demonstrating for participants how to think aloud; and
4) giving participants time to ask questions about this method.

Appendix C outlines how Teacher T and the students were instructed to use the think-aloud method.

3.3.6 Data-Collection Procedures

This section provides some important explanations about data collection (3.3.6.1) and details the data-collection procedures (3.3.6.2).

3.3.6.1 Some Explanations

Before describing the procedural steps, it is necessary to make the following explanations. First, all the teacher tasks (except Teacher T's think-alouds) were carried out in an office on the City Campus of KEY and all the student tasks were carried out in an office on the Suburban Campus of KEY. Both offices were quiet as they were not in use during the semester when this study was conducted. Second, all the interviews and think-aloud tasks were conducted primarily in Chinese according to Teacher T and the students' preferences, and for the purpose of ensuring their accurate articulation of their thoughts and perceptions. Third, all interviews were audio-recorded. Generally, I used two audio recorders for the same interview and think-aloud just in case one of them did not work properly. Fourth, all interviews were one-to-one interviews and one-off events. Before the interviews with the student participants, drinks and anything else (e.g., pen, hard copies of teacher feedback) participants might have needed were prepared.

Basically, all my interviews involved the following seven steps:
1) explaining the purposes of the interview, the topics to be covered, and the interviewee's rights (e.g., to refuse to answer some questions) so as to establish "a relaxed, non-threatening atmosphere" (Dörnyei, 2007, p.140);
2) giving the participants time to ask questions;
3) switching on the recorder and entering the interview sessions under the participants' permission;
4) proceeding with questions as naturally as possible;
5) expressing gratitude to the interviewee at the end of the interview;
6) checking and labeling the audio file; and
7) making copies of audio files after the interview.

In addition, the interview and think-aloud sessions were guided by the following principles. First, when conducting interviews, I followed Richards' (2003) recommendation to avoid sticking rigidly to the interview schedule. I followed this recommendation for the purposes of providing the interviewees with sufficient "thinking space" (Bitchener & Basturkmen, 2006, p.8) and encouraging them to offer extensive responses. Second, Walker (as cited in Nunan, 1992, p.152) suggested that sitting side-by-side could often result in a more productive interview than sitting face-to-face. My study followed this principle. However, when the students were thinking aloud, I sat down on a sofa beside the table the student was using. Because of this, the students were less aware of my presence, but I could still hear what they were saying clearly and could observe them. To keep the recording devices unobtrusive when recording interviews and think-alouds, they were positioned where I could easily control them, but out of the interviewee's direct line of vision.

3.3.6.2 Data-Collection Steps

This sub-section describes the procedural steps I took to collect data over the 18-week semester.

1) **When the new semester just started, I conducted the background interview with Teacher T and showed her how to think aloud.**

   Before the background interview, I made a brief presentation of my study again, answered Teacher T's questions, and shared with her my idea of going to her classrooms to recruit the student participants. As time was a concern for Teacher T, we agreed that she could perform the think-aloud tasks at home on her own and then sent her recordings to me via email. Teacher T also said that she preferred using Chinese (her mother tongue) when thinking aloud and during interviews. She believed that using Chinese was much easier, and she thought in Chinese as well when writing feedback. Additionally, Teacher T allowed me to go into her class to recruit the student participants.

Then, the background interview and think-aloud protocol training were carried out respectively. Both were guided by the steps designed in advance. During the interview, the presence of a tape recorder did not trigger Teacher T's anxiety since she did not seem to be aware of it. During the think-aloud training session, she did not seem to have difficulty with thinking aloud and she quickly understood how it worked.

2) **The next day I visited Teacher T's classrooms to recruit the student participants** (See Section 3.3.2 for details).

3) **Then, I had a conversation with each potential student participant.** Immediately after the potential student participants showed their willingness to join my study, I booked an appointment with each of them so that we could meet and get to know each other better. During our first meeting, all the students confirmed their participation. Student A felt excited as she knew that her experience would be part of a study; Student B said that she would like to offer any help I needed; and Student C believed that she could use this opportunity to improve her writing ability for the CET-4 and CET-6 tests (See Section 3.3.3 for details about these two tests).

4) **I conducted background interviews with the student participants and trained them to do think-alouds.**
Then, the background interviews with the students and the students' think-aloud training were arranged respectively at the weekends. All students chose to finish these two activities at one time, and each meeting lasted about two hours. To ensure that the students could better carry out think-aloud tasks, I also asked them to consider whether they failed to say what

they had thought of when thinking aloud. Only Student C told me that she felt she had such problems. To solve Student C's problem, I suggested that she could practice the think-aloud method when she was performing some daily routine tasks and try to report all her thoughts during that process. I told her to contact me at any time if she had more inquiries about this method afterwards. In fact, I shared the suggestions I gave to Student C with Students A and B as well. At the initial meetings, all students agreed to send me their writing assignment when they finished it each time.

5) **I collected student writing three times (nine pieces in total).**

Each time when submitting their assignment to Teacher T, Students A, B, and C sent their writing to me as well. Teacher T and I always received Student B's writing first. In Student B's opinion, since the writing tasks were not very difficult for her, they usually did not take her a lot of time.

6) **I collected Teacher T's think-aloud audio files (nine in total) and comments on student writing.**

Each time after Teacher T received student writing, she commented on it and thought aloud at home. Then, she sent me her think-aloud verbalization recordings via email. Together with the think-aloud audio files, I received the student writing she had annotated. Here, I want to point out that the feedback Teacher T provided was **electronic, computer-delivered feedback** (e-feedback) instead of feedback written on paper with red pen. She felt that these two modes were not different. She said she used computer-delivered e-feedback just because it was more convenient and efficient. For example, when using computer to add comments, she thought it was handy to use online dictionaries.

7) **I recorded student think-aloud tasks (nine files) and conducted retrospective interviews and ongoing interviews with each student**

participant (nine files).

Each time after Teacher T sent me her feedback and think-aloud audio files, I always contacted Students A, B, and C immediately to schedule appointments for think-alouds and interviews. Due to their busy schedules, Students A, B, and C preferred seeing me on weekends, and they wanted to have these three activities in one meeting. Please note the students had no opportunity to read the teacher feedback until they did the think-aloud tasks.

Generally speaking, Students A, B, and C were able to talk continuously each time as they were reporting their thought processes, and it seemed that they did not care too much about my presence and the presence of recorders. However, when Student A was thinking aloud for the first and second time, I had to remind her to raise her voice. Student B was prompted once not to just read the teacher feedback while thinking aloud, but afterwards she told me that that was what she was thinking about at that time. Comparatively speaking, Student C could clearly and continuously verbalize her thoughts and had no difficulty with think-alouds.

8) **I also conducted retrospective interviews and ongoing interviews with Teacher T.**

In total, I collected nine retrospective and ongoing interview files from Teacher T.

9) **Before the students left school for summer holidays, I conducted the final interview with each of them.**

10) **During summer holidays, I conducted the final interview with Teacher T.**

In brief, the total resulting data sets I collected are shown in Table 3.4.

Table 3.4 Resulting Data Set

Data	Purposes	T	A	B	C
1. Background Interview (Audio File)	Contextualizing the Study	1 file	1 file	1 file	1 file
2. Think-Aloud (Audio File)	RQ1 & RQ2	9 files	3 files	3 files	3 files
3. Retrospective & Ongoing Interviews (Audio File)	RQ1 & RQ2 & RQ3	9 files	3 files	3 files	3 files
4. Final Interview (Audio File)	RQ3	1 file	1 file	1 file	1 file
5. Teacher Feedback (Text File)	RQ1 & RQ2	9 files			
6. Student Notes (Text File)	RQ2		3 files	3 files	3 files

3.3.7 Data Treatment: Transcribing, Translating, Coding, Categorizing, and Analyzing Data

As mentioned above, my study collected think-aloud, interview, and document data. This section explains how these data were handled (3.3.7.1–3.3.7.3).

However, before I proceed, it is necessary to note the following issues. As retrospective interview was used as a supplementary method to supplement think-aloud data in my study, it provided masses of repetitive data. As such, I first compared retrospective interview data with its corresponding think-aloud data to check and specify which portions of retrospective interview data I could leave out. In addition, my study utilized NVivo11, a computer software designed to assist the analysis of qualitative data (Bazeley & Jackson, 2013, p.2), to code and analyze data.

NVivo11 was used to deal with data mainly because it could help me see "at a glance, which codes have been used where" (Welsh, 2002, p.5). That is to say, by using it, I could easily link the codes, the coded feedback segments and their sources by just clicking a node from a node tree in NVivo (In NVivo, codes are stored in a virtual container which is called "node".).

3.3.7.1 Handling Think-Aloud Data

As McKay (2009) provided a practical step-by-step way to organize think-aloud data, my study roughly followed the process and stages she recommended to organize the think-aloud data. The following describes the stages through which I organized and analyzed the think-aloud data (for RQ1 and RQ2).

1) Transcribing the Think-Aloud Data

As discussed previously, the think-aloud data I collected were to provide insight into participants' cognitive decision-making thought processes. According to Bowles (2010), studies framed in cognitivist approaches do not need to use a very detailed transcription system and it is not necessary to give special attention to details such as intonation, timing, pauses, or non-verbal cues. Thus, my transcription of the think-aloud data was a verbatim record of the talk, which was not concerned with detailed features like intonation, sighs of relief, and other information including non-verbal cues. When my transcription was completed, I listened to the recordings several times and double-checked the transcriptions.

2) Translating the Think-Aloud Data

At this stage, I tried to keep a verbatim record of the transcribed data. Following Tsui (2003), I conducted a flexible semantic translation when literal translation affected the meaning of an utterance. After translation was completed, I gave Teacher T a portion of my translation and its original Chinese version to read in order to see whether there was any misunderstanding in the transcription and translation. She verified the appropriateness of the content.

3) Dividing the Data into Individual Thought Units or Segments, Each of Which Reflected a Single Thought or Idea

I then divided my data into segments so that each segment corresponded to a unit that stated a single complete idea. According to Ericsson and Simon (1993), a segment may be a single sentence, a clause, a phrase, or even a single word. In my study, I segmented three types of data. Table 3.5 summarizes them and provides an example for each type of data.

Table 3.5   Types of Data and Examples

Data Types	Examples
1. The segment which contained several sentences that expressed one complete idea	Student C's writing is a mixed writing of narration and argumentation. Yes, narration and argumentation. It is a mixture of these two types.
2. The segment which was one sentence/phrase/clause/incomplete sentence that expressed one complete idea	Today I have already made an explanation of it in class.
3. The segment which was a coordinate clause (linked by a conjunction such as "and" "or" "but" or "yet") that expressed two complete ideas	I carefully read her writing yesterday, and now I wrote feedback on her writing.

After segmentation, I numbered each segment with the coded names of the participants and numerals. Take the following excerpt of Teacher T's think-aloud verbalizations that I segmented and numbered as an example. In this example, "T" referred to the teacher participant; "C" represented Student C; the first number represented it was Student C's first writing assignment; and the second number represented the sequence of the segments.

> "This is Student C's writing. **(T-C-1-1)** I carefully read her writing yesterday, and now I write feedback on her writing. **(T-C-1-2)** First, it is the problem of writing genre. **(T-C-1-3)** Today I have already made an explanation of it in class. **(T-C-1-4)** Student C's writing is a mixed writing of narration and argumentation. Yes, narration and argumentation. It is a mixture of these two types."

4) Importing Data into NVivo11

After numbering each segment, I imported the data into the NVivo software. According to Creswell (2013), a computer program may create a distance between the researcher and data due to the fact that there is a machine between them. To avoid this disadvantage of using software, I usually familiarized myself with the data and tentatively devised codes on paper first.

5) Reviewing Previous Feedback-Related Studies that were Focused on Decision-Making to Find Whether There were Existing Coding Labels for My Study

According to the Literature Review Chapter, it seems that several previous studies had some relevance to my search. In these studies, labels to code teachers/students' or test raters' thought process were constructed (e.g., Brice, 1995; Cumming, Kantor, & Powers, 2002). However, most of the labels devised in these studies were too general. For example, Brice (1995) coded her students' think-aloud data as "Reading comments/texts" "Describing" "Explaining" "Responding" "Goal Setting", and "Assessing". Because of a lack of information about what the students were "explaining" "responding to", or "assessing", I could not just apply them to my data analysis. Furthermore, in my study, the teacher's and the students' decision-making thought processes were reasoning, emotional, and behavioral processes. There were no existing coding labels I could use to code the emotional and behavioral processes the participants experienced. As such, inspired by previous studies (e.g., Cumming, Kantor, & Powers, 2002; Han, 2016), I created my own coding tags based on "the information contained in each segment itself" (Ericsson & Simon, 1993, p.266).

6) Labelling the Numbered Thought Units

As mentioned above, the labels I used to code the segmented thought units mainly came from my own data. In fact, I spent months labelling data with codes. To code them, I repeatedly read through the segments of data, and (re)coded the data over and over again. For the segments that were ambiguous or confusing, I usually consulted the context (i.e., the preceding and following segments) and Teacher T to determine how to encode them. The following two examples in Table 3.6 and Table 3.7 indicate how I segmented the think-aloud data from Teacher T and Student A (See Appendices G and H for the codebook used in my study to label the think-aloud data).

Table 3.6 Labelling Teacher T's Think-Alouds: A Sample

Sample of Data Segmentation	Codes
This is Student C's writing. **(T-C-1-1)** I carefully read her writing yesterday, and now I wrote feedback on her writing. **(T-C-1-2)** First, it is the problem of writing genre. **(T-C-1-3)** Today I have already made an explanation of it in class. **(T-C-1-4)** C's writing is a mixed writing of narration and argumentation. Yes, narration and argumentation. It is a mixture of these two types. **(T-C-1-5)** So, from opening paragraph to the arrangement of the paragraph… **(T-C-1-6)** Certainly, the arrangement of paragraphs can have nothing to do with the issue of genre. **(T-C-1-7)** But the style of some sentences she wrote is problematic. **(T-C-1-8)** Then, I will write a general comment first. That is, pay attention to your style. <{I'm afraid you mixed, misunderstood the style, the genre of this writing task.}> Let me put a crying face emoticon here. <☺> Then, it is, <It is still an argumentation.>	**(T-C-1-1)** read student writing **(T-C-1-2)** point out genre problem **(T-C-1-3)** reflect on class instruction **(T-C-1-4)** point out genre problem **(T-C-1-5)** evaluate student writing **(T-C-1-6)** interpret student writing **(T-C-1-7)** point out genre problem **(T-C-1-8)** make a feedback decision

Table 3.7 Labelling Student A's Think-Alouds: A Sample

Sample of Data Segmentation	Codes
Let me open the word document from the teacher about feedback. **(A-1-1)** "The campus activity that benefits the most. Our lives at college cannot be colorful unless we get rid of boring courses." **(A-1-2)** "*Try your best to avoid negative comments when writing, and make greatest efforts to convey	**(A-1-1)** read the text **(A-1-2)** read teacher feedback

Continued

Sample of Data Segmentation	Codes
a positive attitude*." **(A-1-3)** I didn't convey negative messages. **(A-1-4)** What I meant, using a, using a double negative, using a sentence with "unless". **(A-1-5)** This, this is, this should be, this is an issue of language; it is my way of expressing myself. **(A-1-6)** "Your writing could reflect your state of mind or life attitude, and your writing would influence the reader." **(A-1-7)** This is how I, how I used techniques to increase the influence and power of my language. **(A-1-8)** Avoid negative comments. **(A-1-9)** [Let your readers understand your attitude towards life].	**(A-1-3)** state disagreement **(A-1-4)** justify self-written text **(A-1-5)** interpret teacher feedback **(A-1-6)** read teacher feedback **(A-1-7)** justify self-written text **(A-1-8)** reread teacher feedback **(A-1-9)** read teacher feedback

7) Asking Teacher T to Check the Codes

To protect the participants, I asked Teacher T, instead of a second reader, to select a portion of the data I had transcribed, translated, and coded to double check it. As Teacher T's research area is discourse analysis, after I explained to her how to check the codes I used to label data, she had no trouble understanding and checking how the think aloud transcripts were coded. In cases of disagreement, we held a discussion until a decision was made. Meanwhile, I coded the data at different times and the coding system emerged from many rounds of recoding, which largely determined the intra-rater reliability (McKay, 2006).

8) Sorting Codes into Categories and Themes

Then, I further sorted the data codes into categories and groups. In summary, Teacher T's and the students' think-alouds were sorted into two themes: "**teacher/student engagement**" (cognitive engagement, behavioral engagement, and affective engagement) and "**interactional**

factors that influence decision-making" (teacher/student factors and contextual factors). The categories I created for grouping codes (e.g., interpreting operations, evaluating operations, justifying operations, etc.) are provided in Appendices G and H due to space constraint.

In my study, two types of acceptance and incorporation of feedback were identified: ① cognitive and behavioral acceptance and incorporation of EA feedback and ② emotional acceptance of EA feedback. From the cognitive and behavioral perspective, I used the following codes to label the extent to which Teacher T's EA feedback was cognitively accepted: accepting EA feedback, semi-accepting EA feedback, not-accepting EA feedback, and noticing EA feedback. Table 3.8 lists the labels and its indications.

Table 3.8   Cognitive Acceptance Categories and Their Indications

Acceptance Categories	Acceptance Indications
Accept EA Feedback	Acknowledgement of Agreement Articulation of Positive Attitudes to EA Feedback Articulation of Emotional Acceptance
Semi-Accept EA Feedback	Acknowledgement of Agreement and Questions Acceptance of EA Feedback and Failure to Act on Acceptance of EA Feedback from One Perspective But Not from Another Perspective Acceptance of Part of EA Feedback
Not Accept EA Feedback	Articulation of Disagreement Inability to Understand EA Feedback Failure to Notice EA Feedback Neither Agreement Nor Disagreement Defensive/Offensive Reaction to EA Feedback
Notice EA Feedback	Reading EA Feedback Translating EA Feedback

In my study, the following behavioral operations the students carried out indicated that they attempted to behaviorally incorporate Teacher T's EA feedback: making mental note (i.e., to make effort to pay attention to something so as to remember it)/memorization, making written note, underlining/highlighting important points, making attempted or actual revisions, and summarizing main points.

9) Carrying out Quantitative and Qualitative Analysis of Data

Generally, the think-aloud data (for RQ1 and RQ2) mainly took the form of text (instead of numbers). That is to say, reporting the qualitative results could provide good answers to RQ1 and RQ2. However, to triangulate perspectives, I also converted the codes under the theme "teacher/student engagement" into percentages and carried out within-case and cross-case quantitative analyses.

3.3.7.2 Handling Document Data

In my study, the document data I analyzed included teacher data: the feedback Teacher T wrote on student writing (for RQ1 & RQ2); student data: the notes Students A, B, and C made during and immediately after interpreting teacher feedback (for RQ2). These two types of document data were organized and analyzed in the following ways respectively.

- **Handling Document Data from Teacher T: Teacher Feedback**

In my study, Teacher T's feedback built the basis for understanding the participants' decision-making. According to Straub (2000), feedback focus identifies what the teacher writes on (e.g., on wording, organization, ideas, the writer, etc.), and feedback delivery approaches describes how the teacher writes feedback (e.g., criticism, advice, praise, etc.). Thus, in my study, analyzing Teacher T's feedback referred to looking for the patterns of Teacher

T's feedback foci and feedback delivery approaches. I took the following steps to organize and analyze Teacher T's written feedback.

1) **Translating Teacher Feedback**

   I translated Teacher T's comments that were written in Chinese into English.

2) **Segmenting Teacher Feedback**

   Then, I segmented Teacher T's feedback into individual feedback points according to the messages and meaning being conveyed through them (See Table 3.9 for examples). The utterance(s) that expressed one meaning/idea constitute(s) one feedback point. Feedback points in my study usually ranged from a phrase to several sentences in length.

3) **Numbering Segmented Teacher Feedback**

   I numbered all feedback points with names and numerals. For example, "T-A-1-8" represents it was Teacher T's feedback on Student A's first writing and "8" represents it was the eighth feedback point.

4) **Importing Data into NVivo11**

   Although NVivo software cannot "do the analysis for the researcher" (Bogdan & Biklen, 2011, p.187), I imported data into it because it has the advantage of allowing researchers to manage and retrieve data easily and efficiently.

5) **Labelling the Feedback Points**

   I labelled all the feedback points I had numbered. To label Teacher T's feedback focus, I used the feedback checklist Ferris (2007) created for L2 writing teachers, Straub's (2000) classification of feedback foci, and the checklist Ma (2010) developed for analyzing feedback foci as the guidelines for building my own code list. Overall, I used five codes to group Teacher T's feedback foci ("organization-related EA feedback" "content feedback" "style/conciseness feedback" "others", and "error feedback") and six sub-codes to identify her various EA feedback ("feedback on **thesis statement**" "feedback on **topic sentence**" "feedback on **cohesion and coherence**" "feedback on **supporting evidence**" "feedback on **conclusion**", and "feedback on **overall organization**"). Table 3.9 provides a sample of how Teacher T's feedback foci were coded.

Table 3.9   Segmenting and Labelling Feedback Focus: A Sample

Feedback Focus Segmentation	Feedback Focus Codes
Literature is always full of deep thoughts and ideas (T-B-2-1) (["Ideas" and "thoughts", it is somewhat repetitive.]). It is overt **(T-B-2-2)** (it is great to practice using the words we have learned) that reading literature is an essential part of learning and living. So, it is significant for us to read literature. (T-B-2-3) the first paragraph goes directly to the point☺ (T-B-2-4) However, I am a bit confused about the logic relationships of the first several sentences. [Based on your logic, we can say reading literature is important because it is a necessary part of learning and everyday life. It is necessary, and then it is important. It seems that this is not logical enough. Besides, why is it necessary?] Try this: Literature is a collection of wisdoms and deep thoughts and the significance of reading literature is wildly recognized. The importance can be illustrated as follows.	**(T-B-2-1)** feedback on style/ redundancy **(T-B-2-2)** error feedback **(T-B-2-3)** EA feedback on thesis statement **(T-B-2-4)** EA feedback on cohesion and coherence

After that, I applied labels to each feedback point to mark Teacher T's feedback delivery approaches. My preliminary labels were based on the categories proposed by Straub (2000). However, when these labels were revisited again and again, I adjusted nearly all of them. Altogether, I used 13 codes to label the feedback points I had segmented (e.g., strengths/problems identification, suggestion, See Chapter 5 for all codes). Table 3.10 is an example of how I coded Teacher T's feedback delivery approaches.

Table 3.10 Segmenting and Labelling Feedback Delivery Approaches: A Sample

Sample of Data Segmentation from T's Feedback	Codes
Literature is always full of deep thoughts and ideas (T-B-2-1) (["Ideas" and "thoughts", it is somewhat repetitive.]). It is overt (T-B-2-2) (it is great to practice using the words we have learned) that reading literature is an essential part of learning and living. So it is significant for us to read literature. (T-B-2-3) the first paragraph goes directly to the point☺ (T-B-2-4) However, I am a bit confused about the logic relationships of the first several sentences. [Based on your logic, we can say reading literature is important because it is a necessary part of learning and everyday life. It is necessary, and then it is important. It seems that this is not logical enough. Besides, why is it necessary?] Try this: Literature is a collection of wisdom and deep thoughts and the significance of reading literature is wildly recognized. The importance can be illustrated as follows.	(T-B-2-1) feedback identifying problems directly (T-B-2-3) feedback identifying strengths (T-B-2-4) feedback combining problems identification, explanation, and revision, indirect feedback

However, I drew upon Straub's (2000) idea for grouping codes. From the perspective of orientation, I grouped Teacher T's feedback modes into "evaluator-response comments" "instructor-response comments", and "reader-response comments". From the perspective of degree of scaffolding, I followed Straub as well and used his classification "single-statement comments" and "combination comments" to group Teacher T's feedback delivery approaches. By "combination comments", Straub (2000) meant the joining of two or more feedback comments the teacher places next to a writing issue (e.g., praise-criticism pair, Hyland & Hyland, 2001). By single-statement comments, Straub (2000) meant the teacher responds to a writing issue with only one feedback comment, instead of one feedback comment followed by another in sequence.

When coding feedback data, I also clearly indicated the language Teacher T used. This is because, in Teacher T's view, her choice of language (feedback in English or in her native language, Chinese) was a striking characteristic of her feedback and she quite often used Chinese to construct feedback. Moreover, Teacher T often used emoticons, underlining, and highlighting to deliver her feedback as well.

6) Reviewing the Feedback Points

Then, I asked Teacher T to review the feedback points I had segmented and coded. In cases of disagreement, we held a discussion until an agreement was achieved.

7) Carrying out Quantitative Analysis of Data

As mentioned above, the purpose of analyzing feedback data involved looking for patterns and building the basis for analyzing think-aloud and interview data. For this reason, it was enough to only conduct a quantitative analysis of data to identify patterns. To achieve this end, I identified code/sub-code occurrences, counted code/sub-code frequencies, and summarized the statistical results related to Teacher T's overall, cross-student and cross-assignment feedback patterns.

- **Handling Document Data: Student Notes/Memos**

As mentioned in Section 3.3.4, the data in the form of student notes were limited. Meanwhile, the notes or memos the students wrote were rather brief. Students B and C mainly just used short phrases to keep record of their questions and/or the key points about teacher feedback. Student A's notes were relatively longer (See Appendix J for Student A's notes) and it contained her exploration of the reasons behind her writing problems about argumentation, her reflections on how to better manage argumentation in new writing, and her insights into how to improve English writing.

3.3.7.3 Handling Interview Data

I analyzed data obtained from background interviews (to understand the course context and personal context), the reduced retrospective interview data (for RQ1 and RQ2), ongoing interviews (for RQ3), and final interviews (for RQ3). What follows are the steps I took to analyze the interview data.

- I used the same steps to transcribe and translate think-aloud data to treat the interview data.
- I conducted "topic coding" (Richards, 2015, p.110). That is to say, I first divided the interview materials into passages according to the topics they discussed. Then I coded the passages according to their topics. After that, I brought the passages that had been labelled by similar topics together and used them to answer RQs. Listed in Table 3.11 are the coding topics I applied to my interview materials.

Table 3.11 Handling Teacher/Student Interview Data: Topic Coding

Types of Interview Data	Topics Ascribed to Passages
Background Interview	(1) participant profiles (2) participants' understanding of feedback (3) students' previous experiences of receiving teacher feedback (4) feedback provision/interpretation beliefs (about feedback focus and delivery approaches) (5) feedback provision/interpretation plans for this semester (6) participants' motivation and confidence (7) teacher-student relationship
Retrospective Interview	(1) Teacher T's feedback beliefs (2) factors influencing teacher/student decision-making
Ongoing/Final Interview	(1) effectiveness of the feedback-and-interpretation process (2) helpfulness of feedback on various EA issues (3) helpfulness for student ability to deal with teacher feedback (4) reasons behind their opinions

3.3.8 Researcher Roles

According to Johnson (1992), in case studies, the researchers' role ranges from being "a detached observer, to a participant observer, to an active change agent" (p.94). In my study, I simply aimed to document the data I obtained through verbal reports, interviews, and document collection. Thus, when collecting and analyzing data, I consciously acted as a detached investigator.

Duff (2008) pointed out that researchers need to clarify their role in the research process. Before the study commenced, I clearly explained my roles in this project to the participants. However, during the process of data collection, the student participants sometimes asked me questions or asked for my opinions about their writing and teacher feedback. So, although I tried to adopt a detached role as a researcher, I cannot claim absolute detached objectivity. In addition, I aimed to avoid ethical issues in my study. This role I played is to be discussed in the following section.

3.3.9 Research Ethics

According to Duff (2008), case study research requires rigorous attention to the issues of research ethics. To ensure my study was ethical, I implemented the following three principles.

In the first place, I put the principle of informed, voluntary and consented participation into practice. Prior to conducting the study, the participants were informed of the methods, procedures, and research aims through my explanation, the Participant Information Sheet, and my answers to their questions. The participants, who voluntarily agreed to be involved in this study, clearly understood that their role in this project was to provide data through verbal reports, interviews and what they wrote.

Secondly, I used a list of principles to protect participants at various stages. When recruiting the participants to join the study, I informed the participants that there would not be any negative consequences if they withdrew from the study at any time. During the study, I often reminded the participants that "If you happen to talk about this study with anyone, please remember not to mention any specific person associated with this study by name". When gathering data, I tried to establish a relaxed, comfortable, and trusting relationship with the participants, and offered the participants help at any time when necessary. I was always mindful to avoid causing discomfort or embarrassment or straying into sensitive topics as a result of the study. In general, to ensure their full participation and that they would remain in the study as planned, I treated the participants as "'people' who had feelings, values, and needs" (Elbaz, as cited in Tsui, 2003, p.76) instead of treating them as research "subjects". When using the data, the principle that all data were confidential was followed, and the anonymity of the participants and their school was preserved by using code names. To ensure that the study did not in any way compromise the participants, I also invited them to read a portion of the data I had analyzed. They could specify the parts they did not want me to include in the final report. When reporting data, I kept alert to the possible harm caused by the publication of results as well.

What is equally important, I applied the principle of collaborative partnership to achieve mutual benefit. Apart from its own intrinsic benefits for the participants (e.g., gaining a deeper insight into personal feedback beliefs and practices, developing a better understanding of the importance of teacher feedback and making better use of it in their future study), the students benefited from my special long-term attention to them and their special attention to the practice of English writing. As for Teacher T, I always tried my best to offer aid when and where help was needed. For example, I read the research proposals and research articles she wrote and provided comments to compensate for the time I requested from her.

3.3.10 Issues of Validity and Reliability

To be evaluated as a high-quality case study and to yield valid and dependable results, my study engaged in the following strategies:

1) using multiple methods to collect data;

2) conducting a one-semester pilot study to trial the data collection

methods, instruments, and procedures;

3) continuing the data collection over an 18-week semester;

4) presenting the participants with a portion of data I transcribed, translated, coded, and organized for member checking;

5) coding and recoding data at different times and many times to ensure intra-coder reliability;

6) using NVivo software to increase intra-coder reliability; and

7) reporting sufficient details about the research site, course context, the case study participants, and every methodological decision to the research audience.

According to case study and qualitative study methodologists (e.g., Creswell, 2013; Duff, 2008; Gall, et al., 2005), to augment the trustworthiness and credibility of findings, researchers need to use sound research methods, thoroughness of data collection and analysis (e.g., comprehensiveness of description of setting), and sensitivity to readers' needs (e.g., documentation of entire process). My study gave attention to all these crucial issues concerning the validity and reliability of a case study.

3.4 Chapter Summary

To ensure the results of a case study "'make sense' to others" (Duff, 2008, p.179), it is necessary to offer rich information related to the philosophical stance this case study builds upon (more positivist or more interpretative), its cases and their boundaries, the research instruments, methods, and procedures it uses to collect and handle data, and its way to resolve the issue of validity and reliability. This chapter, in turn, has described and explained in detail all these fundamental issues involved in this case study. The next chapter presents the results obtained through this research design and research process.

Chapter 4 The Construction of Non-error Feedback

4.0 Introduction

In this book, Chapter 4 presents findings in response to RQ1 (*When constructing feedback, how does the Chinese EFL teacher decide what EA concerns to focus on and how to deliver EA feedback?*). As explained in the Methodology Chapter, when writing feedback, Teacher T typed her feedback directly into the computer and she provided Microsoft Word feedback via the computer (rather than feedback in pen and paper format). As such, in my study, RQ1 revolved around Teacher T's decision-making when she was constructing computer-delivered electronic feedback (e-feedback). On RQ1, the following findings emerged from teacher feedback, background interview, think-alouds, and retrospective interviews:

- what Teacher T brought to the feedback process: contextual information (4.1);
- the entire process Teacher T went through when she typed in feedback: contextual information (4.2);
- the EA issues teacher feedback focused on (4.3);
- teacher decision-making: how Teacher T decided which EA issues to

focus on (4.4);

- the feedback delivery approaches the teacher used (4.5); and
- teacher decision-making: how Teacher T decided on feedback delivery approaches (4.6).

This chapter reports the above findings from teacher data (4.1–4.6). A chapter summary is offered in Section 4.7.

4.1 What the Teacher Brought to the Feedback Process: Contextual Information

In the Methodology Chapter, general information about the school context, course context, and personal context in which my study was situated has been provided. To more fully contextualize the study and research findings, a background interview with Teacher T was conducted. It captured more particulars of the micro-level personal and classroom contexts within which Teacher T's feedback practices took place. As Teacher T also articulated some of her general thoughts (e.g., feedback beliefs) about the construction of feedback in the retrospective interviews, this section reports some findings from the retrospective interviews as well. This section is concerned with the following issues:

- Teacher T's personality traits (4.1.1),
- Teacher T's teaching approaches (4.1.2),
- Teacher T's teaching plans and objectives (4.1.3),
- Teacher T's relationship with the students (4.1.4),
- Teacher T's beliefs about feedback foci (4.1.5), and
- Teacher T's beliefs about feedback delivery approaches (4.1.6).

Chapter 4　The Construction of Non-error Feedback

4.1.1　Teacher T's Personality Traits

Regarding her personality traits, Teacher T said that she was an extroverted person. As she was straightforward and outspoken in personality, she said she usually spoke at a very fast rate and was pretty direct with students and people. Jokingly, Teacher T associated her openness and directness with being "rude" and "impolite":

> I tend to be an 'impolite' person. ... I'm simply being direct when speaking in Chinese, and there's no difference when I communicate with people in English. ... But I always try to protect their [the students'] self-esteem and prevent them from losing face. But my style is too direct. I often can't help pointing out their problems bluntly, including the problems irrelevant to their English study.

4.1.2　Teacher T's Teaching Approaches: Discourse Analysis- and Textbook-Oriented

About her teaching approaches and objectives, Teacher T made the following points. She said that her writing instruction was discourse analysis- and textbook-oriented, which normally included the following steps:

1) using the writing samples in the textbook to explain the writing technique covered in each unit of the textbook (e.g., the technique to argue by using the cause-effect analysis method),
2) asking the students to discuss the writing task given in the textbook and then write an outline for it in class,
3) discussing the outline the students write in class,
4) giving the writing assignment topic (usually a CET-4 writing topic) near

the end of the class,

5) collecting student writing and writing feedback on it,

6) returning commented student writing, and

7) orally responding to student writing in class.

Apart from these steps, Teacher T said that she also spent one or two 50-minute class session(s) every month analyzing CET-4 model writing; but during this/these session(s) she usually focused on language issues to explain choice of words, diversification of sentence patterns, and other language techniques and issues to prepare her students for the CET-4 test.

On her teaching methodology (a textbook-oriented approach), Teacher T commented on the practical constraints she worked under, and how she dealt with those constraints in her teaching situation:

> I need to ask my students to write multiple drafts. But there're so many things to do in class, and the class sessions seem so short. In order not to fall behind in our teaching schedule (completion of teaching six units of the textbook in one semester), it's impossible to adopt a process approach to writing instruction. Anyway, … I usually just follow the textbook, … It's just impossible to ask my students to write beyond one draft.

4.1.3 Teacher T's Teaching Plans and Objectives: Test- and Competence-Oriented

In the semester when my study was conducted, Teacher T said that the objective of her teaching would be test-oriented, as well as competence-oriented:

> Considering a new reform of CET-4 and CET-6 is to be launched and the tests are becoming similar to IELTS and TOEFL tests,

> I'm going to give a lecture on IELTS writing and TOEFL writing this semester. Of course, all my classes aim to lead the students in the right direction for studying English and improve their writing ability.

4.1.4 Teacher-Student Relationship

In the background interview, Teacher T mentioned that she did not know the three students well enough although she taught them reading and writing last semester as well. Among the three students, Teacher T felt Student A was not active and responsive in class. She had a sense that Students B and C held a positive attitude toward her and her teaching, and felt she that her relationship with Student B was the closest. In her eyes, Student B always behaved very cooperatively in class, and Student C's engagement and motivation in class were active. However, in Teacher T's opinion, Student B's writing and overall language ability were not as high as that of Students A and C.

4.1.5 Teacher T's Beliefs Regarding Feedback Foci

Teacher T's Beliefs: General Distribution of Her Feedback Foci

In the background interview, Teacher T clearly pointed out her attention on EA-related issues would exceed that of lexicon-grammar:

> I usually don't give much attention to surface-level language issues when writing feedback on student writing. I just underline the students' grammatical errors, although I often carefully look at their choice of words and building of sentences. I usually give a lot of attention to the discourse-level features such as organizational structure and logic.

Here, it is necessary to detail the explanations Teacher T made about "logic".

She said she used the word "logic" as an umbrella term that embraced issues related to logical organization of ideas and logical flow of ideas at different levels. About its importance, Teacher T associated it with expository writing's readability and comprehensibility:

> As to expository writing, logic is so important that I want my students to be aware that their writing must be logical. Otherwise, their readers can't understand them.

Teacher T's Beliefs: Specific Distribution of Her Feedback Foci

In the background interview, Teacher T said that her focus of attention covered a range of issues at various levels. At the macro level of the whole text, she said she usually looked at *the overall organizational structure*, *completion of task requirements*, *genre*, and *cohesion and coherence*:

> I look at the overall organizational structure, looking for whether it's a three-paragraph text that includes the opening, body and concluding paragraph. ... I also holistically look at whether the student writing meets the task requirements, whether it conforms to the exposition genre, and whether it's written cohesively and coherently.

When it comes to her focus at the paragraph level, Teacher T stated she focused her comments on the body and conclusion and she mainly looked at two issues when commenting on the opening paragraph (i.e., information redundancy and thesis statement):

> I look at each paragraph as well, including the body paragraph, the conclusion paragraph as well as the opening paragraph. For example, I'll see whether there's too much lead-in information provided in the opening paragraph, and whether this paragraph lacks a sentence summary at the end [i.e., thesis statement].

Teacher T believed that there were more issues to attend to within paragraphs. She pointed out the coherence and supporting evidence issues within a paragraph drew her attention particularly:

> I feel they [students] have problems with issues like coherence and logic at the local level. Sometimes they use too many connective words, and their writing reads very awkwardly because of it. Sometimes, they can't organize the supporting evidence under each topic and subtopic sentences very well. I'm sure I'll point out these local-level problems. They [These writing problems] are really annoying.

Generally, when providing EA feedback, Teacher T believed that she would constantly focus on ① overall organizational structure of student writing, ② the opening, body, and conclusion paragraphs, ③ thesis statement and topic sentences, ④ supporting evidence, ⑤ cohesion and coherence, and ⑥ other issues related to "logic". In general, Teacher T had confidence in her ability to deal with her students' logic, EA-related problems. She said in the background interview: "*I'm confident in writing feedback on these issues.*"

Teacher T's Beliefs: Sources of Her Beliefs Regarding Feedback Foci

In my study, a qualitative analysis of teacher interview data (background and retrospective interviews) produced another layer of findings: the sources of Teacher T's beliefs about her feedback foci. The interview data revealed that Teacher T's beliefs about focusing on "logic issues" was directly associated with ① her research area and interest, ② her knowledge of Chinese EFL writers' writing difficulties and students' writing abilities, and ③ her beliefs about what to teach in her writing class.

In the background interview, Teacher T directly pointed out that her feedback beliefs might be influenced by her research area and interest:

> You know, my PhD work was based on discourse analysis. Although it was a study in Chinese, my research area and interest probably have a relationship with my focus of attention when I provide feedback on student writing in English.

The background interview data revealed that Teacher T's knowledge of the students' writing problems and difficulties was the other reason why she chose to focus on issues related to "logic". In her mind, the Chinese and English way of writing and thinking were different, and the difference between them was that *"the Chinese way is circular while the English way is direct and logical."* Due to this difference, she believed that Chinese EFL students were used to composing English writing in a circular Chinese way, and thus it was not easy for them to produce English writing that was logically structured. As to why Teacher T focused on "logic" and "directness" issues when providing feedback, it could be inferred from the following comments she made about students' writing problems and difficulties associated with the English way of writing and thinking:

> Most often, they [students] write in a poetic indirect Chinese way. It's illogical, absurd, and incompatible with English expository writing. ... I always provide feedback on these issues, but it seems that there're always such problems.

In one retrospective interview, Teacher T related her belief about focusing on cohesion and coherence to students' difficulties with use of connective words. She said:

> It seems that a proper use of cohesive devices is very easy and every student can use them very well, but in fact it's hard [to use

them very well]. So, I frequently mark them in my feedback.

(From the retrospective interview for Student C's third piece of writing)

Moreover, Teacher T connected her feedback belief to the students' inability to make generalizations. For example, in the retrospective interview for Student A's first piece of writing, she said that students seemed to lack the ability to give their readers a specific point to focus on and it was difficult for them to create appropriate (sub)topic sentence. About this lacking, what she said in the background interview was as follows:

> [I focus on this sub-topic sentence] because they often don't write topic sentence or subtopic sentence at the beginning of a paragraph, or I can't find them within a paragraph. The reason behind this is that they're unable to give their readers a specific point to hang onto.

As to the other source of her feedback beliefs, the following is what Teacher T said in the background interview, which showed that her teaching belief determined her focus on "logic" when she commented on student writing:

> My students often hear me say these things in our reading and writing class or when we discuss their writing in class. ... I feel they've begun to realize that the logic issues are important since they're the main concerns of my instruction and feedback.

Teacher T's Beliefs About Focus Changes Across Time, Students, and Writing Tasks

When asked whether there would be any changes in her focus of attention during the semester of my data collection, Teacher T answered: "*I have no plan to change my way of teaching and providing feedback this semester. I've used this pattern for years.*"

4.1.6 Teacher T's Beliefs Regarding Feedback Delivery Approaches

Teacher T's Beliefs Regarding Provision of Evaluator-Response Feedback (e.g., Problem/Strength-Oriented Feedback)

In the background interview, Teacher T described herself as an evaluator and stated she would provide negative, positive and advisory comments:

> When responding to student writing, I usually look at its negative and positive aspects first, and then based on my evaluation, I'll write down something negative or good, give advice and suggestions, and so on.

Although Teacher T believed that she mainly used feedback to show her students where their writing problems lay, she also said: *"On the strengths of their work, I don't withhold genuine praise."* In Teacher T's opinion, positive feedback could motivate student writers, especially when she felt there were quite a few problems in student writing.

Teacher T repeated that she tended to write advisory comments directly and concisely:

> I tend to point out their problems directly. Of course, I don't want to hurt their feelings, but I'm inclined to write 'You should…' or 'Pay attention to your brevity' instead of 'It'd be better if you…'

As a non-native English speaker, Teacher T thought her English was not perfect, so she could just offer students suggestions and help them get some ideas of how to write better. About this, she said: *"I don't think I can use feedback to teach my students to write perfectly. I can only point them in the right direction."*

Chapter 4 The Construction of Non-error Feedback

Teacher T's Belief Regarding Provision of Instructor-Response Feedback (e.g., Explanation)

In the background interview, Teacher T stated that students might be "*on the defensive*" and could not think carefully about their problems if teachers only pointed out problems but did not provide explanations. She believed explanatory comments could help the students better understand their problems and accept teacher feedback more easily.

Teacher T's Beliefs Regarding Provision of Combination Comments

In a retrospective interview (for Student A's first writing assignment), Teacher T said that comments that contain a sequence of strength/problem identification, explanation, suggestion, and revision were quality comments because such comments were logical, clear, informative, systematic and complete. In her own words, "*This way of commenting means I'm pointing out the problem, analyzing the problem, and providing solutions. Good comments should include this set of information.*"

Teacher T's Beliefs Regarding Providing Feedback Comments in English/ Chinese

In the background and retrospective interviews, Teacher T provided the following reasons for her choice of using the Chinese language to write EA feedback (or "logic" feedback in her own words). First, she felt it could help her students better understand her feedback on EA-related issues. In Teacher T's opinion, feedback comments in Chinese could have a deeper impression on the students and raise their attention to their problems. Second, Teacher T believed it was difficult and troublesome for her to clarify the complicated logic issues in English. As such, she asked in class whether she could comment on EA issues mainly in Chinese, and she found no disagreement with her students in providing Chinese EA feedback.

Teacher T's Beliefs Regarding the Changes of Her Feedback Delivery Approach

In the background interview, Teacher T pointed out that she might write feedback according to student personality and their relationship. She provided the following explanation:

> I'll use more hedges if the students are shy and introverted, and if our relationship isn't very close. I'd also like to provide them with more suggestions. If our relationship is close, I have less worries about writing something negative. As to how to deliver my feedback, it depends. It depends on who is the student writer.

Particularly, Teacher T pointed out that she might treat Student A somewhat differently: *"I'll be more careful when writing feedback on Student A's work."* She related this to Student A's class performance and their relationship: *"Since she isn't active and responsive in class, I have no idea about how she thinks about me and my class; I don't feel I know how to communicate with her very well."*

Teacher T's Beliefs in the Usefulness of Emoticons (☺)

In the retrospective interview for Student B's first piece of writing (about practicing cause-effect writing techniques), Teacher T explained the reasons why she mainly used the smiling emoticon (☺), and seldom used the crying one (☹). She believed that the smiley face could demonstrate her recognition of the strengths of student writing and motivate students to write better in a powerful way. In her own words: *"I used it to directly and clearly show my recognition of their strengths and achievements. It's very impressive."*

Teacher T's Beliefs Regarding the Location of Feedback

Teacher T expressed her dislike of using the Review Mode in Microsoft Word and her unwillingness to insert comments in the document margin. She said, *"Using it [the Review Mode] looks neat and tidy, but I feel it's overwhelming and it's difficult to track and connect the comments with the writing problems."* Teacher T said she would just type her comments throughout the student writing and put them in the position that was within the students' line of sight.

4.2 The Entire Feedback-Constructing Process the Teacher Went Through: Contextual Information

Before Teacher T typed in her comments, she usually had already carefully read student writing several times. When she began to add comments to student texts via computer, she was used to scanning the student's whole text again and articulated her general impression. Then, based on her general impression, she first provided general comments at the end of the text (i.e., typed in end comments). After writing end comments, Teacher T started re-reading the student writing sentence by sentence from the first paragraph so as to insert in-text comments related to each sentence and each paragraph. When she was typing in in-text comments, new ideas that she believed should be added to the end comments sometimes occurred to her. To make sure that no new idea was forgotten, Teacher T usually went back to the end comments immediately to write down a completely new piece of feedback or edit the comments she had already written out.

4.3 The EA Issues the Teacher Actually Focused on

In this section, the following findings are reported:

1) the general distribution of Teacher T's feedback,
2) Teacher T's non-error feedback and EA feedback, and
3) cross-assignment and cross-student changes in Teacher T's EA feedback.

Teacher T's Feedback: Its General Distribution

A comprehensive analysis of the feedback Teacher T presented on student writing showed that over a semester she provided 380 feedback comments on the three student participants' nine pieces of writing. Of these comments, 15.3% focused on surface-level language issues and 84.7% focused on issues beyond language. Table 4.1 below shows the general distribution of Teacher T's feedback, with error feedback and non-error feedback in the proportion about 1:5.5.

Table 4.1   Teacher Feedback: Its General Distribution

Teacher Feedback	Number	Proportion
Error Feedback	58	15.3%
Non-error Feedback	322	84.7%
Total	380	100%

Teacher T's Non-error Feedback and EA Feedback

Table 4.2 below presents the issues that were targeted in Teacher T's non-error feedback and EA feedback.

Table 4.2   Teacher T's Non-error Feedback and EA Feedback

Foci of Non-error Feedback and EA Feedback		Number	Proportion
EA Feedback (210, 65.2%)	Supporting Evidence	103	32%
	Cohesion & Coherence	42	13%
	Thesis Statement	19	5.9%
	Overall Organization	17	5.3%
	(Sub)Topic Sentence	16	5.0%

Continued

Foci of Non-error Feedback and EA Feedback		Number	Proportion
	Conclusion	13	**4.0%**
Content	Ideas	35	10.9%
Style	Conciseness/Redundancy	36	11.2%
Others	Task Completion, Genre Appropriateness, Register, etc.	41	12.7%
Total		**322**	**100%**

Table 4.2 indicates that Teacher T's non-error feedback (322) was spread across **organization, content, style** and **other issues** like genre appropriateness, register, and task completion. Of these, **EA feedback related to organization issues** had the highest percentage (65.2%), followed by **content feedback** (10.9%), **style feedback** (11.2%), and **feedback on other issues** (12.7%).

As demonstrated in Table 4.2, Teacher T's **EA feedback** included **feedback on supporting evidence** (e.g., relevance and development of supporting evidence), **cohesion and coherence** (e.g., connectives, pronominal cohesion), **thesis statement** (e.g., its style/directness), **overall organizational structure** (e.g., paragraphing), **(sub)topic sentence** (e.g., its style/directness), **and conclusion**. Among these feedback comments, Teacher T's **feedback on supporting evidence** constituted the largest part (32% of non-error feedback) and the percentages of the rest, in descending order of frequency, were 13%, 5.9%, 5.3%, 5.0%, and 4.0%.

In addition to EA issues, content was another concern (10.9%) of Teacher T. Her **content feedback** was mainly about the ideas in student writing. Teacher

T's **style feedback** related only to the issue of **conciseness/redundancy**. In total, Teacher T provided 36 (11.2%) **style comments**. Also, Teacher T gave 12.7% feedback on issues like **register** (e.g., academic formal word choice and informal word choice), **genre appropriateness** (e.g., expository genre of writing or narrative genre of writing), and **task completion** (e.g., achievement of writing requirements).

Teacher T's Non-error Feedback and EA Feedback: Cross-task changes

The findings, presented in Table 4.3, showed that Teacher T provided 67, 83, and 60 EA comments on writing task one (W1, **cause-effect writing**), writing task two (W2, **exemplification writing**), and writing assignment three (W3, **free-technique writing**) respectively. It seemed that, over the course of a semester, the total number of Teacher T's EA comments on each set of writing assignments remained relatively stable. However, we can still see a rise from W1 to W2 and a drop from W2 to W3 in feedback amount.

Table 4.3 Teacher T's Non-error and EA Feedback: Cross-task Changes

Non-error Feedback	W1	W2	W3
EA Feedback (210)	67 (65.7%)	83 (73.4%)	60 (51.2%)
Content (35)	10 (9.8%)	12 (10.6%)	13 (12.1%)
Style (36)	10 (9.8%)	8 (7.1%)	18 (16.8%)
Others (41)	15 (14.7%)	10 (8.8%)	16 (15%)
Total (322)	102 (100%)	113 (100%)	107 (100%)

(Note: W1=the first cause-effect writing task; W2=the second exemplification writing task; W3=the third free-technique writing task)

Teacher T's EA Feedback: Cross-student Changes

An examination of the cross-student changes indicated that Teacher T focused on EA issues when commenting on Students A, B, and C's writing tasks (75.2%, 65.4% and 50.6% respectively; more than half of non-error feedback in general). However, Teacher T gave less non-error feedback on Student C's writing (79 comments) but it seemed she that provided more feedback on the "Others" (See Table 4.4 below) of Student C's writing (e.g., genre appropriateness, task completion, register).

Table 4.4   Teacher T's Non-error and EA Feedback: Cross-student Changes

Non-error Feedback	A	B	C
EA Feedback	85 (75.2%)	85 (65.4%)	40 (50.6%)
Content	13 (11.5%)	13 (10%)	9 (11.3%)
Style	13 (11.5%)	14 (10.8%)	9 (11.3%)
Others	2 (1.8%)	18 (13.8%)	21 (26.6%)
Total	113 (100%)	130 (100%)	79 (100%)

4.4   Teacher Decision-Making: How the Teacher Decided Which EA Issues to Focus on

Qualitative and quantitative analyses of teacher think-aloud and retrospective interview data indicated that Teacher T's feedback focus decisions were mainly influenced by

   1) her feedback beliefs,

2) her heightened awareness of what to focus on, and

3) the teacher-context interaction (i.e., the interaction among the examination orientation of her classroom instruction, the role she played as a test assessor when giving EA feedback, and the traditional Chinese educational culture).

This section presents an explanation of these three results.

The Influence of Feedback Beliefs

Teacher data obtained in my study showed that, to a large extent, Teacher T had already decided what EA concerns to focus on before she set out to deliver feedback on student writing. Each time when thinking aloud, Teacher T usually just reported what she would focus on according to the ideas that had already been formed in her mind and there was no real reasoning behind her focus decisions. Her automatic decision-making indicated that her focus decisions were mainly belief-informed and her feedback practices could be distilled down to an issue of teacher belief/cognition. For example, after Teacher T scanned Student A's W1 (the first cause-effect writing assignment) and spoke aloud her thoughts and feelings about it, she immediately announced her focus decisions. Without much formal reasoning, Teacher T stated: *"Now let me write comments on her writing; first on the whole text in general and then on paragraphs."*

At the same time, connecting Teacher T's feedback beliefs (reported in Section 4.1.5) with her actual performance (reported in Section 4.3), it is not difficult to see that there was a match between Teacher T's feedback beliefs and practices. In general, it seemed fair to say Teacher T's beliefs regarding feedback foci were inherent in her decisions and her actual feedback practice, and her focus decisions stemmed from what she believed.

Teacher T's retrospective interview data also showed her decision-making was guided by her beliefs and her decisions to focus on these EA issues had already been made in advance. In each retrospective interview, when asked what non-error and EA issues Teacher T had written on, she always repeated the same answer: *"Just as I tell you all the time: on global issues like organization, logic, cohesion and coherence and on the local-level issues."*

The Influence of Heightened Teacher Awareness: Teacher T's Changing Feedback Beliefs

Teacher T's beliefs about feedback focus were found to be relatively stable over the course of one semester. However, after commenting on the students' W1, she came to realize that the argumentation issue in student writing was more problematic than she thought and her awareness to focus on argumentation issues was heightened. This finding highlighted the following points. First, Teacher T's focus beliefs were changing over time, although the change was relatively slight. Second, Table 4.3 shows that there was an increase in the amount of Teacher T's EA feedback from W1 (65.7%) to W2 (73.4%). Probably informed by her changing beliefs, Teacher T gave more EA feedback on the students' W2.

The Influence of the Interaction Among Teacher and Contextual Factors

During the retrospective interview for Student A's W1, Teacher T said:

> [When providing feedback,] First I look for whether the general Introduction-Body-Conclusion format is appropriately used because using this structure to organize writing is a basic requirement of the CET-4 test and the CET-4 test raters usually look at it first. Look at her writing, … to see whether there're five paragraphs. For a piece of CET-4 test writing, three or four

paragraphs are enough and five-paragraphs is too long. So, I decided to comment on it; there are too many paragraphs.

The statement Teacher T made above confirmed that she had a strong motivation to use her EA comments to help her students achieve good scores on the CET-4 examination and she seemed to assume the role of a test assessor. As discussed in literature review chapter and this chapter (Sections 4.1.2 & 4.1.3), Chinese education is examination-centric and Teacher T's teaching objectives and plans were closely related to preparing her students for the upcoming CET-4 test. As such, Teacher T's responding foci pointed to the interactional effect of teacher factor (teacher role), sociocultural context (examination-oriented culture), and pedagogic context (examination-oriented teaching belief/approach) on her focus choices and decisions.

4.5 The Feedback Delivery Approaches the Teacher Used

Out of text analyses of the feedback data, the following perspectives on Teacher T's delivery approaches emerged:

1) the perspectives of orientation and language channel,
2) the perspective of scaffolding degree, and
3) the cross-assignment and cross-student perspective.

This section presents the findings from these three perspectives (4.5.1–4.5.3).

4.5.1 Feedback Delivery Approaches: From the Perspectives of Orientation and Language Channel

Table 4.5 exhibits in detail the different delivery approaches Teacher T used to provide EA feedback.

Table 4.5　Teacher T's Feedback Delivery Approaches: From the Perspectives of Orientation and Language Channel

Feedback Delivery Approaches			Number
Evaluator-Response Comments (241, 74.8%)	Revision (60)	Direct Revision	22
		Suggested Revision	38
	Problem Indication (61)	Direct Indication	28
		in English	6
		in Chinese	22
		Hedged indication	33
		in English	11
		in Chinese	22
	Strength Indication (65)		65
	in English		41
	in Chinese		24
	Advice (48)	Imperative Advice	32
		in English	16
		in Chinese	16
		Suggestion	16
		in English	2
		in Chinese	14
	questions in Chinese (7)		7
Instructor-Response Comments (68, 21.1%)	Descriptive/Interpretative Comments		11
	in English		2
	in Chinese		9
	Explanatory Comments (57)		57
	in English		16
	in Chinese		41
Reader-Response Comments (13, 4.0%)	Reader-Response Comments (13)		13
	in English		10
	in Chinese		3
Total (322, 100%)			**322**
in English			164
in Chinese			158

Table 4.5 shows, from the perspective of orientation, Teacher T provided 75% "**evaluator-response feedback**", 21% "**instructor-response feedback**", and 4% "**reader-response feedback**". More specifically, in Teacher T's evaluator-response feedback comments, there were a large number of **strength-oriented comments** (65), **problem-oriented comments** (61), and **advisory comments** (48) while her **questioning comments** were limited (7). It seemed that Teacher T frequently pointed out what the students had achieved (strength-oriented comments) and she provided a similar number of strength-oriented comments (65), problem-oriented comments (61), and revision comments (60). Findings presented in Table 4.5 also revealed, instead of directly writing feedback, Teacher T used more hedges (33) when commenting on the negative aspects of student writing and providing revisions. She usually preceded her revisions with words like "*Here, a possible revision can be: ...*" to mitigate the imposition of her revisions.

Teacher T's "**instructor-response feedback**" centered around **explanatory comments** (57), which were mainly used to explain why she considered student writing to be problematic or impressive, and why she commented on or revised student writing in the way she did. Sometimes, Teacher T also used **descriptive/interpretative comments** to describe/interpret student writing in her own words (11). Occasionally Teacher T responded to student writing as a reader (4%), instead of acting as an evaluator or an instructor. Moreover, from the perspective of language channel, Teacher T commented both in English and in Chinese. Table 4.5 indicates she gave a similar number of English comments (164) and Chinese comments (158).

4.5.2 Feedback Delivery Approaches: From the Perspective of Scaffolding Degree

From the perspective of scaffolding degree, Teacher T's feedback delivery approaches were divided into **single-statement comments** and **combination comments** (e.g., the praise-criticism-suggestion triad; criticism-suggestion pair). Findings obtained from teacher feedback indicated that she wrote out 50 **single-statement comments** and 94 **combination comments**. Table 4.6 shows the number and percentage of each type of comments.

Table 4.6 Teacher T's Feedback Delivery Approaches: From the Perspective of Scaffolding Degree

Feedback Delivery Approaches		Number
Single-Statement Comments (34%)		49
Combination Comments (95, 66%)	Two-Statement Pairs	46
	Three-Statement Triads	21
	Four-Statement Quaternity	14
	Comments Containing More Statements	13
Total		**144**

4.5.3 Feedback Delivery Approaches: Cross-assignment Changes

Cross-assignment Changes: From the Perspective of Orientation

Table 4.7 below presents the results about the cross-assignment changes of Teacher T's feedback delivery approaches from the perspective of orientation.

As can be seen from Table 4.7, there were two typical cross-assignment changes in Teacher T's delivery approaches. First, Teacher T provided many more strength-oriented comments on W2 (26) and W3 (30) than on W1 (9). Second, there were fewer explanatory comments on W2 (17) and W3 (17) than on W1 (23).

Table 4.7 Cross-assignment Changes: From the Perspective of Orientation

Feedback Delivery Approaches			W1	W2	W3
Evaluator-Response Comments (241)	Revision	Direct Revision	10	6	6
		Suggested Revision	9	13	16
	Problem Indication	Direct Indication	13	9	6
		Hedged Indication	8	15	10
	Strength Indication		9	26	30
	Advice	Imperative Advice	14	9	9
		Hedged Suggestion	5	5	6
	Questions		3	2	2
	Total		71	85	85
Instructor-Response Comments (68)	Descriptive/Interpretative Comments		5	4	2
	Explanatory Comments		23	17	17
	Total		28	19	19
Reader-Response Comments (13)	Reader-Response Comments (13)		3	7	3
	Total		3	7	3
Total (322)			102	113	107

Cross-assignment Changes: From the Perspective of Scaffolding Degree
From the perspective of scaffolding degree, the following cross-assignment findings were obtained (See Table 4.8 below).

Table 4.8   Cross-assignment Changes: From the Perspective of Scaffolding Degree

Feedback Delivery Approaches	W1	W2	W3
Single-Statement Comments (49)	16	16	17
Combination Comments (95)	28	32	35
Total (144)	**44**	**48**	**52**

As shown in Table 4.8, the quantity of single-statement comments Teacher T wrote on the students' W1, W2, and W3 were almost identical (16, 16 & 17), and the quantity of combination comments on W1, W2, and W3 appeared quite similar (28, 32 & 35). In general, from the perspective of scaffolding degree, Teacher T's feedback delivery approaches did not seem subject to change according to writing assignments.

4.5.4   Feedback Delivery Approaches: Cross-student Changes

Cross-student Changes: From the Perspective of Orientation
From the perspective of orientation, Table 4.9 shows how Teacher T gave EA feedback on Students A, B, and C's writing over a semester.

Table 4.9   Cross-student Changes: From the Perspective of Orientation

Feedback Delivery Approaches			A	B	C
Evaluator-Response Comments (241)	Revision	Direct Revision	6	7	9
		Suggested Revision	14	18	6
	Problem Indication	Direct Indication	9	14	5
		Hedged Indication	17	10	6
	Strength Indication		**16**	**30**	**19**
	Advice	Imperative	14	13	5
		Suggestion	9	5	2
	Questions		4	3	0
	Total		89	100	52
Instructor-Response Comments (68)	Descriptive/Interpretative Comments		4	3	4
	Explanatory Instruction		18	21	18
	Total		22	24	22
Reader-Response Comments (13)	Reader-Response Comments (13)		2	6	5
	Total		2	6	5
Total (322)			**113**	**130**	**79**

Table 4.9 indicates that there was a cross-student variation in Teacher T's feedback delivery approaches. First, she provided more EA feedback and more positive feedback on Student B's writing. Second, she gave a smaller amount of EA feedback on Student C's writing. However, considering that Teacher T gave Student C only 79 EA comments in total, the number of

instructor-response comments she gave to her were relatively large (22, about 30%).

Cross-student Changes: From the Perspective of Scaffolding Degree

From the perspective of scaffolding degree, Table 4.10 below summarizes the cross-student findings. Teacher T's EA feedback delivery approaches did not seem to change considerably from student to student from this perspective.

Table 4.10   Cross-student Changes: From the Perspective of Scaffolding Degree

Feedback Delivery Approaches	A	B	C
Single-Statement Comments (49)	15	21	13
Combination Comments (95)	36 (71%)	34 (62%)	25 (66%)
Total (144)	51	55	38

4.5.5 More Feedback Delivery Approaches: Emoticons, Highlights, and Underlines

When Teacher T provided EA feedback, she often used emoticons (e.g., ☺; ☹), highlights (with colors or in boldface), and underlines. Generally speaking, Teacher T mainly used smiling faces and she usually placed them at the end of a feedback comment. Regarding highlights and underlines, Teacher T mainly used them to indicate the issues her comments addressed.

4.6 Teacher Decision-Making: How the Teacher Decided on Feedback Delivery Approaches

As indicated in 4.4, Teacher T's decisions about her feedback foci were mainly belief-informed and had often been made before she commented on student texts. As to Teacher T's decisions about how to deliver EA feedback, my study found that they were usually made in the moment when she was re-reading/re-scanning the student's writing and adding her electronic comments to student writing. In relation to how Teacher T's feedback delivery approaches were determined, the following key findings emerged from teacher data.

1) Teacher T's decisions were produced through **the interaction** among her **cognitive, behavioral**, and **affective engagement** during feedback provision;
2) Teacher T's decisions were formed as a result of **her intense social cognitive engagement**; and
3) **The interaction between teacher factors and contextual factors** influenced the formation of Teacher T's decisions about how to deliver EA feedback.

In this section, the above-mentioned findings are reported in turn (4.6.2–4.6.4). Before it, I first explain Teacher T's cognitive, behavioral, and affective engagement (including her social cognitive and metacognitive engagement) when she was deciding how to deliver and type in her EA feedback (4.6.1). This explanation contextualizes the answers reported in the sub-sections following it.

4.6.1 Making Feedback-Delivery-Approach Decisions: An Explanation of Teacher T's Cognitive, Behavioral, and Affective Engagement

In this section, to be clear, I first use an example to explain Teacher T's cognitive, behavioral, and affective engagement when she was deciding on her feedback delivery approaches and adding feedback. Then, I present quantitative and qualitative findings about the cognitive, behavioral, and affective operations Teacher T performed to make her feedback-delivery-approach decisions.

Deciding on Feedback Delivery Approaches: An Example of Teacher T's Cognitive, Behavioral, and Affective Engagement

Here is the example, which shows how Teacher T's feedback delivery approaches were decided. In this example, the comments Teacher T wrote down read as follows:

> This opening could go straight to the point, but not very attractive. Try this: "Campus activities play an indispensable and active part in the college life. Among these various activities, social practice benefits me the most." (Is it much more concise?) ☺
> (Notes: The words enclosed by the round brackets were originally written in Chinese. The translation is mine. From Teacher T's comments on Student A's W1)

The comments, taken from Teacher T's feedback on Student A's W1 (See Appendix I for the whole piece of writing with Teacher T's feedback comments), were written on the EA-related issue of **thesis statements**. The comments indirectly pointed out Student A's writing problems (*"This opening could go straight to the point, but not very attractive."*), and provided a suggested revision ("*Try this: 'Campus activities play an indispensable and active part in the college life. Among these various activities, social practice benefits me the most.'*"), a question comment to make explanation ("*Is it much more concise?*"), and a smiley face (☺).

To type in the comments given above, Teacher T made the following cognitive, behavioral, and affective investment. To decide to make the hedged problem-oriented comment provided above ("*This opening could go straight to the point, but not very attractive.*"), Teacher T first articulated her negative feelings about Student A's opening paragraph (**affective engagement**): "*Oh..., I don't feel this opening paragraph is good.*" Then, she read the opening paragraph again, re-evaluating it and saying that the language and idea of Student A's writing were both problematic (**cognitive engagement, interpretative and evaluative operations**). Teacher T thought aloud: "*besides, 'get rid of' used here is not appropriate; and the idea 'our life is colorful' isn't appropriate either.*" Then, based on her re-reading, interpretation, and evaluation of the opening paragraph, Teacher T decided to point out Student A's writing problems in her comments. The decision she articulated was (**cognitive engagement, decision formed**): "*Let me point them out.*" However, just before typing in her problem-oriented comment, Teacher T stopped to decide whether to use English or Chinese to compose her comments (**cognitive engagement, identification and selection operations**). The final decision she made was that she preferred using English (**cognitive engagement, decision formed**): "*I'll do it in English since it's clear enough for her to follow me.*"

After reading the introduction, evaluating it, deciding to point out problems, and selecting the response language, Teacher T moved on to the acting stage of putting down her decisions by using her keyboard (**behavioral** engagement). At first thought, she decided to type in her problem-oriented comment as follows: "*This opening is not very attractive.*" However, she changed her decision immediately (**cognitive engagement, identification and selection operations**). Considering Student A might feel uncomfortable when receiving negative feedback (**social cognitive engagement, evaluative operations**), she rephrased her problem-oriented comment by beginning her feedback with something positive (**social cognitive engagement, identification and selection operations**) and put down the following hedged feedback comments on the computer: "*This opening could go straight to the point, but not very attractive* (**behavioral engagement**)." Then, Teacher T carried out **review operations (cognitive engagement)**, thinking that "*It's much better to confirm her achievement first* (**social cognitive engagement**)." After that, Teacher T re-reviewed her comment by re-reading the opening paragraph and re-evaluating student writing. She thought aloud with a feeling of unsatisfaction with student writing: "*Yeah, it's [the opening paragraph] ok, but it isn't good enough.*" (**cognitive and affective engagement**)

Furthermore, Teacher T's review of her feedback comment inspired her to provide revision. After reviewing her comment "*This opening could go straight to the point, but not very attractive.*", Teacher T reported her decision to provide a suggested revision (**cognitive engagement, decision formed**) and typed "*Try this: ...*" into the computer (**behavioral engagement**). Then, she stopped to re-consider how to provide a suggested revision (**cognitive engagement, identification and selection operations**). Feeling difficulty in giving a better suggested revision, Teacher T said: "*Oh..., my Goodness, how to revise it?*" (**affective and cognitive engagement**). As will be explained in the following section (4.6.2), she compared several sentence stems and language expressions she could use when writing down comments (**cognitive engagement, identification and selection operations). Finally, she gave up her idea to use the phrases she attempted to use at the beginning (**cognitive engagement, identification and selection operations**) and decided to use the simplest way to construct her revision (**cognitive engagement, decision formed**). While typing in her revision, Teacher T also articulated her belief that she would like to keep most of what Student A wrote originally (**behavioral and cognitive engagement**). After Teacher T finished her revision (*"Campus activities play an indispensable and active part in the college life. Among these various activities, social practice benefits me the most."*), she reviewed it by reading her revision (**cognitive engagement, review operations**).

Once again, inspired by her review operations, Teacher T decided to add a question comment (*"Is it much more concise?"*) and a smiley emoticon (☺). Regarding her addition of feedback points, Teacher T thought aloud as follows: *"It's necessary to let her know why I made the revision, and I also need to add a smiley emoticon (☺) to let her know that she did a job that wasn't bad* (**behavioral and social cognitive engagement**).*"* According to what Teacher T said here, she used her question comment to provide an explanation instead of using it to ask a question.

In the end, Teacher T reviewed the whole set of feedback comments she had put on the computer and articulated how to construct her comments in future (**cognitive engagement, reflection operations**). With her students' affective response to her feedback in mind, Teacher T planned to use the positive and negative pair as a feedback strategy in the future (**social cognitive engagement, reflection operations**). About this, she said:

> I'd feel very uncomfortable if I received a lot of negative comments. Who wants to be judged and criticized? And no one wants to

have their work revised too much. It'd be much better to confirm their achievements first before pointing out their problems. I'll continue to use this way to provide comments.

(From Teacher T's think-aloud for Student A's W1)

In general, when Teacher T was writing feedback on the thesis statement (behavioral engagement), she mainly went through a cognitive process during which she spent much of her effort on cognitively interpreting and evaluating Student A's writing, considering students' response (social cognitive engagement), and deciding how to type in her comments. Meanwhile, in the act of typing in feedback (behavioral engagement), Teacher T was also found to make choices and decisions regarding which sentence stem or language expression to use in her comments and revisions (cognitive engagement). In addition, the example given above showed that Teacher T felt that it was hard to offer revisions (affective engagement). Although she did not often express her feelings about experiencing difficulties when revising student writing, it is undeniable that the feedback-providing process she engaged in was not easy and it had an affective and social dimension. To summarize, Teacher T usually went through (social) cognitive, affective, and behavioral processes when completing EA feedback-typing activities, during which her decisions about how to deliver feedback were formed. As to Teacher T's cognitive, behavioral, and affective engagement, more details are reported in the following from the quantitative and qualitative perspectives.

Quantitative and Qualitative Findings: Teacher T's Cognitive, Behavioral, and Affective Engagement

Table 4.11 below demonstrates the number and percentages of the cognitive, behavioral, and affective investment Teacher T made during feedback provision.

Table 4.11 Teacher T's Cognitive, Behavioral, and Affective Engagement

Teacher T's Engagement	A	B	C	Average
EA Feedback Provision (Feedback Provision 100%)	95.3%	88.5%	87.7%	90.6%
Cognitive Engagement (EA Feedback Provision 100%)	70.0%	69.6%	72.2%	70.4%
Behavioral Engagement (EA Feedback Provision 100%)	24.4%	22.1%	21.8%	22.9%
Affective Engagement (EA Feedback Provision 100%)	5.6%	8.3%	6.0%	6.8%
Error Feedback Provision (Feedback Provision 100%)	4.7%	11.5%	12.3%	9.4%
Total (100%)	451	561	324	1336

Table 4.11 shows that Teacher T's think-aloud and retrospective interview data could be divided into 1366 segments, among which more than 90% were related to EA feedback provision and about 10% were related to error feedback provision. According to the table, Teacher T demonstrated a very high level of cognitive engagement (about 70% of the process to respond to EA issues), a low level of affective engagement (about 7% of the process to respond to EA issues), and a relatively high level of behavioral engagement (about 22% of the process to respond to EA issues). In addition, a cross-student examination indicated that Teacher T's cognitive, behavioral, and affective engagements during feedback provision was consistent across students, each of which was about 70%, 22% and 7%.

Regarding Teacher T's high-level cognitive involvement, Table 4.12 shows the type, number, and percentages for the cognitive operations she utilized during EA feedback provision.

Table 4.12 The Cognitive Decision-Making Process Teacher T Involved in

Teacher T's Cognitive Engagement	A	B	C	Total
Cognitive Engagement	**301**	**346**	**205**	**852**
Planning and Monitoring Operations	0.7%	2.3%	1.0%	1.4%
Interpretation Operations	21.6%	16.8%	20.0%	19.2%
Evaluation Operations	19.6%	22.0%	21.5%	21.0%
Identification and Selection Operations	11.0%	15.3%	8.3%	12.1%
Review Operations	20.9%	18.8%	22.4%	20.4%
Reflection Operations	1.3%	3.2%	3.4%	2.6%
Decisions and Reasons	24.9%	21.7%	23.4%	23.2%

(Note: Teacher T's monitoring operations, or her metacognitive operations, mainly refer to her regulation of emotions.)

Table 4.12 indicates that, to decide how to provide EA feedback, Teacher T mainly carried out the following cognitive operations: "interpretive operations" "evaluative operations" "identification and selection operations" "review and reflection operations", and "metacognitive operations (i.e., planning and monitoring operations)". She spent great effort reading and interpreting student texts (about 20% of cognitive engagement), making evaluations (about 20% of cognitive engagement), and carrying out reviewing operations (about 20% of cognitive engagement). Additionally, the table shows that Teacher T's cognitive, behavioral, and affective engagement did not vary greatly across students.

As shown in Table 4.11, the percentage values of Teacher T's affective involvement (about 7%; including her affective responses to student writing, her emotional states aroused by responding to student texts, and her attitude towards her own comments) and metacognitive operations (i.e., planning and monitoring operations, 1.5% of cognitive engagement; e.g., Teacher T's regulation of her emotions) were relatively low. However, this low percentage indicated that to look at Teacher T's decision-making during feedback only from the perspective of thinking was still not enough. My study found that Teacher T's cognition, affect, and act were inseparable, and it is the cognition-affect-behavior interaction/integration that led to the formation of her decisions about how to deliver EA feedback. Now, this finding is to be detailed in the following sub-section (4.6.2).

4.6.2 Teacher T's Decision-Making: The Interaction Among Her Cognitive, Behavioral, and Affective Engagement

In this section, several examples are provided to illustrate how Teacher T's affect, cognition, and behaviors were intertwined and how her decisions about feedback delivery approaches were produced as a result of this interrelatedness.

The first example illustrated the affect-(meta)cognition interaction and Teacher T's decisions to offer explanatory comments. As Teacher T's evaluation of Student A's argumentation in her W1 was completely negative, Teacher T felt rather bad (cognitive and affective engagement). She thought aloud: *"Hang on; be patient. Let me handle the problem paragraph by paragraph and give her explanations."* That is to say, in this example, along with Teacher T's cognitive interpretation of the student writing was her negative emotion (impatience). However, Teacher T used a metacognitive strategy (*"hang on"*) to remind herself to shift her attention from her negative emotion (impatience) to the cognitive task itself (i.e., deciding how to add feedback), and then her decision to provide explanation feedback (*to "handle the problem paragraph by paragraph" and to "give her explanation"*) was made. Obviously, this example showed that teacher affect was deeply interwoven with teacher cognition/metacognition, which interactively led to the formation of teachers' feedback-delivery-approach decisions.

The following is a simple example, which clearly showed the relationship between the affect-behavior-cognition interaction and Teacher T's decision-making. When in the act of entering her "revision" of student writing, Teacher T was found to stop typing again and again so as to re-consider and re-decide how to offer a better version of revision (interaction between cognition and behavior). Finally, because she felt it was too cognitively demanding and affectively stressful to provide a "revision" without appropriating student texts, Teacher T decided with reluctance and regret to delete and remove her half-finished revision (affect-cognition-behavior interaction and a decision made). In this example, it is easy to see that Teacher T's act (typing in and deleting comments), thinking (reconsidering and remaking her decisions about how to revise student texts), and feeling (e.g., feeling difficult to revise student texts and feeling regretful for giving up providing revision) were inseparable, which merged to guide her decision-making as she revised student texts.

In fact, the example I used in Section 4.6.1 to illustrate Teacher T's cognitive, behavioral, and affective engagement (*"This opening could go straight to the point, but not very attractive. Try this: ..."*) also clearly showed Teacher T's decisions to offer revision were made as a result of the interaction among her cognitive, behavioral, and affective engagement. In that example, when Teacher T was revising student writing and writing down the following words: "*Try this:*", she had difficulty in giving a really good revision (behavior-affect interaction). However, even though she felt bad, in her mind Teacher

T kept making comparisons and choices among several sentence stems and language expressions she thought she could use (affect-cognition interaction). For example, she made a selection between two expressions: "*as far as I am concerned*" and "*for me*." As she preferred a concise, direct way to express herself, she decided to use "*for me*" in her revision sentence. She said when thinking aloud: "*I choose to be concise and direct; it's better to construct my revision sentence in this way.*" However, at last, she gave up her idea of using "*for me*" and decided to use the simplest way (deletion of "*for me*") when resuming typing in her revision (cognition-behavior interaction and a decision formed). Clearly, The research evidence shows behind Teacher T's revision decisions was the workings of a cognition-behavior-affect interaction.

4.6.3 Teacher T's Decision-Making: High Level of Social Cognitive Engagement

In addition, my study found that it was through Teacher T's ongoing, intense social (re)interactions with the students (i.e., Teacher T's high level of social cognitive engagement in my study) that her decisions about how to deliver EA feedback were made. The focus of this sub-section is on the contribution of the social interactions Teacher T experienced during her feedback provision to her decision-making.

To decide how to deliver EA feedback during feedback provision, my study found that Teacher T engaged in six types of operations: interpretation operations, evaluation operations, identification and selection operations, review operations, reflection operations, and planning and monitoring operations (See Sub-section 4.6.1). As shown in Table 4.12, my study found that Teacher T often invested considerable time and effort into (re)reading and (re)interpreting student texts (**interpretation operations**), and then she could make up her mind to provide evaluator-response comments (e.g., problems/

strengths-oriented feedback). Considering Teacher T's investment of time and effort in interpretation operations was big (about 20% of her cognitive engagement), my findings revealed that, basically, the formation of her decisions about how to deliver feedback was the result of her interaction with student texts. However, usually beginning as a cognitive process, Teacher T's responding engagement and decision-making then often became a social process which involved her interaction not only with student texts but also with their writers.

When carrying out (re)reading and (re)interpretation operations, Teacher T responded not only to student writing, but also to student writers. For example, sometimes Teacher T was found to be engaged in a deep-level interpreting process. During this process, she made attempts to identify the student's writing intention, uncover what the students attempted but failed to write into texts, and interpret student texts at a deep level in order that she could justify her decision to provide positive EA feedback or to accompany her problem-oriented comment with positive remarks.

As Teacher T's evaluation of student writing was usually negative, her evaluation of student writers when she performed evaluation operations usually justified her decisions to add something positive to her combination comments. When carrying out evaluation operations (20% of her cognitive engagement), Teacher T often evaluated the following student factors:

- students' abilities,
- students' writing attitude,
- students' efforts devoted to the writing task,
- students' development as L2 writers,
- students' acceptance of and affective reactions to EA feedback,

- students' writing process,
- students' application of classroom instruction to writing, and
- the differences and changes in students' writing (differences with previous writing attempts and cross-student differences).

In other words, when carrying out evaluation operations and providing positive comments, Teacher T frequently "interacted" with students who are feedback receivers/users (e.g., as shown by her consideration of student reaction to feedback), classroom participants (e.g., as shown by her consideration of student application of classroom instruction), writers (e.g., as shown by her consideration of students' writing process), learners (e.g., as shown by her consideration of students' ability, changes and development) and people who have emotions (e.g., as shown by her consideration of student affect).

Teacher T also carried out the following **identification and selection operations** during feedback addition (12% of her cognitive engagement) on the computer screen:

- identifying the exact idea she intended to convey in her feedback,
- selecting a better way to convey her ideas and messages, and
- selecting the most appropriate lexical items, language expressions, sentence structures, feedback language channels (Chinese or English), feedback sequence (e.g., positive feedback placed before negative feedback), and symbols (e.g., highlight or underline; use of liking/ disliking face or not) to provide high-quality EA feedback.

As shown above, Teacher T carried out a number of identification and selection operations to decide on what ideas to convey, how to exactly convey ideas, and which lexical items/language expressions/sentence structures/feedback language channels (Chinese or English)/feedback location/symbols (e.g., highlight or underline; use of sad face or not) to use. When thinking aloud, Teacher T was always active in making selections so that she could accurately convey ideas about good writing to feedback recipients. For example, when wording her feedback comments and selecting the most appropriate verb (*"improve"*, or *"promote"*, or *"enhance"*) to use in her feedback, Teacher T spoke aloud: *"improve their…, promote their…, or enhance their…"* After translating the three verbs into Chinese and making comparison, she eventually decided to use *"enhance"* in her comments. Simply put, when using identification and selection strategies, Teacher T kept interacting with herself as a feedback giver and an instructor. However, as the optimal comments she attempted to write down were intended to tell her students what the best pieces of writing were like and model ideas about good writing for her students, Teacher T actually was also experiencing a high level of social engagement when she phrased her comments and monitored her feedback practice.

In my study, Teacher T devoted considerable energy to reviewing the decisions she had made about how to deliver EA feedback (about 20% of her cognitive engagement). As to Teacher T's **review operations**, they were found to include her

- rereading and reviewing student writing,
- reading and evaluating her own feedback,
- re-evaluating student ability,
- comparing student writing and her revision of student writing,
- articulating (dis)satisfaction with her own work, and
- considering student understanding/incorporation/application of her EA feedback.

Sometimes, Teacher T went further and carried out **reflection operations**

(2.6% of her cognitive engagement) as well. During and after typing in comments, now and then she reflected on:

- student problems with dealing with EA issues and the causes,
- student progress in argumentation and the causes of student progress,
- her own feedback purposes (i.e., to give students explicit instructions),
- the effective feedback delivery approaches (e.g., confirmation of student strengths and progress),
- student affect, student acceptance of teacher feedback, and student application of classroom instruction concerning EA issues.

Generally, the above findings showed that teacher decision-making is inherently interactional and interactive. This conclusion was drawn because Teacher T's review and reflection operations embraced her re-interaction with student texts (e.g., as shown by her re-reading and reviewing of student writing), and with herself as a feedback giver (e.g., as shown by her reading of her own feedback), a critic (e.g., as shown by her evaluation of her own feedback and by her comparison of student writing and her own revision), an instructor (e.g., as shown by her consideration of her own feedback purposes), and an emotional decision maker (e.g., as shown by her articulating (dis) satisfaction with her own feedback). More importantly, as enlisted above (e.g., evaluating/comparing student ability, considering student reaction, assessing student progress), when reviewing and reflecting on her own work concerning feedback decision-making, Teacher T also needed to socially (re)interact with students and treat them as writers, feedback receivers/users, learners and people who have emotions.

At the outset of this section (4.6), an example was provided to illustrate Teacher T's cognitive, behavioral, and affective engagement. In that example, one observable action Teacher T took was typing in her comments. In fact, during feedback provision, there was another observable action (behavior) Teacher T undertook from time to time. That is, she sometimes consulted online dictionaries/resources to ensure the words and expressions she used in her feedback comments were accurate and appropriate or to find a model text to read. When thinking aloud, she gave two reasons for her behaviors: ① an inadequate stock of vocabulary, and ② her expectations to write better comments to explicitly convey and model ideas about high-quality writing and to positively affect students' writing performance. The second reason (her high expectation to provide feedback) once again indicated how Teacher T decide on her feedback deliver approaches was through her interaction with students.

4.6.4 Teacher T's Decision-Making: Teacher-Context Interactions

My study also found that underlying Teacher T's decisions about how to deliver EA feedback was the interplay of teacher and contextual factors. This sub-section reports these findings.

The Interaction Between Teacher Beliefs and Interpersonal Context

In the background interview, my study found that Teacher T believed that she would provide positive, negative, advisory, and explanatory EA comments, and she believed in the usefulness of praise, combination comments, and comments provided in Chinese. Consistent with her beliefs, she did provide these types of EA feedback in her actual practices (See Table 4.5). In general, the consistency between Teacher T's beliefs and the outcomes of her decisions showed that, to a certain extent, her beliefs about how to provide EA feedback underpinned her feedback decision-making.

However, my study also found that Teacher T's final decisions/responding practices did not completely conform to her beliefs. In the background interview, Teacher T repeated that she tended to write direct and concise feedback comments; but in practice, instead of writing direct feedback, she used more hedges when commenting on the negative aspects of student writing and providing revisions (See Table 4.5). In some retrospective interviews, Teacher T ascribed this to her consideration of the acceptability of teacher feedback and establishing a good relationship with her students. She said in the retrospective interview for Student B's W1: "*I hedged because of considering its acceptability, and ... probably, teacher-student relationship.*"

In addition, in the background interview, Teacher T reported that there was a high level of trust between Student B and herself, and she felt their relationship was closest. Although she believed that she would provide students with more negative feedback if their relationship were good (as shown in Section 4.1.6), Teacher T wrote more positive EA feedback on Student B's writing in actual practice (as shown in Table 4.5). Her explanation for her decisions to provide a larger amount of positive, encouraging EA comments on Student B's text also pointed to the influence of a good teacher-student relationship: "*Because it was her [Student B's] writing; I don't do it on others*'." As is the above-given cases, it was the interaction between Teacher T's feedback beliefs and interpersonal contexts (i.e., constructing/ maintaining the teacher-student relationship) through which she came to her decisions concerning her provision of EA feedback.

The Interaction Between Teacher Image and Sociocultural Context
As mentioned above, Teacher T often provided EA feedback in a hedged way. In the retrospective interview for Student B's W2, Teacher T provided another reason for her decision to use hedges. She said that she felt afraid of "losing face" for responding directly but in fact she misunderstood students' writing intentions and provided feedback that might be inappropriate. About this,

Chapter 4 The Construction of Non-error Feedback

Teacher T's remarks made in the retrospective interview were:

> I'm afraid that I provided wrong comments, or I misunderstood these two sentences, so I used 'seem' in here. If I didn't understand her writing correctly, at least my feedback wasn't completely wrong. This is an issue of 'face-saving'.

In Teacher T's view, hedges created a higher probability of face saving in front of her students and cultivating an image of a good teacher. It is generally believed that people from collective societies (like Chinese people) are more concerned with loss of face (Waterman, 1984). From this perspective, Teacher T's decision to provide hedged feedback was indeed shaped by the interaction of creating a good teacher image and the contextual factor of society and culture.

The Interaction Between Teacher Role and Sociocultural Context
In my study, Teacher T often inserted emoticons (e.g., ☺) into her feedback on student writing. As to this choice, she said that it was influenced by her frequent use of emoticons when using *WeChat* (a mobile app widely popular in China) to text messages and communicate with people. At the same time, Teacher T pointed out that emoticons, especially the smiley face (☺), could directly, easily, and efficiently express her supportive attitude and build students' motivation and confidence in writing. This piece of evidence from my study reflected the interactional effect of the sociocultural context (i.e., the social media age) and teacher role (i.e., the role of a facilitator) on Teacher T's decision-making about how to provide EA feedback.

The Interaction Between Teacher Role and the Teacher's Personal Circumstances
Teacher T's think-alouds indicated that she considered provision of reliable revisions important, and she always tried to provide reliable comments and

161

revisions. For example, to help Student C better revise the conclusion of her second writing assignment, Teacher T searched the Internet and consulted a piece of model writing she got online. However, she found the conclusion of the "model writing" available to her was too simple and indeed not well-written. When verbalizing her thinking, Teacher T said: "... *Or how to write a conclusion for her?... Let me read the conclusion of the model writing. ... It's very simple.*" Eventually, for lack of a reliable way of providing revision and lack of motivation and energy, Teacher T decided not to add a suggested revision to Student A's writing. After writing a "praise-criticism-explanation triad" comment on the concluding paragraph, she said, "*I'll stop here [and not write revision comments]. Let her make revisions on her own.*" To summarize what has been reported so far, concerning Teacher T's decision-making about constructing EA feedback, it might not be the result of a single factor, but of the link between her considerations of the role she took on and her personal circumstances/context (e.g., lack of reliable resources and motivation).

As to the influence of the teacher role-personal circumstance link on Teacher T's choice not to revise the students' conclusion, here is another example. In the retrospective interview for Student B's W1, Teacher T said she commented on Student B's conclusion too simply and did not provide revision (*Teacher T's Chinese comment on the student text was:* "*It restated the key point, but it was a paragraph that wasn't attractive.*"). With regards to its reason, Teacher T said that she had spent too much effort and time on commenting on other issues and she had no energy to consider how to revise the student's concluding paragraph. Likewise, when she was typing in conclusion feedback on Student A's W1, she said that cognitive overload happened as well. The following was what she said in the retrospective interview: "*I also felt very tired when writing feedback on Student A's conclusion, and I felt I had no spare energy to make a revision at that time.*" Teacher T's remark implied that the link between her role (as a feedback provider who should not provide simple feedback) and her personal circumstance (cognitive overload) made her provision of revision possible/impossible.

The Interaction Between Teacher Personality and the Teacher's Personal Circumstances

In my study, Teacher T chose not to frequently provide questioning comments. In a retrospective interview, she related her decision not to question the student to her personality and personal preference. About this, she said:

> "I rarely use questions when writing feedback; I choose to directly express my ideas. ... I'm straightforward in personality. I prefer telling you what your problems are instead of putting forward questions. I just want to show you problems directly. (Teacher T, retrospective interview for Student B's W2)

To write revision comments, Teacher T's choice was also influenced by her personality and personal preference to express herself concisely and directly. As the example used in Section 4.6.1 illustrates, when deciding how to revise the opening paragraph of Student A's W1, Teacher T preferred a concise, direct way to express herself. According to her retrospection, commenting on student writing in a concise, direct way also saved her time and trouble. When this comment was given by Teacher T in the retrospective interview, it meant it was the interrelatedness of teacher factor (i.e., teacher personality, personal preference) and contextual factor (e.g., personal contexts such as busy life and stressful work) that could explain Teacher T's decision formation.

The Interaction Between Teacher Affect and the Pedagogic Context

During the background interview and the retrospective interview for Student A's W1, Teacher T said that, in class, she and her students had already achieved an agreement to provide/receive EA feedback in Chinese. Moreover, Teacher T's decision to provide Chinese comments could also be linked to what was emphasized in her class. For example, she explained her decision to provide a Chinese comment on supporting evidence as follows:

> The issue about the relevance of supporting evidence is our focus in class. Here, my English comment and Chinese comment expressed the same idea. I chose to use the Chinese comment to repeat what I've already said in English; this is because I want to stress the importance of the relevance of supporting evidence.
>
> (Teacher T, retrospective interview for Student B's W2)

In actual practice, my study showed that Teacher T provided an equivalent number of English (50%) and Chinese (50%) comments (See Table 4.5). This was because Teacher T felt worried that she could not create an ideal English-learning environment if she frequently used Chinese comments. These quantitative and qualitative results indicated that the teacher-student common decision only partially influenced Teacher T's feedback decisions; it is the interaction between Teacher T's affect (i.e., anxiety) and the contextual factors (i.e., the teacher-student shared decision and focus of classroom teaching) that determined her choice of language channels.

4.7 Chapter Summary

This chapter reported findings related to the following issues:

1) what the teacher brought to the feedback-adding process,

2) the general feedback-adding process the teacher went through,

3) the EA issues teacher feedback focused on,

4) the approaches the teacher used when typing in EA feedback, and

5) teacher decision-making that underlay the teacher's feedback foci and feedback delivery approaches.

In my study, a quantitative and qualitative analysis of Teacher T's feedback indicated that her feedback was closely related to argument construction and mainly focused on *supporting evidence, cohesion and coherence, thesis statement and topic sentence (chiefly from the angle of whether the topic and topic sentences were stated directly and concisely), conclusion,* and *the overall organization.* My study also found that Teacher T's feedback foci were relatively stable.

In my study, the following findings related to Teacher T's approaches to deliver EA feedback emerged:

- From the perspective of orientation, Teacher T used **evaluator-response feedback** (74%; e.g., *feedback indicating problems/strengths, advice/ suggestion, revision*), **instructor-response feedback** (22%; e.g., *feedback making explanations*), and **reader-response feedback** (4%) to deliver her EA feedback; and Teacher T's EA feedback tended to be delivered in a hedged manner.

- From the perspective of scaffolding degree, one third of Teacher T's comments were delivered as **single-statement feedback** while two thirds were **combination feedback,** which usually consisted of problem/strength indication, explanation, advice/suggestion, and/or revision.

- From the perspective of language channel, Teacher T's comments were delivered **half in English and half in Chinese**.

- From the perspective of cross-assignment/student differences, Teacher T's feedback delivery approaches remained relatively stable across writing assignments and students. The clearly observable differences across writing tasks were **the steady increase** of Teacher T's positive feedback and hedged feedback, and **the decrease** of her explanatory feedback and direct feedback. In terms of cross-student differences, **Student B** was found to receive more comments in total and more positive feedback than Students A and C, among whom Student C received the least amount of EA feedback in total.

With regards to the decision-making behind Teacher T's feedback foci, my study found how Teacher T decided on her feedback foci was shaped by:

- **teacher beliefs** about feedback foci,
- heightened **teacher awareness** of what to focus on, and
- **the interaction among teacher role, the examination orientation of the traditional Chinese educational culture and Teacher T's classroom instruction**.

As to how Teacher T's feedback delivery approaches were determined, the following key findings emerged from teacher data:

- Teacher T's decisions were formed as the result of the **interaction** among her **cognitive** (e.g., interpreting student writing), **behavioral** (e.g., consulting online dictionary), and **affective** (e.g., affective response to student writing) **involvement** in feedback addition;
- The process of teacher-student interactions Teacher T opened up guided the decisions she made as she typed in her EA feedback;

- The **interaction between teacher factors** (e.g., teacher belief) and **contextual factors** (e.g., sociocultural context, pedagogic context, personal circumstance) was found to underlie the formation of Teacher T's decisions about how to deliver EA feedback.

Now, with the teachers' provision of EA feedback in mind, I turn to RQ2 and focus my attention on the students' interpretation of EA feedback in the following chapter.

Chapter 5 The Interpretation of Non-error Feedback

5.0 Introduction

As explained in the Methodology Chapter, to answer RQ2 (*When processing the teacher's EA feedback, how does the Chinese EFL student decide the extent to which it is accepted and incorporated?*), I collected and analyzed student data obtained from background interviews, think-alouds, retrospective interviews, and student notes. For RQ2, the following findings emerged:

- what the students brought to the feedback process: contextual information (5.1);
- Student A's acceptance and incorporation of EA feedback (5.2);
- Student B's acceptance and incorporation of EA feedback (5.3);
- Student C's acceptance and incorporation of EA feedback (5.4); and
- Student decision-making: how the students' acceptance and incorporation of EA feedback were decided (5.5).

This chapter reports the findings from student data. Finally, a chapter summary is offered (5.6).

Chapter 5　The Interpretation of Non-error Feedback

5.1　What the Students Brought to the Feedback Process: Contextual Information

In this section, what Students A, B, and C brought to the feedback process is reported respectively (5.1.1–5.1.3). It is mainly concerned with each student's personality and motivation for learning English, their feedback beliefs, their plans and goals to deal with teacher feedback, and their views about the teacher-student relationship.

5.1.1　Student A

Student A: Personality Traits and Self-Image as an English Learner and Writer
In the background interview, Student A described herself as highly self-disciplined and self-motivated. She thought that she could study independently and keep a high level of concentration while studying. Student A also said that she was a learner who kept adapting her learning strategies, study plan, and learning pace so as to find the way that best suited her personality.

As an English learner, Student A said she had a passion for learning English and English is a useful tool for horizon expansion, communication and future career:

> … I feel English is charming. I love it especially when the speaker seems to be saying one thing on the surface, but all his listeners understand what was implied in his remarks. English is also a tool that's so widely used in the world. We need it to expand our horizon, communicate with the world, and help us have a better future career.
> … I'm not good at memorization and I need a lot of practice to learn something new, but I'm willing to spend time on it.
>
> (From the background interview with Student A)

In Student A's opinion, her English writing ability was at an upper intermediate level and she liked writing in both Chinese and English.

Student A: Feedback Beliefs

In the background interview, Student A said that in the past she had few chances to receive written feedback from her teachers; but she acknowledged the importance of teacher feedback, saying "*I think teacher feedback is the second round of teaching, while in-class teacher instruction is the first round. ... So, I think teacher feedback is a very important step of teacher instruction.*" Concerning her acceptance of teacher feedback, she commented: "*In general, I felt teachers' evaluation of student writing was accurate and their feedback was constructive. I'd like to take all of the feedback I got from my teacher.*" However, the background interview with Student A also showed that she would exercise her agency when processing teacher feedback. She said: "*We should question teacher feedback if we don't think it's right. I'll keep my own opinion if it isn't persuasive enough.*"

Concerning language, content and organization feedback, Student A said she tended to fully accept her teacher's organization feedback because she believed "*the biggest difference between English and Chinese is organizational structure*" and she was prone to making errors in that regard. As for the acceptance of Teacher T's feedback on content and language, Student A said: "*I feel, if you can deal with the structure issue very well, you won't have big problems with content and language issues.*" What Student A said implied that she valued organization feedback and the degree of her acceptance of it might be high.

Student A: Plans and Goals to Deal with Teacher Feedback in the Semester She Participated in My Study

In the semester she participated in my study, Student A thought she would read all the teacher comments, and pay particular attention to the comments on the issue of logic and the natural ways of expressing herself in English---two major problems in her writing. At the same time, she said she would give attention to the parts that she felt were poorly written and carefully read teacher comments on them.

Based on teachers' suggestions and comments, Student A said she would rethink her writing problems, and try to work out the writing skills and techniques implied in the teacher feedback. Also, she said that she would spend time on positive feedback, as she could make use of it to understand what was working for writing and would continue to use the criteria underlying teacher praise in new writing. Student A also reported it was easier to follow direct feedback.

Student A: Teacher-Student Relationship

Student A thought that she trusted Teacher T's capability as a language teacher and considered Teacher T to have a serious attitude toward teaching. Also, she thought Teacher T could provide her with suggestions on what she most needed to improve and Teacher T's feedback would be explicit enough for her to follow. In addition, Student A considered her relationship with Teacher T to be good: "*She knows my name and who I am, ... she doesn't know the names of most of the class.*"

5.1.2 Student B

Student B: Personality Traits and Self-image as an English Learner and Writer

Student B considered herself observant and eager to learn. "*However*," she said, "*as far as English learning is concerned, I'm a lazy learner.*" In her opinion, rote learning was an easy way to learn English, so she was good at and fond of rote memorization.

Regarding language ability, Student B had felt that her English was at an intermediate level before entering KEY, but she had since realized that she was a low-intermediate level English learner and writer compared with the other freshmen at KEY. Furthermore, it seemed that Student B needed a confidence boost: "*It appears that I'm not as confident as them. It'd be much better if I were placed in the C-level class [basic-level class; As indicated in the Methodology chapter, Student B was placed in the intermediate B-level class after the placement test.].*"

For Student B, English, especially spoken English, was very important. She said that she would take part in an interview in English soon to transfer to the best school at KEY. Regarding writing in English, Student B claimed she had never received formal writing instruction. She said at secondary school she was only asked to recite some typical sentence patterns, and to produce writing that consisted of three parts: paragraph one (stating there is a phenomenon), paragraph two (explaining the reasons behind the phenomenon), and conclusion (providing solutions). Even so, Student B said,

> I hope my teacher teaches me writing moves, typical structures and useful sentence patterns; I'd like to do mechanic drilling and just directly use these moves and sentence patterns [without thinking] when writing.
>
> (From the background interview with Student B)

Student B felt that her writing sounded unnatural to native English speakers and was full of Chinglish. She felt "cause-effect" was the only method she could use when writing in English. However, Student B did not think she could distinguish between "cause" and "effect". "*I only know this method, but I can't flexibly use it,*" she said.

Student B: Feedback Beliefs

Student B said that at secondary school the feedback she received was usually just a grade. At KEY, she said she mainly got feedback from the website *pigai.org*. She thought she preferred teacher feedback since feedback from *pigai.org* focused only on language and sentences: "*We need feedback on both macro- and micro-features of a text.*"

Student B believed that it was necessary to read every error her teacher pointed out, and it was not difficult for her to understand teacher feedback. However, she also believed that she would consider whether teacher feedback was reasonable before deciding whether to accept it or not. According to Student B, she might accept most of teacher feedback (60-80%).

Specifically, Student B believed that it was necessary to consider whether the teacher's **content feedback** was reasonable before deciding whether to accept it or not. About this, she said: "*if what my teacher said in her feedback doesn't sound reasonable, I won't accept it.*" Talking about the possibility of accepting teachers' content and organization feedback, Student B said she was more likely to take her teacher's organization feedback.

Student B said that giving feedback was to instruct, and she believed direct/ directive feedback was more effective to achieve this purpose:

> I can't follow teachers if their feedback is somewhat indirect. They should directly tell their students what they need to do. Then I'll

quickly remember what the teachers tell me and try to use it next time. It's also good if teachers directly provide us with revision.

(From the background interview with Student B)

Apart from revision, Student B thought feedback that pointed out her writing problems and advisory comments were crucial, and she tended to accept these two types of comments. In addition, Student B said she did not consider positive feedback useful and would not pay much attention to it. According to her, "*Teachers use praise comments just to be polite.*"

Student B: Plans and Goals to Deal with Teacher Feedback in the Semester She Participated in My Study

In terms of plans and goals in the semester she participated in my study, Student B aimed to learn how to write and how to improve her writing ability. She said:

> There'll be nothing I'll particularly focus on and I'll read all teacher comments. Then, I'll bear them in mind, and try to figure out the writing methods my teacher intends to teach me through her feedback. My purpose of processing teacher feedback is to find out the way to produce better writing in similar future tasks, instead of just improving the current one.
>
> (From the background interview with Student B)

Student B: Teacher-Student Relationship

Student B thought that teachers were the people who imparted knowledge and who directed the students to do what they should do. In Student B's mind, her relationship with Teacher T was a normal teacher-student relationship, but they could talk with each other like friends when out of class.

5.1.3 Student C

Student C: Personality Traits and Self-Image as an English Learner and Writer
Student C said that she had a bright, outgoing personality. She believed that she was a good learner of English because she had a great interest in and strong motivation for learning English. She said:

> As a language learner, I'm a really good one. I started learning English at five. My interest in English began when I watched 'Growing Pains' and 'Family Album USA' as a child. These American TV series were fascinating. I think my childhood experience laid a good foundation for me to stay motivated to learn English.
>
> (From the background interview with Student C)

However, Student C felt her written proficiency was only fair. She said, when writing, she usually made a mental draft in Chinese first, and then translated it into English. In Student C's view, she still did not have a good grasp of English writing, since she felt she did not know how to fully translate her ideas from Chinese into English.

Student C: Feedback Beliefs
Student C considered teacher feedback important: "*If there were no teacher feedback, I wouldn't know why we were asked to write.*" However, regarding her acceptance of teacher feedback, Student C believed she was a semi-resistor who was easily put on the defensive. About this, she said:

> I believe most students are semi-resistors. When interpreting teacher feedback, we partly accept teacher comments and partly insist that our writing is good. In our mind, we justify what we write and feel defensive about why the teacher only looks at our

problems but ignores the strengths of our writing.

(From the background interview with Student C)

Furthermore, Student C explained under what circumstances she did not accept teacher feedback:

> I wouldn't accept my teacher's feedback if I followed the instructions of my high school English teacher or what I had learnt from some books to compose my text but my teacher [at the university] considered my writing problematic; I'll insist on using what I've learnt in the past.

(From the background interview with Student C)

Regarding teachers' language, content and organization feedback, Student C said that there was no difference in her tendency to incorporate these three types of feedback and she might accept all of them. Moreover, she said it was easier for her to accept feedback that used the connective "but", because it indicated the strengths of her writing before pointing out her problems. Revision was another type of feedback Student C believed she might easily accept and imitate. In the background interview, she also mentioned her willingness to accept comments that both indicated the major problem of her writing and gave her advice and suggestions as to how to improve her writing ability.

Student C: Plans and Goals to Deal with Teacher Feedback in the Semester She Participated in My Study

According to Student C, if she got specific comments rather than just a grade or general comments, she would read the specific comments from the first to the last to ensure that she did not miss anything. She also thought she would read teacher feedback two times, since it was possible that she could not fully understand it if she just read it once. She felt that it was good to understand what the teacher wanted to tell her via feedback, carefully think about it, and remember it. However, Student C did not think she would write in English after graduating from KEY and beginning to work. She only considered English writing to be important because she needed to take the CET-4 and CET-6 tests.

Student C: Teacher-Student Relationship
In Student C's eyes, Teacher T's English class was interesting and informative. She also felt that Teacher T was a teacher with whom she could have a talk, although she felt that they seldom had the opportunity.

5.2 Student A's Acceptance and Incorporation of EA Feedback

This section begins with a brief description of how Student A approached teacher feedback (5.2.1). Then, Student A's acceptance and uptake of EA feedback is reported from two perspectives: the cognitive and behavioral perspective (5.2.2), and the affective perspective (5.2.3).

5.2.1 How Student A Approached Teacher Feedback: A General Description

Student A's think-alouds showed that she processed teacher feedback in the following way. When writing was returned with teacher comments, Student A usually immediately began to process the teacher feedback. She usually went through three rounds of the feedback-interpreting process. In the first round, she processed all the feedback Teacher T provided on her writing and went through the teacher feedback from start to finish in sequence. In the retrospective interviews, Student A said: "*I read every piece of Teacher T's feedback, from the one written at the beginning to the one at the end; I don't want to miss anything."*

Then, Student A went into the second round of feedback interpretation. She pointed out that in the second round she interpreted teacher feedback at a deeper level:

> After I went through Teacher T's feedback and had ideas about where my problems lay, I began to think deeply about Teacher T's feedback and tried to summarize what I could learn from it. Again, I went through all feedback on my writing.
>
> (From the retrospective interview with Student A for her W2)

Student A was also found to write down notes while she was re-interpreting teacher feedback. She said she mainly wrote down her thoughts and reflections. The notes Student A wrote down were usually a paragraph long (See examples later in Section 5.2.2).

Student A's third round of feedback-interpretation was short. During this process, she usually used key words to summarize the teacher feedback. For example, she summarized that Teacher T's comments on her W1, W2, and W3 focused on organization, clarity, and conciseness respectively.

5.2.2 Student A's Cognitive and Behavioral Acceptance and Incorporation of EA feedback

Based on analyses of Student A's think-alouds and retrospection, Table 5.1 presents an overview of her acceptance and incorporation of Teacher T's EA feedback from the cognitive and behavioral perspectives. The "√" in Table 5.1 represents the way Student A accepted and incorporated EA feedback, which might be "accepted and incorporated" "semi-accepted" "noticed", or "not-accepted". In this section, the information summarized in Table 5.1 is explained.

Table 5.1 Student A's Acceptance and Incorporation of EA Feedback

EA Feedback	Accepted and Incorporated	Semi-Accepted	Noticed	Not-Accepted
Supporting Evidence	√ (W1 & W2)		√ (W3)	
Cohesion & Coherence (Conjunction)	√ (W1 & W2)		√ (W2 & W3)	√ (W2)
Thesis Statement	√ (W1)		√ (W2 & W3)	
(Sub)Topic Sentence	√ (W1 & W2)		√ (W3)	
Conclusion	√ (W2)	√ (W1, W3)		
Overall Organization	√ (W1 & W2)		√ (W3)	

(Note: W1=the first cause-effect writing task; W2=the second exemplification writing task; W3=the third free-technique writing task)

Student A: Widespread Acceptance and Incorporation of EA Feedback

Table 5.1 indicates that Student A widely accepted Teacher T's EA feedback on her W1 and W2. As mentioned in Section 5.2.1, Student A usually went through three rounds of feedback interpretation. After three rounds of interpretation, she generally accepted and incorporated Teacher T's EA feedback on her W1 and W2. In fact, when dealing with teacher feedback on her W1 and W2, Student A often expressed her acceptance or appreciation of it (e.g., *"really good" "inspiring"*). In addition, as can be seen from the notes Student A took down, she deeply understood, agreed with, and assimilated Teacher T's feedback on her W1 and W2 (See examples later in this section).

Regarding Student A's non-acceptance of feedback on cohesion and coherence, she just occasionally rejected Teacher T's feedback on her use of connectives. For instance, when responding to Teacher T's feedback adding *"For example"*, Student A thought aloud: *"it's OK without it."* In the retrospective interviews, she explained:

> When writing, I focused my attention on coherence of meaning. Using conjunctives to create coherence in form isn't that important. ... I don't think I need to pay much attention to teacher feedback on connectives.
>
> (From the retrospective interview with Student A for her W2)

Student A semi-accepted teacher feedback on the conclusion of her W1 and W3. Teacher T's feedback on the last paragraph of Student A's W1 reads as follows:

> This paragraph is not clear. ... You're still arguing with cause and effect. This is actually one of the body paragraphs. So, you did not conclude your writing appropriately. ... A real conclusion is still needed.
>
> (From Teacher T's comments on Student A's W1, originally in Chinese)

When responding to these comments, Student A only accepted Teacher T's advice (*"A real conclusion is still needed."*) but refused to accept her criticism (*"...you did not conclude your writing appropriately."*). She said:

> This is one of my body paragraphs. I didn't write a concluding paragraph. Teacher T misunderstood me. I agree with her that a conclusion is needed, but I disagree that I concluded my writing inappropriately.
>
> (From Student A's think-alouds for her W1)

When dealing with Teacher T's conclusion feedback on her W3, Student A agreed with Teacher T's criticism that coherence was lacking in her conclusion, but she did not accept Teacher T's revision. In her words, *"I didn't mean that I refused to accept this feedback. I feel her revision is a concise version, but it wasn't coherent either."*

Student A: Decreasing Incorporation of EA Feedback

Table 5.1 also shows that, when interpreting Teacher T's EA feedback on her W3, Student A mainly acknowledged she noticed it. Furthermore, after interpreting Teacher T's feedback on her W3, Student A did not write down any words or compose written notes as she had done before. These differences indicated that Student A's uptake of Teacher T's EA feedback was decreasing. Student A said in the retrospective interview that she only *"marked up the issues about conciseness and wordiness"* when dealing with Teacher T's feedback on her W3. She also said that the EA-related knowledge Teacher T intended to teach through feedback on her W3 had already existed in feedback on her W1 and W2.

Student A: Self-regulated, Deep-Level Incorporation of EA Feedback

As indicated in Table 5.1, Student A cognitively and behaviorally incorporated most of Teacher T's EA comments. Qualitative analyses of student data showed the depth of her incorporation of Teacher T's EA feedback on her W1 and W2.

When interpreting teacher feedback on her W1, Student A accepted Teacher T's feedback on supporting evidence during the first round. She thought Teacher T's feedback on supporting evidence was clear and understandable so that she agreed with what Teacher T said in her comments. However, Student A could not incorporate it because she had no idea how to act on it and how to develop arguments. So, during the second round of feedback interpretation,

Constructing and Interpreting Non-error Feedback:
From the Perspective of Sociocognitive Theory

Student A searched the internet to find out whether there was a model text to consult and whether she could learn from it how to back up arguments and how to write conclusion. She found one model text and her critical analysis of the text helped her deeply understand how to deal with issues like supporting evidence, the concluding paragraph, cohesion and coherence, and the overall organization in new writing. For example, when thinking aloud, Student A said, "*Yes, he [the writer of the model text] didn't just list empty ideas like me; there're concrete explanations in his writing.*"

When going over Teacher T's feedback on her W1 and W2, Student A took down notes related to supporting evidence, cohesion and coherence, topic sentences, overall organization, and conclusions. She wrote down ① what she learnt from Teacher T's comments, ② her writing problems and strengths, ③ her ideas about how to develop arguments, and ④ her reflection about how to plan writing and improve it. In general, the content of Student A's notes was insightful, and her comments were long. The following is an example of her end notes:

> Major writing problems: 1. Structure of my writing: To produce a well-structured text, it is necessary to have a logical and clear outline before writing. And it is needed to argue from various perspectives and use concise sentences to ensure the topic is elaborated thoroughly and strongly. 2. What is exceedingly important is the organizational structure of the body paragraphs. The topic sentence should be elaborated by two or three supporting arguments. It could be argued from the perspective of the how and the why.
>
> (From Student A' notes written on her W1; Originally in Chinese)

The above quote showed Student A accepted and assimilated Teacher T's comments on supporting evidence, topic sentences, and organization. It seemed that teacher comments also provided Student A with inspiration on how to plan writing (having an outline). Student A's thinking about how to produce well-organized expository texts and how to plan writing revealed that she accepted what Teacher T said not only on the surface but also at a deep level.

When going over Teacher T's EA feedback on her W1 and W2, Student A often mentally considered how to make the revision. For instance, when Teacher T pointed out Student A failed to provide supporting evidence for one of her subtopic sentences in her W1 (*"Be involved in social practice found a platform for us to communicate and cooperate with others"*), Student A attempted to revise it: *"Then, what do I need to write to support it? I can write..."* The process Student A went through to make mental revision also reflected that her acceptance and uptake of Teacher T's EA feedback on her W1 and W2 did not lack depth.

5.2.3 Student A's Emotional Acceptance of EA Feedback

Emotionally, Student A's attitude towards Teacher T's EA feedback underwent a major change. When dealing with Teacher T's EA feedback on her W1, Student A sometimes said: *"Teacher T's suggestion [on my topic sentence] is really good, and I also like the revision she made."* Sometimes, she said that Teacher T's feedback on supporting evidence was *"clear"* and *"impressive"*. Similarly, Student A highly valued and appreciated Teacher T's feedback on her W2. In her own words, Teacher T's feedback on her topic sentence and the relevance of supporting evidence was *"detailed"* and *"enlightening"*. However, Student A felt that Teacher T's EA feedback on her W3 was *"simple"* and *"wasn't as helpful as before"*. In her opinion, she had already been able to apply Teacher T's feedback on her W1 and W2 to new writing and Teacher T's EA feedback on her W3 provided no new knowledge and insight regarding how to deal with EA issues and how to produce better expository writing. Overall, Student A's emotional acceptance of Teacher T's EA feedback is marked by a shift from her appreciation of it to her dissatisfaction with it.

5.3 Student B's Acceptance and Incorporation of EA Feedback

Like Section 5.2, this section is organized around three aspects of the findings: a brief description of how Student B approached teacher feedback (5.3.1), Student B's cognitive and behavioral and affective acceptance and incorporation of EA feedback (5.3.2 & 5.3.3).

5.3.1 How Student B Approached Teacher Feedback: A General Description

When commented writing was returned to Student B, she usually began to process the teacher feedback immediately and went through three rounds of the feedback-interpreting process as well. In the first round of interpretation of feedback, aside from cognitively processing Teacher T's comments, Student B highlighted some of Teacher T's comments with colors or jotted down the questions she had when she interpreted the feedback. Student B described her second round of feedback interpretation as a process of scanning Teacher T's feedback and her own writing and taking down notes:

> I re-read it, from the beginning to the end. I scanned Teacher T's feedback again and re-thought about my writing problems. Re-reading is my habit; I think this does me good. I also wrote down Teacher T's key points, my questions and problems, but mainly questions and problems.
>
> (From the retrospective interview with Student B for her W1)

Student B's third round of feedback-interpretation was short. When dealing with teacher feedback on her W1, at the final stage, Student B wrote down the following notes, the longest one she wrote while participating in my study:

> I think the entire organizational structure of my writing is good; it is necessary to revise the body structure; and the relevance of the support to the subtopic sentence is my problem.
>
> (From Student B's notes; Originally in Chinese)

In her notes, Student B first confirmed the strengths of her writing and then began to accept Teacher T's feedback on supporting evidence by admitting the existence of one weakness in her writing (irrelevance of the support to the subtopic sentence).

5.3.2 Student B's Cognitive and Behavioral Acceptance and Incorporation of EA Feedback

Table 5.2 summarizes Student B's acceptance and uptake of EA feedback from the cognitive and behavioral perspectives. This section explains the findings contained in Table 5.2, as well as the findings from qualitative analyses of student data.

Table 5.2 Student B's Acceptance and Incorporation of EA Feedback

EA Feedback	Accepted and Incorporated	Semi-Accepted	Noticed and Incorporated	Not-Accepted
supporting evidence	√ (W2)	√ (W1, W2)	√ (W2, W3)	√ (W1)
cohesion & coherence	√ (W2)		√ (W1, W2, W3)	√ (W1)
topic statement	√ (W2)		√ (W3)	√ (W1)
(sub)topic sentence			√ (W2, W3)	√ (W1)
conclusion			√ (W1, W2)	
overall organization	√ (W1)		√ (W2, W3)	

Student B: Slow, Passive, Superficial Acceptance and Incorporation of EA Feedback

Table 5.2 reveals that, regarding Student B's acceptance of EA feedback on her W1, she did not accept most of it. For example, when Teacher T pointed out in her feedback on Student B's W1 that Student B just repeated the main point she made in the topic sentence but provided no supporting evidence, Student B voiced her disagreement, stating that it was not a repetition of the topic sentence but a writing technique she used purposefully to reinforce the claim she had made in the topic sentence. However, when dealing with teacher feedback on her W2, Student B's acceptance and uptake of it showed modest increase. She accepted a number of teacher feedback on supporting evidence, cohesion and coherence, and topic statements. Moreover, Table 5.2 shows that in most cases Student B just **noticed** (read and translated) Teacher T's EA comments on her W2 and W3; and then based on her reading of them or her reading and translation (from English to Chinese) of them, she incorporated Teacher T's EA feedback (by making mental notes, memorization, and marking up key points). In the third retrospective interview, Student B said that she incorporated all of Teacher T's EA comments: "*I solved all the problems Teacher T pointed out in her comments on the previous two pieces of writing.*" Generally, from the cognitive and behavioral perspectives, Student B experienced a change in her acceptance and uptake of EA feedback (from non-acceptance to notice and uptake of it). This change reflected that it took Student B time to accept and incorporate EA feedback, and her notice-based incorporation of EA feedback could only help her make superficial advances regarding her learning of EA issues.

There was more evidence from my study that pointed to Student B's superficial acceptance and incorporation of EA feedback. First, sometimes,

Chapter 5　The Interpretation of Non-error Feedback

her acceptance and uptake of Teacher T's EA feedback was based on her understanding of it from the perspective of language. For example, Teacher T wrote down the following coherence comments on Student B's W2:

> ***Student B's original writing:***
> *In the process of her writing, literature served as a guide to provide inspiration.*
> ***Student B's writing with Teacher T's comments:***
> In the process of her writing, literature (**A possible revision: 'the literature work read previously'. This change is made for the purpose of emphasizing previous reading experience.**) served as a guide to provide inspiration.
> (From Teacher T's comments on Student B's W2; Originally in Chinese)

In the retrospective interview, Student B said:

> I memorized this piece of feedback. I feel pointing this out is really good. Previously, I've never paid attention to language issues like this. Look, adding some modifiers to emphasize previous reading experience improves my writing a lot. ...
> (From the retrospective interview with Student B for her W2)

In this example, to a large extent, Teacher T used the revision she suggested in her comments to construct the semantic coherence of Student B's writing. However, what Student B said in the retrospective interview clearly indicated that her acceptance and incorporation (memorization) of it was at a superficial level. This is because she interpreted Teacher T's coherence feedback from the perspective of language and there was a lack of understanding of the intention of teacher feedback.

Second, the actions Student B carried out during the process of interpreting teacher feedback also showed that her acceptance and incorporation of EA feedback was superficial. At the first and second rounds of the feedback-interpretation process, Student B took notes from time to time. In general, she chiefly noted down her questions. For example, Student B often wrote down the following notes: *"What's the problem?"*, *"Details?"*, and *"Is there a problem?"* Student B also wrote down the knowledge she learnt from Teacher T's EA feedback, such as *"Use 'as follows' to connect paragraphs"*, and *"Use modifiers to show your writing sticks to the topic."* These examples provided here indicated that the notes Student B generally took were not only brief and short, but also lacked depth.

Student B also either made mental notes to incorporate Teacher T's EA feedback or just memorized it. When thinking aloud, sometimes Student B spoke aloud: *"Keep this in mind"* *"Pay attention to this when writing next time"* *"Use connectives to be concise next time"*; and so forth. In addition, Student B kept highlighting the key words (e.g., *"logical structure"* *"cohesion and coherence"* *"well-developed argumentation"*, and *"clear overall organization"*) contained in Teacher T's EA comments when she was interpreting teacher feedback. In Student B's opinion, highlighting the key words in teacher comments was also a type of memorization. Generally, these approaches Student B often used to incorporate EA feedback showed that her cognitive and behavioral acceptance and incorporation of teacher feedback was limited.

Regarding Student B's non-acceptance to acceptance of teacher feedback on EA issues, it seemed that there was a turning point. When commenting on a supporting example in Student B's W2, Teacher T explained why she considered that the example Student B used was not argumentative as follows:

... Besides, the logic in your sentence was not clear: There is no logical relationship between the two facts that Michael Yu got something new from literature and that he changed from a farmer's son to a person well known in the world.

(From Teacher T's comments on Student B's W2; Originally in Chinese.)

In the retrospective interview for her W2, Student B said that, in the first round of feedback interpretation, she did not understand what Teacher T meant by commenting *"The logic ... was not clear"*. In her mind, "logic" was a construct too abstract to be understood. However, in the second round of feedback interpretation, by re-reading Teacher T's explanatory comment *"There is no logical relationship between the two facts ..."*, Student B suddenly realized that there was a lack of a cause-effect relationship between "the two facts" she mentioned in her writing and that cause-effect relationship was "the logic" Teacher T referred to in her feedback. Based on this realization, Student B accepted Teacher T's feedback on her supporting example about Michael Yu and considered Teacher T's feedback *"enlightening and inspiring"*. After that, Student B seemed to become receptive to teacher feedback.

5.3.3 Student B's Emotional Acceptance of EA Feedback

Like Student A, Student B's emotional acceptance of EA feedback also underwent a change. When responding to teacher feedback on her W1, she said that she was *"surprised" "stuck" "confused"*, and *"defensive"*. As can be seen in the example quoted in Section 5.3.2 (the example about Student B's understanding of EA feedback from the perspective of language), Student B highly valued some of Teacher T's feedback on her W2, saying that *"I feel pointing this out is really good."* From the emotional perspective, Student B's acceptance of Teacher T's EA feedback moved from resistance to continuous acceptance of it.

5.4 Student C's Acceptance and Incorporation of EA Feedback

Similar to Sections 5.2 and 5.3, this section is organized according to the following headings: a general description of how Student C approached teacher feedback (5.4.1), Student C's cognitive and behavioral and affective acceptance and incorporation of EA feedback (5.4.2 & 5.4.3).

5.4.1 How Student C Approached Teacher Feedback: A General Description

The first step Student C usually took when interpreting teacher feedback was to go through her own writing first. She said: "*I need to read my writing first to refresh my memory.*" Then, Student C went through three rounds of the feedback-interpreting process. During this process, she did not want to miss any teacher comment. She said:

> I'm sure that Teacher T commented on my writing from the beginning to the end; so, I want to follow the same sequence she went through when she commented on my writing. By reading in this way, I'll miss nothing from teacher feedback.
> (From the retrospective interview with Student C for her W1)

In the second round of feedback interpretation, Student C said that she summarized her thoughts and ideas that arose from her first round of feedback interpretation and wrote down the greatest problems of her writing. In addition, Student C said: "*I also marked the notes I took down with numbers.*" Then, during the third round of feedback interpretation process, Student C usually corrected some of her language mistakes. At the last stage, Student C sometimes also noted down where a revision was needed and planned to "*fix the major flaw of my [her] writing*" afterwards (Student C rewrote her W1

Chapter 5 The Interpretation of Non-error Feedback

before Teacher T assigned the second writing task to the class.).

5.4.2 Student C's Cognitive and Behavioral Acceptance and Incorporation of EA Feedback

Table 5.3 displays Student C's acceptance and incorporation of Teacher T's EA feedback from the cognitive and behavioral perspective. This section illustrates the findings summarized in this table and reports qualitative findings.

Table 5.3 Student C's Acceptance and Incorporation of EA Feedback

Focus of EA feedback	Accepted	Semi-Accepted	Noticed	Not-Accepted
	Semi-Incorporated			
Supporting Evidence	√ (W2)	√ (W1, W3)		
Cohesion & Coherence	√ (W1, W2, W3)	√ (W1)	√ (W2)	
Topic Statement	√ (W2, W3)	√ (W1)		
(Sub)topic Sentence	√ (W3)			
Conclusion	√ (W3, W2)	√ (W1)		
Overall Organization		√ (W3)		

Student C: Other-Regulated, Semi-Acceptance and -Incorporation of EA Feedback

Table 5.3 indicates that Student C was relatively stable in her general acceptance and incorporation of teacher feedback. She chiefly accepted or semi-accepted the feedback. In the final retrospective interview for teacher feedback on her W3 (the free-technique writing), Student C said that she accepted almost all of Teacher T's EA comments that pointed out her major writing problems and the comments focused on logic issues. Student C, like Teacher T, used "logic" as an encompassing term that referred to both macro- and micro-level "logic" issues such as relevance of supportive arguments, logical sequence of argumentation, and a clear logical flow from one idea/ sentence to next.

However, Student C's data indicated that she mainly semi-incorporated Teacher T's EA feedback. This is because sometimes her acceptance and incorporation of it was based on her assumption about what Teacher T intended to tell her. Here is an example. Teacher T made the following comments on Student C's W1:

> ***Student C's writing:***
>
> *In order to ..., I referred to many books and websites. These resources not only enrich my knowledge but also broaden my horizons.*
>
> ***Student C's writing with Teacher T's comments:***
>
> *In order to ..., I referred to many books and websites. These resources **(The learning process)** not only enrich my knowledge but also broaden my horizons.*

When thinking aloud and responding to this revision Teacher T made, Student C said:

> Teacher T told me to revise "These resources". Probably what Teacher T wanted to tell me was that it isn't the inanimate resources that enriched my knowledge, but the process of learning through resorting to resources that could enrich my knowledge.
>
> (From Student C's think-alouds for her W1)

Furthermore, in the retrospective interview, Student C made the following explanation about her think-alouds:

> At the beginning, I was unable to understand why my writing needed to be modified to 'the learning process'. But I tried to

understand it from Teacher T's perspective and tried to find out the reasons behind her revision. I felt I got her point, though not quite sure about it.

(From the retrospective interview with C for her W1)

To a large extent, Teacher T's revision ("*the learning process*") made that sentence and its preceding sentence ("*In order to ..., I referred to many books and websites*") better connected in meaning; so, it seemed that Teacher T used her revision to help Student C construct cohesion and coherence. However, the above-provided quote showed that although Student C made great effort to understand teacher revision, she did not feel that her understanding of it was adequate and thorough. As such, it is not possible to say this assumption-based interpretation could lead to Student C's full acceptance and incorporation of Teacher T's feedback on cohesion and coherence.

Moreover, Student C also just semi-incorporated Teacher T's feedback on supporting evidence, cohesion and coherence, topic statements, and conclusions because she often did not know how to act on the feedback and she still needed further clarification from the teacher. For example, when thinking aloud, Student C said: "*Teacher T wanted me to insert [conjunction] 'since', but where to insert it?*" She also said: "*then, how to write it to make it supportive?*". Moreover, when taking notes, Student C wrote down her questions about how to act on teacher feedback, such as "*How to revise, and how to open an expository writing?*"

Student C's semi-incorporation of teacher feedback is also reflected in how she took notes. Like Student B, Student C's notes were generally brief and short (e.g., "*1. Pay attention to logic!!!*"). Sometimes, she only used punctuation or marks or underlines to indicate the part of comments she considered important/difficult to act on and to remind herself what could be incorporated into her new writing.

5.4.3 Student C's Emotional Acceptance of EA Feedback

In the retrospective interviews for her W2 and W3 (the exemplification and free-technique writing assignments), Student C stressed that she took a more accepting attitude when interpreting teacher feedback. She gave the following explanation:

> Unlike interpreting Teacher T's feedback on my first writing assignment, I didn't feel defensive this time. To tell the truth, I didn't tell myself that I shouldn't be defensive before reading Teacher T's feedback. This time, the more comments I read, the happier I felt; my teacher often used "or" in her comments and gave me choices.
>
> (From Student C's think-aloud for her W2)

The above quote indicated that, similar to Student B, Student C experienced a change in her emotional acceptance of teacher feedback. That is, emotionally, her reaction to Teacher T's EA feedback changed from defensiveness to receptiveness.

5.5 How the Students' Acceptance and Incorporation of EA Feedback were Decided

My study found how the students' acceptance and incorporation of EA feedback were decided was related to

1) the depth of students' cognitive processing of EA feedback,
2) the interaction among their cognitive, affective, and behavioral

engagement, and

3) student-context interactions.

These findings are reported in Sub-sections 5.5.2, 5.5.3 and 5.5.4. Before presenting these findings, first I explain Students A, B, and C's cognitive, behavioral, and affective engagement with Teacher T's EA feedback separately (5.5.1). This explanation contextualizes the findings reported after it.

5.5.1 The Students' Cognitive, Behavioral, and Affective Engagement with EA Feedback

A quantification of the think-aloud and retrospective interview data obtained from Students A, B, and C revealed that the process they went through to interpret teacher feedback was a cognitive, behavioral, and affective process. Table 5.4 summarizes the percentages of their cognitive, behavioral and affective engagement with Teacher T's EA feedback.

Table 5.4 The Students' Engagement with EA Feedback

Students' Engagement with EA Feedback	A	B	C
Cognitive Engagement	86.0%	74.2%	77.8%
Behavioral Engagement	6.0%	18.5%	10.7%
Affective Engagement	8.0%	7.3%	11.5%
Total	100%	100%	100%

Table 5.4 indicates that, when Students A, B, and C were processing Teacher T's EA feedback, they (especially Student A) spent a great deal of effort on cognitive operations (e.g., reading teacher feedback). In comparison,

Student B devoted more effort to taking actions (18.5%, e.g., typing in notes, highlighting with colors the key points of teacher feedback). Furthermore, the percentage of Student C's affective engagement with Teacher T's EA feedback was the highest among the three students (11.5%).

In my study, although the students were only asked to cognitively process Teacher T's feedback, Students A, B and C unexpectedly carried out a number of behavioral operations (6%, 18.5% and 10.7% of total engagement respectively). Their behavioral operations included help-seeking operations (e.g., consulting dictionaries installed in mobile phone), (mental/written) note-taking, minor revision, memorization, and key points highlighting.

According to Table 5.4, it seemed that Student A employed far fewer behavioral operations than Student B. The cause of this difference was that Student B frequently highlighted, underlined or marked the key points in the teacher feedback so the frequency count of her behavioral operations was much greater. By comparison, Student A usually wrote longer notes, but seldom just highlighted problems or teacher comments with colors or in boldface. The behavioral operations Student A deployed usually took a long time, but the frequency of occurrence was much less.

Overall, Students A, B, and C's affective engagement with the teacher feedback mainly involved the emotional feelings that were aroused by their affective responses to teacher feedback (e.g., overwhelmed, overjoyed), their affective evaluation of their own writing (e.g., confident), and their affective evaluation of the teacher feedback (e.g., excellent feedback). For example, when commenting on one of Teacher T's feedback comments on cohesion and coherence, Student B said: "*I feel pointing this out is really good.*" Table 5.4 shows that Student C's feedback interpretation was marked by her affective engagement with it (11.5%). In my study, Student C often articulated her emotional responses when responding to Teacher T's EA feedback (e.g., *"Teacher T praised me; I'm overjoyed."*). Student B also often articulated her emotional feelings that arose from interpreting teacher feedback, but Student A chiefly articulated her affective evaluation of the teacher feedback and showed her appreciation of the teacher feedback when thinking aloud.

As for the students' cognitive engagement, Table 5.5 summarizes the percentages of the different cognitive operations the three students carried out.

Table 5.5   Students A, B, and C's Cognitive Engagement with EA Feedback

Cognitive Engagement	A	B	C
(Re)-Reading (A Stretch of Self-Written Text & Feedback)	30.6%	44.7%	30.6%
Processing Operations (E.g., Processing Self-Written Text)	15.3%	0.0%	5.6%
Evaluation Operations (E.g., Evaluating Teacher Feedback)	15.0%	30.6%	26.5%
Analysis Operations (E.g., Analyzing Teacher feedback)	9.6%	2.1%	15.3%
Justification Operations (E.g., justifying Self-Written Text)	4.7%	7.4%	11.2%
Review Operations (E.g., Re-analyzing Teacher Feedback)	10.0%	9.2%	1.5%
Metacognition Operations (E.g., Control of Emotion)	3.7%	1.8%	6.1%
Incorporation Decisions	11.3%	4.2%	3.1%
Total	100%	100%	100%

In Table 5.5, it can be found that several figures stood out (marked in bold). First, the table shows that, comparing with Students A and C, Student B spent a large amount of time and effort on reading Teacher T's EA comments and her own writing (44.7%). Unlike Students A and C, she never analyzed her own writing (0.0%). What is more, although the percentage value of Student B's evaluative operations was comparatively high (30.6%), most of her evaluation operations were her articulation of her disagreement with or inability to understand Teacher T's EA feedback.

According to Table 5.5, Student C's feedback engagement was characterized by the evaluation and interpretation operations (26.5% & 15.3%) she carried out. It seemed that she spent much more time and effort on these operations than Student A did (9.6%). However, this was not exactly the case. Like Student C, a major portion of Student A's time and effort was devoted to analyzing Teacher T's EA feedback. This was found because Student A not only interpreted her own writing (15.3%) and Teacher T's EA feedback (9.6%) but also further analyzed it when she carried out analysis and review operations (10% respectively).

In general, when Student A processed or interacted with Teacher T's EA feedback to decide how to accept and incorporate Teacher T's EA feedback, she usually

- closely read teacher comments and her own writing (**reading operations**),
- critically analyzed her own writing problems **(processing operations)**,
- thoroughly evaluated teacher feedback **(evaluation operations;** e.g., articulating (dis)agreement with Teacher T**)**,
- made great effort to identify and summarize the focus, key points, and implications of Teacher T's EA feedback **(analysis operations)**, and
- reviewed the useful information, key points, and messages implied in Teacher T's EA feedback **(review operations)**.

My study found that Student B's cognitive engagement with EA feedback mainly involved her superficial **(re-)reading and evaluation operations** (about 75% of her cognitive engagement). When going about Teacher T's EA feedback, she usually just (re-)read teacher feedback and responded to it chiefly by asking simple questions (e.g., *"why on earth is it problematic?"*), showing her disagreement with Teacher T (e.g., *"I don't think it's problematic."*), or interpreting Teacher T's EA feedback from the linguistic perspective (e.g., interpretation of coherence feedback as Teacher T's help to improve her use of English).

Similar to Student A, Student C made great efforts to understand why Teacher T provided EA feedback in the way she did, how Teacher T revised her writing, and what was behind Teacher T's EA comments (**evaluation and analysis operations**) so as to accept and incorporate teacher instruction. However, as she often ended her feedback interpretation with questions like *"[if what I wrote were problematic], then what should I do?"* and employed operations to justify her writing (**justifying operations**), she usually processed Teacher T's EA feedback at a moderately deep level.

In summary, Students A, B and C's cognitive, behavioral and affective operations involved their (re)interaction with teacher feedback (e.g., identifying key points of teacher feedback; making connections between feedback; identifying the "what" of teacher feedback), themselves (e.g., articulating expectation for teacher feedback; articulating confidence in writing cohesively and coherently), their teacher (e.g., articulating trust of teacher) and their own writing (e.g., considering writing process). When interactively responding to Teacher T's EA feedback, the students usually assumed the role of a superficial/deep feedback receiver (e.g., when reading and interpreting teacher feedback), a writer (e.g., when reading their own writing), a critic (e.g., when evaluating teacher feedback), a superficial/deeper learner (e.g., when reviewing the useful messages), or a rational decision-maker (e.g., when taking control of their feelings).

5.5.2 Student Decision-Making: The Depth of Students' Cognitive Processing of Teacher Feedback

As shown in Table 5.5, Student B spent a lot of effort on reading Teacher T's EA feedback aloud and reading her own writing (44.7%) but spent a rather limited amount of time and effort on analyzing teacher feedback during feedback interpretation (2.1%). Considering Student B could only superficially and slowly accept and incorporate Teacher T's EA feedback, these numerical results, to some extent, indicated that student decision-making about acceptance and incorporation of teacher feedback somewhat was related to the depth of their processing of it.

The following qualitative analysis of Student A's retrospective interview for her W2 also indicated that there was a connection between the depth of the students' interaction with teacher feedback and their acceptance and incorporation of it. When being interviewed retrospectively, Student A said:

> ... Then I read the comment "Pay attention to the coherence of the supporting details which should go closely around the topic." This means that you need to let your readers see that your details do revolve around your topic [topic sentence], and you need to use sufficient details to illustrate your topic [topic sentence]. Use details appropriately, and then your readers can deeply and comprehensively understand your topic [topic sentence]. This is all that I thought about and realized [when thinking aloud for Teacher T's advice].
>
> (From the retrospective interview with Student A for her W2)

Chapter 5   The Interpretation of Non-error Feedback

Here, by constantly stating "you need ...", it can be seen that Student A accepted and incorporated Teacher T's feedback on supporting evidence and coherence as advisory messages. However, her repeated mention of "readers" showed that she did not simply accept Teacher T's advice as advisory messages. As she interpreted the feedback from the perspective of audience, Student A also accepted and incorporated the implication of Teacher T's intention. That is, the aim of one's writing should be *"your readers can deeply and comprehensively understand your topic."* Moreover, she summarized a rule about what to do when composing new writing (*"use sufficient details to illustrate your topic"*). In general, in this instance, Student A's deep-level processing of Teacher T's EA feedback played an important part in her full acceptance and incorporation of it.

As to Student C's semi-acceptance and -incorporation of teacher feedback (See Section 5.4.2), my study found that it was related to her reading and processing of the feedback at a relatively deep level. For example, Student C sometimes sensed a negative meaning in Teacher T's positive comments on supporting evidence. On Student C's W3, Teacher T commented: *"The structure of this paragraph is fine: statement + exemplification."* From this comment Student C received the following implied message: *"The structure is fine. It means there's still room for improvement. I don't think this [teacher feedback] is real encouragement. But how to improve it [Student C's writing]?"* This quote showed that Student C did not fully accept and incorporate Teacher T's positive feedback (for not receiving real positive feedback and not knowing how to make improvement) largely because she based on the implications of teacher feedback and the depth of her interaction with teacher feedback to make acceptance and incorporation decisions.

In my study, the students read Teacher T's EA feedback in two other ways:

repeated reading of the same piece of teacher feedback and multiple rounds of reading of teacher feedback. These two ways of interacting with teacher feedback, more or less, added depth to the students' processing of the feedback, which then contributed to the students' acceptance and incorporation of it. For example, during thinking-aloud and interview sessions, Student A mentioned from time to time her re-reading of Teacher T's EA feedback and its effect: "*I read the sentence **again** and found it [what Teacher T said in her feedback] was right*"; and "*To tell the truth, at this point I read it **again** and then understood where the problem was.*" These quotes clearly indicated that re-reading and a deeper-level of processing of teacher feedback played a decisive part in Student A's acceptance and uptake of teacher feedback.

As indicated in Sub-sections 5.2.1, 5.3.1, and 5.4.1, Students A, B, and C all went through three rounds of feedback processing. Multiple rounds of reading and interpreting Teacher T's feedback, for example, had a significant effect on Student B's acceptance of Teacher T's comments on supporting evidence. In Sub-section 5.3.2, the example about Michael Yu showed that Student B came to understand, accept, and incorporate Teacher T's feedback on supporting evidence when she re-interacted with it during the second round of feedback interpretation.

5.5.3 Student Decision-Making: The Cognition-Affect-Behaviour Interaction

As indicated at the beginning of this section (5.5), my study found that the three participants' decision-making regarding their acceptance and uptake of EA feedback were related to the integration of their cognitive, behavioral, and affective engagement during feedback interpretation. This finding is illustrated by the following examples. In the retrospective interview for her W2, Student

Chapter 5 The Interpretation of Non-error Feedback

A recalled what was going through her mind when she was thinking aloud for the following teacher feedback:

Student A's Writing:
Literature is just like blooming flowers and its prosperity and diversity if an essential part of development of our civilization.

(From Student A's W2)

Student A's Writing with Teacher T's Comments:
Literature is just like blooming flowers and its prosperity and diversity if an essential part of development of our civilization. (The prosperity and diversity of literature is essential for civilization development. It seems that this sentence is logically problematic. It can be deleted. Using less modifiers to be concise.)

(Originally in Chinese)

The following remarks were Student A's retrospection about her interpretation of the above comments:

Teacher T said that the sentence "The prosperity and diversity of literature is essential for civilization development" seems to be logically problematic. At the first sight of it, it put me on the defensive. I didn't think my writing was problematic and I believed it was logical. But I didn't pass it [teacher feedback] over. I kept focusing on it. I kept thinking. Very shortly, I realized that it was problematic. And then I wasn't defensive any more. Yes, it was problematic. ...

(From the retrospective interview with Student A for her W2)

The above quote clearly indicated the way the cognition-affect and the affect-(meta)cognition interactions contributed to the formation of Student

203

A's decision to accept Teacher T's hedged negative feedback (on cohesion and coherence). Student A first said that Teacher T's negative feedback immediately put her on the defensive, which indicated the influence of the cognition-affect interaction on Student A's refusal to accept and incorporate teacher feedback. Then, she told herself to rationalize her negative emotional reactions and not skip over it. That is to say, the affect-metacognition interaction led to her decision not to move on and to keep carrying out cognitive operations. Overall, on the basis of these cognition-affect and affect-(meta)cognition interactions, Student A's decision to accept teacher feedback ("*Yes, it was problematic.*") was formed. In fact, then, Student A provided a revised version of the problematic sentence. Her revision read as follows:

> The prosperity and diversity of literature contribute to the development of our civilization. We can never neglect the weight of reading literature.

This revision indicated that Student A accepted and incorporated the teacher feedback. To be concise, she deleted *"Literature is just like blooming flowers"* and broke down the original long sentence into two short coherently connected ones. Meanwhile, the revised thesis statement directly stated the importance of literature. This revision Student A made reflected that she cognitively, affectively, and behaviorally accepted and incorporated Teacher T's feedback. Her final decision was made because she was involved in a process during which her (meta)cognition, affect, and behavior were intertwined and inseparable.

Here is another example about the effect of the cognition-behavior-affect interaction on the formation of the students' acceptance and incorporation decisions. As reported in the Methodology Chapter, Teacher T's students were asked to write CET-4 writing tasks. As free model texts for the CET-4 writing

Chapter 5 The Interpretation of Non-error Feedback

tasks are usually available online, the students had access to them if they wanted to consult them. After reading teacher feedback, Student A felt she still had questions about how to use evidence to support topic sentences and how to conclude a piece of writing. She then took some actions (cognition-behavior interaction). She looked up online resources to find model texts and critically analyzed one model text to locate answers to her questions (behavior-cognition interaction). While she cognitively processed the model text she found online, from time to time she pointed out what made her feel excited and what made her feel disappointed (cognition-affect interaction). Then, Student A incorporated a way of writing (using evidence to support topic sentence) she felt excited about (affect-cognition interaction) and intended to save the online document for future reference (affect-cognition-behavior interaction). On the whole, the formation of Student A's decision to accept and incorporate Teacher T's feedback on supporting evidence and conclusions were based on her cognition-behavior-affect.

Students B and C's acceptance and incorporation of Teacher T's EA feedback were also based on their inseparable cognitive, behavioral, and affective engagement with it. For example, when Student B received teacher feedback, she exclaimed: *"Oh, my God, so many problems."* In the retrospective interview for her W1, Student B recalled:

> I was overwhelmed by it [teacher feedback]. I felt I got stuck in Teacher T's feedback. All I thought about at that time was Teacher T's criticism that I just repeated what I said in the topic sentence. I couldn't think straight at all. ... My defensiveness prevented me from accepting Teacher T's feedback, although 'defensiveness' may not be the exact word to describe what I felt at that time.
>
> (From the retrospective interview with Student B for her W1)

In the retrospective interview for her W2, Student C said:

> To tell the truth, if I got 'sugar-coated pills' [e.g., praise-criticism paired feedback], I would feel very cheerful and could accept teacher feedback more easily. The teacher's criticism immediately created a feeling of resistance in me.
> (From the retrospective interview with Student C for her W2)

The above two examples showed that the cognition and behavior that the two participants experienced during feedback interpretation were heavily emotion-involved and their interrelatedness determined their acceptance and incorporation of Teacher T's EA feedback. Due to her negative feelings, Student B could not even think, let alone accept the feedback and act on it. Student C's expectation for "sugar-coated pills" (a type of hedged feedback) and her dislike for "criticism" (that is, direct negative comments) controlled her thinking and behavior as well, and were inseparable to influence her cognitive and behavioral and emotional acceptance and incorporation of teacher feedback.

5.5.4 Student Decision-Making: Student-Context Interactions

In my study, the students' feedback beliefs were found to correlate with their acceptance and incorporation of Teacher T's EA feedback in general. In the background interview, Student A said that she valued organization feedback and would willingly and widely accept feedback on this issue. In practice, there was a consistency between what she said in the background interview and her widespread acceptance and incorporation of Teacher T's organization-related EA feedback. In the background interview, Student B believed that she was "a lazy learner" who preferred rote learning. Her frequent use of memorization to incorporate teacher feedback was also consistent with her belief about herself. Student C believed that she was a semi-resistor to teacher feedback. It seemed that her actual semi-acceptance could be linked to what she stated in the background interview.

However, the students' acceptance and incorporation of teacher feedback was not always informed by their beliefs. For example, Student B believed that she would not spend too much time on positive feedback; but in fact, her acceptance and incorporation of teacher feedback was greatly influenced by her expectation to receive more positive feedback. As noted at the outset of Section 5.5, the students' decision-making regarding their acceptance and uptake of EA feedback was also mediated by various student-context interactions (including student interactions with text-level contexts, personal contexts, interpersonal contexts, and sociocultural contexts). An explanation of these interactions behind the students' decision-making toward their acceptance and incorporation of teacher feedback makes up this sub-section. It is organized around the following themes: student-feedback interaction (5.5.4.1), student-self interaction (5.5.4.2), student-teacher interaction (5.5.4.3), student-writing interaction (5.5.4.4) and student-sociocultural/ instructional background interactions (5.5.4.5).

5.5.4.1 Student Decision-Making: Student-Feedback Interaction

As reported in Sub-section 5.5.1, when the students' feedback-processing procedures were in operation, they kept interacting with teacher feedback (e.g., reading, evaluating, analyzing and reviewing teacher feedback). This section gives an overview of the students' acceptance and uptake of Teacher T's EA feedback through their interactions with the text-level contexts (feedback content, feedback delivery approaches, feedback intensity, feedback clarity, and feedback location).

Student Interaction with Feedback Content

My study found there was a close relationship between student-feedback content interactions and the extent to which teacher feedback was accepted and incorporated. For example, Teacher T entered the following comments on the opening paragraph of Student A's W2: "*You go to the point directly ☺; try to combine sentences when necessary or if you can.*" In the retrospective interview, Student A explained her noticing of Teacher T's EA feedback as follows:

> I just had a glimpse at them. The comments are very simple, and there's nothing significant in them. Then I moved on and began to read paragraph two.
> (From the retrospective interview with Student A for her W2)

In this example, Student A's neglect of teacher feedback resulted from the interaction between her expectation for "significant" feedback (student expectation/affect) and the lack of new information in Teacher T's comments. As Teacher T was expected to provide "significant" feedback but failed, Student A then was not greatly engaged in making decisions and her decision (to move on quickly to read the following paragraph) was quickly formed.

Student Interaction with Feedback Delivery Approaches

When Student A was implementing evaluation and analysis operations (See Table 5.5), her processing of Teacher T's explanatory comments was found to directly influence her total acceptance of Teacher T's combination comments. For instance, on one of the supporting examples used in Student A's W2, Teacher T commented:

> This example not clearly stated (originally underlined and in Chinese). Not that effective. Can a description of details

[in literature works] enliven us (originally underlined and in Chinese)? Pay attention to the relevance of the supporting details which should go closely around the topic.

(From Teacher T's comments on Student A's W2)

In the retrospective interview, Student A explicitly talked about the great impact of Teacher T's explanation ("*go closely around the topic*") on her understanding and acceptance of the above comments:

After reading the first two points, I still couldn't gain an insight into my problem. Then I came across the point 'go closely around the topic', with which I immediately realized readers need to see the topic [sentence] is well-supported all the time. ...

(From the retrospective interview with Student A for her W2)

Student C's interaction with Teacher T's hedged comments had a strong influence on her acceptance decisions in general. Regarding the hedged feedback Teacher T provided on her W2, Student C commented:

This time Teacher T gave me choices and it's up to me to choose which one to use. In her comments, she used 'or' quite a lot. Thus, this time I had a less defensive attitude toward her comments.

(From the retrospective interview with Student C for her W2)

This example clearly showed that Student C's willingness to accept teacher feedback was grounded in her appreciative interaction with Teacher T's use of hedges to give students choices.

Moreover, both Students B and C reported, because Teacher T provided more positive and hedged feedback on their W2 and W3 than on their W1, they took a more accepting attitude when interacting with teacher feedback. In the retrospective interview for her W2, Student B said she could patiently and carefully read Teacher T's feedback because it pointed out many strengths of her writing and she felt happy when reading them. Student C similarly recalled that she accepted much more of the EA feedback Teacher T provided on her W2 than on her W1 for Teacher T commented on her W2 like a friend.

Sometimes Student B might have misunderstood Teacher T's feedback on micro-level (e.g., inter-sentential level) coherence as language feedback (misunderstanding-based acceptance and incorporation). To some extent, this was because Teacher T's feedback on micro-level coherence was often delivered in the form of revision and lacked further explanation. That is to say, when the changes Teacher T made via her revision greatly improved the quality of student writing but no explanation was made about these changes, it would be easy for the student to interpret her revision as a type of language feedback. However, Student A (high-level student writer) did not seem to have the same problem; as such, it was probably the interaction of student ability and the teacher's feedback delivery approaches that brought about Student B's problems with acceptance and incorporation of coherence feedback.

Student Interaction with Feedback Intensity

In my study, feedback intensity referred to the degree to which teacher feedback repeatedly targeted the same issue. In relation to student decision-making, my study found that student interaction with feedback intensity was also an important interactional factor. Below are examples.

In Student A's case, feedback intensity appeared to consistently influence her acceptance of teacher feedback. For example, when approaching Teacher T's feedback on supporting evidence the second time, Student A said: *"This problem is the same as the one in the paragraph above"*, which suggested that, to a large extent, she understood and accepted what Teacher T said in her comments at both times. When Student C recognized the same issues were targeted the second time, her interpretation of this type of feedback was fast and her decision to accept it was made quickly as well.

In the retrospective interview for her W2, Student B explained how she accepted and incorporated Teacher T's comment *"Change 'one' to 'you, your'"*: *"One can gradually improve his writing by reading literature."* About it, Student B said:

> At first sight I thought this was the coherence issue that had already been commented on above. I also immediately understood 'his' [highlighted with grey color by Teacher T] in this sentence should be revised as 'your'. Later, I took notes about this in my second round of feedback interpretation.
> (From the retrospective interview with Student B for her W2)

In this example, the rationale behind Student B's quick decision to incorporate Teacher T's revisions into her notes was because she had already processed a similar piece of feedback that addressed the same issue (i.e., cohesion and coherence) before and the intensity of the feedback led to her quick decision (e.g., as shown by her remark *"At first sight I thought this was the coherence issue that had already been commented on above."*).

Student Interaction with Clarity of Teacher Feedback

Student A's interaction with the clarity of teacher feedback enabled her to decide to accept Teacher T's EA feedback as well. On the second body paragraph of Student A's W1, Teacher T wrote the following combination comments in both Chinese (comments underlined) and English (comments not underlined):

> As for this paragraph, the beginning sentence is clear. That is, social practice can provide us with a platform for communication and cooperation. What follows it should further develop this idea and provide relevant supporting evidence. The following sentences should provide details to further explain or illustrate about how or why it helps to communicate or cooperate. But, your following sentences fail to do that. Instead, you didn't give that coherent ideas.
>
> (Teacher T's comments on Student A's W1; The translation is mine.)

In the retrospective interview, Student A provided a simple explanation for her acceptance and incorporation of Teacher T's comments. She said she accepted and incorporated this feedback mainly due to its clarity: "*The key is what Teacher T said is crystal clear, no matter whether it's written in English or in Chinese.*"

Student C tended to semi-accept or just read Teacher T's feedback on supporting evidence when teacher feedback was not clear and she was unable to comprehend it. For instance, when she saw one of Teacher T's suggestions ("*Thus, if revised,* **it** *would discuss three abilities required for debating. The structure could be much clearer and more logical.*"), she just went on reading the next piece of teacher feedback because she was unable to understand what "it" represented. In this instance, Student C's failure to understand the unclear key word "it" stopped her further interacting with teacher feedback and initiating a decision-making process.

Student Interaction with the Suitability of Feedback to the Students' Existing Knowledge/Ability

Whether teacher feedback was suitable to the students' existing knowledge/

ability affected their acceptance of Teacher T's EA feedback on various issues. For example, when interpreting Teacher T's feedback on her W1, Student B often articulated her inability to understand the feedback, saying *"Why is it illogical? This is my question at that time. Then I didn't do anything about it and moved on to the next comment."* The question Student B raised when approaching the feedback clearly indicated that it was beyond her ability to deal with it, and its incomprehensibility led her to decide to ignore it and not accept it.

In Student B's W2, one of Teacher T's comments on cohesion and coherence said:

> In general, the three paragraphs in the body part aren't coherent in terms of your use of personal pronouns. You used 'one' 'his', and 'you' in three paragraphs respectively. It's necessary to be coherent as a whole.

During her think-aloud, Student B responded: *"This is the first time I noticed this issue; I didn't know it before. I must use personal conjunctions coherently. ... I'll pay attention to this issue next time."* This example illustrated how the match between the information contained in teacher comments and Student B's knowledge gap determined her acceptance and incorporation of teacher feedback.

My study found that Students B and C's reaction to Teacher T's feedback on their conclusion seemingly was subject to their knowledge and capability of creating a quality conclusion. For example, Student B acknowledged she just noticed Teacher T's conclusion feedback on her W2 due to her inability to write a conclusion, saying:

> To tell the truth, I don't know how to produce a well-written

concluding paragraph. When interpreting the conclusion
comments, I only thought about my inability to conclude my
writing with a summary, and then I went on to the next comment.

(From the retrospective interview with Student B for her W2)

Student Interaction with Feedback Location

The location of teacher feedback was found to play an interactional part in Student B's acceptance of it. For instance, in the retrospective interview for her W1, Student B explained her non-acceptance of Teacher T's feedback on thesis statements for it was written at the end of the paragraph:

I feel it left me no impression and it was as if I'd never ever read
it before. When thinking aloud, probably I just glimpsed at it. …
Usually, I just shoot a glimpse at the feedback placed at the end of
a paragraph. I finish reading it in a flash.

(From the retrospective interview with Student B for her W1)

Moreover, when Student B felt that it was difficult linking Teacher T's EA comments on her W1 with her writing problems, she chose not to "*give much attention to them*" either. In brief, my study found that two types of feedback locations might shape Student B's acceptance of Teacher T's EA feedback: feedback located at the end of a paragraph and feedback standing alone or far from the issue it addressed. In those cases, Student B might just read it or failed to notice it because of its position.

However, considering Student B only mentioned the influence of feedback location in the retrospective interview for her W1, the location of feedback might not be the single factor that affected her assimilation of teacher feedback. As teacher feedback on her W1 overwhelmed Student B, the reason why he could not link teacher comments and her writing problems was that feedback amount as an integral factor was related to her decision-making.

Student Interaction with Feedback Actionability

In my study, Student C often took feedback actionability into consideration when she was asked to make evaluations. She felt Teacher T's coherence feedback was not that useful because it often merely pointed out problems and she could not act on it. On the other hand, she believed that Teacher T's feedback on topic sentences was quite helpful because of its actionability.

5.5.4.2 Student Decision-Making: Student-Writing Context Interaction

When to decide whether to fully/partly accept, just read, or reject Teacher T's EA feedback, Student C usually took the contexts in which her writing took place into consideration. A clear example of this comes from Student C's think-aloud for her W2. In response to Teacher T's comments on the conclusion ("... *The three concluding sentences are not logical, or lack in logic; they also failed to refer back to the main topic.*"), Student C accepted Teacher T's "criticism" without reservation after considering how her conclusion was written:

> I wrote this concluding paragraph in a self-study English class. My mind wasn't very clear at that time since I just wanted to quickly finish it in class. In haste, I couldn't organize my thoughts well at all.
>
> (From the retrospective interview with Student C for her W2)

This quote illustrated that, by considering the situation in which her writing was composed, Student C seemed to find Teacher T's criticism was acceptable.

5.5.4.3 Student Decision-Making: Student-Self Interaction

In my study, there were instances where Students A, B and C either partly accepted or refused to accept Teacher T's EA feedback because they exercised agency and interacted with their self-regulatory strength when processing teacher feedback. My study found the students' acceptance and incorporation of Teacher T's EA feedback were particularly associated with their interaction with the following three student agency-related factors: ① students' self-efficacy belief (i.e., students' confidence in their writing), ② students' expectations/ preference (for teacher feedback written in a certain way), ③ students' motivation to deal with teacher feedback, ④ students' prior knowledge of their writing problems. The relevant findings are reported below.

Students' Self-Efficacy Belief: Students' Confidence in Their Own Writing
In my study, the students' decisions about their acceptance and incorporation of Teacher T's EA feedback were influenced by their confidence in their own writing and their views about writing. Student A had a great confidence in her understanding and use of cohesion and coherence, which might have been a decisive factor in her decisions to semi-accept or to reject Teacher T's feedback on it. Here is an example. On Student A's W3, Teacher T provided the following suggestion and explanation: *"'Since' is much better. 'while' emphasizes 'happening-together', but here it should be cause-effect relationship."* Student A only semi-accepted this feedback from Teacher T. Her explanation in the retrospective interview was: *"'Since' is better, but 'while' isn't wrong."* Student A's response to Teacher T showed that she had confidence in her use of *"while"* and as a result, she semi-accepted Teacher T's feedback.

Student B's think-alouds and retrospective interviews revealed she was generally satisfied with her own writing, and there was a cause-effect relationship between her confidence in her own writing and her decision to reject Teacher T's EA feedback. During think-aloud sessions related to her W1, Student B often said:

No, this [what Teacher T said in her feedback] isn't right. It [The structure of my arguments] isn't confusing.

I don't think it's [the topic sentence] problematic. This is because I think it connected the opening paragraph and the following paragraphs very well.

(From Student B's think-aloud for her W1)

The above quotes indicated that Student B immediately denied what Teacher T said in her EA comments, and her refusal to take it up was closely associated with her self-confidence as a writer (e.g., as shown by her remark "*I don't think...*").

In the case of Student C, the example given in Sub-section 5.5.2 (about Student C's interpretation of the comment "*statement + exemplification is fine*") showed that one of the main reasons why she was resistant to fully accepting Teacher T's positive comment about her argumentation was that she picked up extra negative messages out of the feedback. In the meanwhile, there was another reason why she decided to partly accept the teacher feedback. She also said the following in the retrospective interview: "*What Teacher T meant was there was room for improvement, but I feel it has already been good enough.*" That is to say, Student C's confidence in her own writing played an interactional role in her refusal to take Teacher T's feedback.

Students' Expectations/Preference

The students' verbal reports during think-alouds and interviews showed that their acceptance of Teacher T's EA feedback was influenced by their expectations. For example, Student A just mainly acknowledged she noticed the feedback on her W3. She associated it with her expectation for helpful teacher feedback:

I must have an expectation. I anticipate that each of my writings exhibits more problems. Or, in this piece of writing, I probably have solved the problems Teacher T identified before. But the teacher should have a higher expectation for their students' writing, and I should be told to do more to improve. This time, by comparison, it [teacher feedback] isn't as helpful for my growth as what I got before.

(From the retrospective interview with Student A for her W3)

In the retrospective interview for her W2, Student B commented: *"Now I just realized I prefer positive feedback. Because of it, I'm interested in reading the last piece of feedback [end comments usually beginning with positive feedback] closely and carefully."* Student B's remarks showed that her expectation/preference for positive feedback shaped her reading of teacher feedback, which would in turn shape her decisions about how to accept and incorporate teacher feedback. In the case of Student C, as mentioned in Sub-section 5.5.3, she expected to get hedged feedback ("sugared pills"). That is to say, if this expectation was matched, her decision to fully accept Teacher T's EA feedback could be made more easily.

Students' Motivation to Deal with Teacher Feedback

The students' acceptance and incorporation of Teacher T's EA feedback were also found to be affected by their motivation to deal with teacher feedback. For example, on Student A's W3, Teacher T commented: *"This connective made your support very well-connected."* In the retrospective interview, Student A said: *"I just read it and moved on. It's unnecessary for me to spend time on it [feedback on connectives]. It [connective feedback] isn't my focus of attention."* In this example, Student A just acknowledged she noticed Teacher T's comment on connectives but she thought that it was of no great

Chapter 5   The Interpretation of Non-error Feedback

importance and her motivation to putting effort into it was not high.

Here is another example of the connection between student motivation and their acceptance and incorporation of teacher feedback. On Student C's W2, Teacher T pointed out that the pronoun *"ones"* she used in her writing should be replaced by the noun *"aspects"*. Student C only read this revision and then moved to the next comment. In the retrospective interview, she explained her actions as follows: *"At that time [when thinking aloud], I felt it was a trivial matter. [Therefore,] I thought almost nothing about it and just scanned through it."* In this instance, it appeared what was crucial to Student C's acceptance of teacher feedback was her motivation.

Students' Prior Knowledge of Their Own Problems

Students B and C's advance awareness of their own problems had a great influence on their acceptance and incorporation of Teacher T's feedback. Sometimes, they fully accepted Teacher T's feedback on cohesion and coherence due to their prior knowledge of their writing problems. As a simple example, on Student B's W2, Teacher T provided an advisory comment: *"Avoid using the same connective repeatedly."* Although Teacher T's comment was written bluntly, Student B accepted it without question. She said: *"I forgot to revise it before submission."* Her explanation suggested that she had realized there was a problem when writing, and her knowledge of it was decisive in her quick decision to fully accept Teacher T's feedback.

Below is an example related to Student C's immediate acceptance of Teacher T's cohesion and coherence feedback. On her W1, Teacher T wrote the following comments: *"'Yourself', revise it as 'debaters' so as to maintain consistency of pronouns."* When thinking aloud, Student C made a split-second decision to completely accept it: *"Absolutely true! It's necessary to revise 'yourself' to 'debaters'."* The rationale behind this decision was also

219

her prior knowledge of her writing problems: *"I have mixed up 'you', 'we', and other pronouns since high school."*

5.5.4.4 Student Decision-Making: Student-Teacher Interaction

Based on the findings of my study, the students' acceptance of teacher feedback might also be determined by their "interaction" with the feedback provider. When Teacher T's feedback was approached, Students A, B and C sometimes took teacher attitudes towards feedback provision into consideration and then decided whether to accept teacher feedback or not. For example, Teacher T wrote the following EA feedback on Student A's W2:

> The supporting examples you used are not relevant enough. ...
> The first example can show the point of 'having a meaningful life', but you lack an example to show the point of 'having a happy life'.
>
> (From Teacher T's comments on Student A's W2)

When thinking aloud and being interviewed for it, Student A said that she had already forgotten why she included two points in her sub-topic sentence (*"Reading literature encourages and helps us to have a meaningful and happy life"*) when composing her writing. She fully accepted it because she believed that the information Teacher T provided in her comments was sufficiently detailed. As illustrated earlier, Student A felt that Teacher T's EA feedback on her W3 was *"simple"* and *"wasn't so helpful as before"*. When she felt that *"probably she [Teacher T] didn't treat it [feedback provision] seriously this time"*, she chose to attend to teacher feedback carelessly.

On the third argument of Student A's W2, Teacher T commented:

> Your argumentation of the third topic sentence is not that

convincing, or it fails to directly support your idea about inspiration. Try this: For example, we can often draw inspiration from the amazing life experiences described in the literature work. ...

(From Teacher T's Feedback on Student A's W2)

In the retrospective interview, Student A made the following explanation for her semi-acceptance of the above comments during the first round of her feedback interpretation:

It didn't take me a lot of time to think about these comments. This was because the same problem had already been pointed out twice. When I read 'it fails to directly support your idea', I knew Teacher T told me again that my support was irrelevant. When writing feedback, she always paid attention to details like this. ... But there was another point: I didn't think Teacher T fully understood what I meant. ... If she were here, I'd like to have a talk with her about it. ...

(From the retrospective interview with Student A for her W2)

Student A's retrospection indicated that, on the one hand, she accepted Teacher T's feedback on supporting evidence because she considered that Teacher T provided detailed feedback and undertook feedback provision seriously. On the other hand, she refused to completely accept Teacher T's feedback for she felt Teacher T failed to understand what she meant. This example showed how Student A's acceptance and incorporation of teacher feedback was influenced by her consideration of the teacher's attitudes toward writing feedback and the teacher's understanding of her writing. However, in the second round of her feedback interpretation, Student A fully accepted and incorporated this feedback by interacting with it from the perspective of teacher intention.

In Sub-section 5.5.4.1, Students A, B, and C all used feedback intensity to judge which EA issue Teacher T treated more seriously, and then, based on teacher attitudes, to decide whether to accept it or not. They all tried to incorporate Teacher T's feedback on supporting evidence and coherence because they felt Teacher T devoted most of her effort to these issues and they frequently encountered feedback on these issues. This finding also showed that feedback factors (feedback intensity) and the students' construction of their teacher are often intertwined and it is hard to single out the feedback itself as the main influencing factor that students might use in deciding how to accept and incorporate teacher feedback.

In addition, the teacher-student relationship was greatly involved in Student C's acceptance and uptake of feedback. Specifically, Student C's acceptance and uptake of Teacher T's EA feedback were influenced by a power-equality relationship and a relationship of trust. According to Student C, she incorporated more teacher feedback when Teacher T commented *"like a kind friend"* and teacher feedback reflected a friendly equal relationship than when Teacher T commented *"as an authoritative teacher"* and she received direct feedback. Student C was also influenced by having a trusting teacher-student relationship. This could be observed by what Student C thought aloud on different occasions: *"Of course, the feedback Teacher T provided is right; after all, she's a university English teacher."*

5.5.4.5 Student Decision-Making: Student-Macro/Micro Context Interaction

As mentioned in Sub-section 5.5.4.1, Students B and C both said they did not know how to conclude her writing. According to them, the set format their

Chapter 5 The Interpretation of Non-error Feedback

high school teacher asked them to follow strictly when writing the conclusion of their exposition had been ingrained in their writing practice, although they knew it was only a technique to gain high scores in the National Tertiary Matriculation Examination. When interpreting Teacher T's conclusion feedback on her W1, Student C did not fully accept it because she thought what Teacher T said (*"The conclusion is not very convincing."*) seemed to contradict the set format that her high school teacher had taught her and could not help her attain high scores in examinations. In this sense, Student C's semi-acceptance of Teacher T's conclusion feedback was in fact the result of the interaction between her sociocultural background (i.e., the traditional examination culture in China), her writing instruction background and the gap of her knowledge and ability related to writing the concluding paragraph.

5.6 Chapter Summary

Based on a quantitative and qualitative analyses of background interview, think-aloud, retrospective interview, and document data, this chapter reports findings related to the micro-level classroom contextual information, the students' acceptance and uptake of Teacher T's EA feedback, and the students' decision-making regarding their acceptance and incorporation of Teacher T's EA feedback.

Concerning Students A, B, and C's acceptance and incorporation of EA feedback, my study reported the following findings:

1) **Student A: self-regulated, deep-level acceptance and incorporation of EA feedback (cognitively and behaviorally)**
    My study found that Student A *understood, and agreed with* most of Teacher T's EA feedback on her W1 and W2, and she also *summarized*

and *internalized* the rhetorical knowledge contained in Teacher T's EA feedback on her W1 and W2 (mainly through her self-initiated thoughts and actions such as searching for a model text online and analyzing it critically). Moreover, after processing the teacher feedback, Student A took down notes which included her summary of the teacher feedback, her reflections on it, and her solutions about how to revise her writing.

2) **Student A: decreasing incorporation of EA feedback (cognitively and behaviorally)**

Student A's incorporation of Teacher T's feedback on cohesion/coherence and supporting evidence gradually decreased after she processed Teacher T's feedback on her W2. This is because she felt that she had mastered the genre/rhetorical knowledge contained in Teacher T's previous EA feedback and Teacher T's EA feedback on her W3 provided no new genre/rhetorical knowledge.

3) **Student B: slow, increasing acceptance and incorporation of EA feedback (cognitively and behaviorally)**

Student B could not understand Teacher T's EA feedback on her W1. She did not begin to understand, agree with, and incorporate Teacher T's EA feedback (especially EA feedback on supporting evidence) until she processed Teacher T's EA feedback on her W2.

4) **Student B: passive, superficial incorporation of EA feedback (cognitively and behaviorally)**

Student B mainly memorized and marked the key points in Teacher T's EA feedback.

5) **Student C: other-regulated acceptance and incorporation of EA feedback (cognitively and behaviorally)**

Student C generally could understand and agree with Teacher T's EA feedback, but after processing Teacher T's feedback, she still had questions regarding how to use the cause-and-effect technique, how to use evidence to support topic sentences, and how to use some cohesion. She still needed the teacher's or others' clarification about EA issues.

6) **Students B and C: misunderstanding/assumption-based acceptance and incorporation of EA feedback (cognitively and behaviorally)**

Students B and C sometimes accepted Teacher T's feedback on micro-level coherence or supporting evidence without a clear understanding of Teacher T's intention. Student B sometimes accepted Teacher T's feedback on micro-level coherence as language feedback or she sometimes disagreed with Teacher T's feedback on supporting evidence. Student C sometimes accepted Teacher T's feedback on micro-level coherence based on guessing Teacher T's intention.

7) **Students A, B, and C: shifting emotional acceptance of EA feedback (emotionally)**

When Student A processed teacher feedback, she changed from expressing appreciation of it to expressing dissatisfaction with it (because she felt she received no new information from Teacher T's EA feedback on her W3). Students B and C did not think they emotionally accepted Teacher T's feedback on their W1, but they thought they emotionally accepted Teacher T's feedback on their W2 and W3.

As to how the students decided to accept and incorporate the various EA comments, my study found that ① it was related to the depth of students' cognitive processing of EA feedback, ② it was associated with the interaction among the students' cognitive, affective, and behavioral engagement with EA feedback, and ③ it was mediated by the student-context interactions.

In my study, the contextual factors that were found to be important in the students' decisions to accept or reject Teacher T's EA feedback were ① text-level contexts (teacher feedback & writing context about when and where writing takes place), ② personal contexts (student belief, student confidence, student expectation, student motivation and student knowledge and ability), ③ social context (e.g., student-teacher relationship) and ④ sociocultural context (examination culture).

In brief, the findings showed that the students' acceptance and uptake of Teacher T's EA feedback varied dramatically from one to the other. In the following chapter, findings on RQ3 indicate more individual variation.

Chapter 6 The Feedback Process: Its Effectiveness and Helpfulness

6.0 Introduction

This chapter provides answers to RQ3 (*According to the student and the teacher, to what extent does the construction and interpretation of EA feedback help students improve, if it is considered effective?*). The data I collected at different points in time (the ongoing and final interview data during and at the end of the study) and from different sources (both the teacher and the students) led to the following answers to RQ3:

1) effectiveness of the construction and interpretation of EA feedback (6.1);
2) student changes as feedback receivers (6.2); and
3) the helpfulness of teacher feedback on various EA issues and positive/ negative EA feedback (6.3).

This chapter ends with a summary of the key findings on RQ3 (6.4), as well as a summary of all findings to paint the picture of the construction and interpretation of EA feedback and its effectiveness (6.5).

6.1 Effectiveness of the Feedback Process

This section contains findings from the ongoing interviews and the final assessment interviews (6.1.1–6.1.2). To a large extent, both confirmed the effectiveness of the construction and interpretation of EA feedback.

6.1.1 Findings from the Ongoing Interviews

Table 6.1 summarizes the participants' ongoing ratings of the effectiveness of the feedback-and-interpretation process over a course of one semester. Teacher T and the students' ratings showed that they perceived the feedback interaction effective in general.

Table 6.1 Effectiveness of the Construction and Interpretation of EA Feedback

Feedback Interaction	Participants' Ratings			
	Teacher T	Student A	Student B	Student C
W1-Related Interaction			80%	80%
W2-Related Interaction	80%–90%	90%	90%	90%
W3-Related Interaction			90%	85%
Helpfulness Percentage	80%–90%	90%	87%	85%

(Note: W1=the first cause-effect writing task; W2=the second exemplification writing task; W3=the third free-technique writing task)

When asked in each of the three ongoing interviews the question about the effectiveness of feedback interactions, Teacher T approached the issue mainly from the perspectives of understandability and the students' understanding of her feedback. Teacher T felt the feedback communication was effective because her feedback was easy to understand and the students could understand most of it. According to Teacher T's assessment, her EA feedback on each of the students' three writing assignments was 80%–90% effective/understandable. For example, in the ongoing interview related to her feedback on the students' W1, Teacher T reported: *"Generally speaking, I don't think*

Chapter 6 The Feedback Process: Its Effectiveness and Helpfulness

the students had a problem to understand 80-90% of my feedback comments."

Student A seemed to confirm Teacher T's assessment. In ongoing interviews, she said:

1) Basically, we [Teacher T and A] could understand each other very well.
(From the W1-related ongoing interview with Student A)

2) I'm certain that I can understand most of my teacher's EA feedback very well. (From the W2-related ongoing interview with Student A)

3) It's easy to follow most of my teacher's EA feedback comments.
(From the W3-related ongoing interview with Student A)

Student A's remarks showed that, similar to Teacher T, she saw the effectiveness of the feedback interactions from the perspective of teacher-student mutual understanding (based on the first quote given above) and the students' understanding of teacher feedback (based on the second and third quotes). She believed that the teacher-student communication went very well. Numerically, Student A reported each time it was 90% effective.

In Student B's mind, the teacher-student interactions she experienced were not equally effective. Student B felt the communication related to the W1 was the least effective (80%), while the other two rounds (related to her W2 and W3) were more effective (90%). Student B used the following example to explain when she felt the teacher-student interaction became more effective:

Take the logic issue for example. My teacher pointed out there was a logic problem in my first writing, but I couldn't understand it until now [when interpreting Teacher T's feedback on her W2]. ... This time I feel it suddenly clicked and I could understand and accept most of Teacher T's EA feedback.

(From the W2-related ongoing interview with Student B)

Student C seemed to equate effective feedback with a two-way dialogue in which both the teacher and the student were involved. In the ongoing interviews related to her W1, W2, and W3, Student C pointed out the three rounds of two-way communication were 80%, 90%, and 85% effective respectively. She believed that W1-related dialogue or communication with Teacher T was not very well established (80%) since Teacher T's EA feedback often *"put her on the defensive"*. To Student C, the communication related to Teacher T's feedback on her W2 was better (90%). She said in the interview: *"I wasn't in a defensive state this time and I strongly felt a sense of involvement."* As to the effectiveness of Teacher T's EA feedback on her W3, Student C said it was in the middle of the previous two (85%).

6.1.2 Findings from the Final Interviews

As explained in the Methodology Chapter, to enhance the reliability and validity of the answers given to RQ3, Teacher T and the students were also asked to evaluate the helpfulness of construction and interpretation of EA feedback in the final assessment interview. Below presents what each participant reported in the final interviews.

Teacher T acknowledged its effectiveness from four perspectives. In the final interview, to the open question *"What do you think of the effectiveness of the feedback-and-interpretation this semester?"*, Teacher T's answer was:

> In my opinion, as to our communication through the feedback, it worked. You see, when commenting on their W2 and W3, I frequently wrote positive comments about the strengths of their writing. In their new writing, what I mentioned before in my feedback wasn't that problematic any more. They, especially Student B, made obvious progress in structure, cohesion and

coherence, and logic, the issues I emphasized in my feedback. I saw the efforts she [Student B] made. In her W2, she followed my feedback on her W1, although it seemed that she just applied my comments mechanically. Students A and C are really good student writers, but they still need help in terms of structure and logic, and they also improved.

(From the final interview with Teacher T)

In this long quote, the four perspectives Teacher T used to support her opinion that the feedback interaction was effective are:

1) the increase in her positive feedback
   (indicated by "*I frequently wrote positive comments…*");
2) the students' cross-assignment improvement (indicated by "*They…made obvious progress*");
3) use of teacher feedback in new writing (indicated by "*I saw the efforts she [Student B] made*" to apply my comments); and
4) satisfaction of student needs (indicated by "*they still need help in terms of structure and logic.*").

In the above quote, Teacher T confirmed the contribution of the feedback interaction to Student B's learning in particular, although she believed Student B could only apply what she said in her EA comments in a mechanical way at first.

However, Teacher T seemed unsure about the extent to which the construction and interpretation of EA feedback was effective since there were no chances to communicate with the students after the commented writing was returned to them. She said:

Constructing and Interpreting Non-error Feedback:
From the Perspective of Sociocognitive Theory

> ... there were no follow-up interactions between us, be it face-to-face or in written form. It's a pity that we didn't have a face-to-face opportunity and none of them gave me a second draft. After their writing was returned to them, no one ever came to me, telling me whether they agreed or disagreed with my comments or sharing with me their ideas about my comments. I felt it's alright even if they came to me to argue for their writing. But I didn't get any direct response from them. I saw the effectiveness of my feedback in their new writing, but I still didn't feel confident about it.
>
> (From the final interview with Teacher T)

Student A believed, via feedback, her interaction with Teacher T was effective overall and she appreciated the way Teacher T wrote feedback. Student A felt Teacher T wrote feedback as if she was creating her own writing, which was clear, systematic and well-structured:

> Without teacher feedback, my pace of improvement would be very, very slow. So, it's really helpful. ... Teacher T not only commented on my specific writing problems but also provide comments at the end of my writing to make a summary. It seemed that she was writing her own article since the comments she wrote from the beginning to the end of my writing seemed to be well connected. I feel this way of writing feedback made her feedback explicit.
>
> (From the final interview with Student A)

However, Student A felt that in some cases Teacher T misunderstood her and their communication did not go very well, but she reported the misunderstandings were not her teacher's fault. They happened because she did not successfully transfer her idea in mind into her English writing. In the final interview, Student A said:

> Generally, there were no communication problems occurring between us. The only problem was that in my writing I failed to get my meaning clearly expressed and Teacher T didn't understand what I wrote. But this didn't happen often, just occasionally.
>
> (From the final interview with Student A)

Student B's answer to the question "*What do you think of the effectiveness of the feedback-and-interpretation process this semester*" was simple. Her response was: "Quite good; a process of becoming better and better." Student B said the communication she and Teacher T engaged in for her W1 was the least effective because what Teacher T wrote and what she could understand did not match: "*It was really difficult to figure out what she meant when reading it for the first time.*" Although unable to thoroughly understand Teacher T's feedback on her W1, Student B said she strictly followed it when writing W2. She believed Teacher T's feedback on her W2 started a good communication cycle: "*the more I could understand, the better our communication became.*" Interestingly, Student B said: "*I feel both Teacher T and I myself grew up.*"

When answering the same open question about the effectiveness of the feedback process, Student C's description showed that she went through interactive processes that changed from being not good to being good:

> When providing feedback on my W1, Teacher T sounded like a critic and director; and the feedback communication between us flew vertically (downward and upward). The following communications were interactive and equal; it was very easy to

accept her feedback on my W2 and W3 when I was reading it.

(From the final interview with Student C)

In short, findings stemming from the final assessment interviews showed that, although sometimes teacher-student miscommunication happened, the participants perceived the construction and interpretation of EA feedback to be effective in the long term.

6.2 Helpfulness of the Feedback Process: Student Changes

In the final review, the students reported that they became better feedback receivers after the feedback sessions in a semester. Students A and C reported that they could quickly identify teacher intent in EA feedback. The following are quotes of Students A and C said in the final interview:

> Now, I can deal with teacher feedback more efficiently and I know how to deal with it. Moreover, I can quickly understand the most important issues in teacher feedback, and quickly come to realize what my core problems are.
>
> (From the final interview with Student A)

> Now, when dealing with teacher feedback, I know what to focus on and pay more attention to my core problems, that is, what my teacher really wants to let me know.
>
> (From the final interview with Student C)

Moreover, Student C said that she did not feel defensive any more when dealing with teacher feedback. She believed that she benefitted greatly from the strategy she used to decipher Techer T's feedback: "*In the past, first, I justified my writing. Now I've already accepted Teacher T's feedback before interpreting it."*

Student B also said she could better deal with teacher feedback. She said in the final interview:

> Now, I have experience in dealing with teacher feedback. I know how to approach it and I've developed more control over dealing with teacher feedback. As I have the criteria and standards to evaluate a piece of writing, now I can give myself feedback.
>
> (From the final interview with Student B)

However, Student B did not think she had more strategies to attend to teacher feedback, such as seeking help from other resources or people.

Apart from what the students directly reported about the changes they experienced as feedback receivers, what they said in the final interviews also reflected that they had improved as feedback receivers. For example, as mentioned in Section 6.1.2, Student A pointed out that it was her failure and fault to express her meaning clearly that led to teacher-student miscommunication via feedback. In the final interview, Student C also mentioned that she should take responsibility for the breakdown in the feedback communication related to her W1. She felt that the failure of communication resulted from the poor quality of her first piece of writing. Being able to distinguish where the responsibility lay suggested that Students A and C seem to have gained deeper insight into teacher feedback, which showed that they became better feedback receivers.

6.3   More Helpfulness of Non-error Feedback

Table 6.2 gives a summary of the participants' evaluation of the helpfulness of various EA feedback provided by Teacher T.

Table 6.2 Helpfulness of EA Feedback

Helpfulness of EA Feedback	T	A	B	C
Feedback on Supporting Evidence	helpful	very helpful	very helpful	very helpful
Feedback on Coherence	helpful	very helpful	helpful	helpful
Feedback on Conjunction	very helpful	helpful	helpful	very helpful
Feedback on Thesis Statement & Topic Sentence	very helpful	helpful	very helpful	very helpful
Feedback on Conclusion	not very helpful			
Positive EA Feedback	Both were needed.	*"hard to say"*	good	not helpful
Direct, Negative EA Feedback		very helpful	bad but helpful	very helpful

Table 6.2 shows that, regarding the helpfulness of the different types of EA feedback, the results varied. However, there was agreement among the participants that the feedback on the concluding paragraph was not very effective and the students made limited progress after processing it. Teacher T offered the following explanation for her evaluation of the helpfulness of her conclusion feedback:

> When commenting on the concluding paragraph, I was usually so tired that I couldn't think straight any more. Now, I know my conclusion feedback on each of the students' writing assignments was not that clear, not that comprehensive, not that, ehh … Probably, ehh… it was also because their [the student']

conclusion was short. The biggest problem was that I failed to provide them with suggestions or just provided them with simple suggestions, and then my conclusion feedback wasn't very clear.

(From the final interview with Teacher T)

In the final assessment interview, Student A expressed a similar opinion: *"Teacher T focused on the body paragraphs. Comparatively, she probably didn't give a lot of attention to it [the concluding paragraph]."* Student B also shared some of Teacher T's ideas about the clarity of teacher feedback, stating *"I don't think Teacher T's conclusion feedback clearly let me know how to write conclusion."* Student C felt Teacher T's conclusion feedback raised her attention to her problem with it, but it was not actionable and thus not very helpful. She said in the final interview:

> For example, Teacher T wrote many comments on the concluding paragraph of my second writing assignment. This raised my awareness that I had problems with it. But as they weren't practically actionable, in my new writing, I'll continue to use the format I learnt from high school.
>
> (From the final interview with Student C)

In general, the above quotes indicated that Teacher T's conclusion feedback was not considered helpful because teacher attention to the final part was lacking and the feedback on it was not clear and not actionable.

In contrast, Table 6.2 shows that there was disagreement as to the participants' evaluation of the helpfulness of positive and direct, negative EA feedback. In the final interview, Teacher T did not give definite answers regarding the helpfulness of positive and negative feedback. She felt that the students needed both positive and direct, negative feedback although positive feedback sounded good and people might like it. Student A said that *"positive feedback wasn't helpful"*, but *"receiving honest, positive feedback is really good."* In general, Student A valued direct, negative feedback. Student B expressed her preference for positive feedback, but she also believed that *"to be helpful, the teacher must point out our problems."* In the final interview, Student C confirmed the significant helpfulness of direct, negative feedback although she felt unhappy when reading it. She said:

> I found that reading positive feedback and feeling happy at that moment had no long-term influence on me. On the contrary, direct, negative feedback raised my attention to my problem because it made me feel so bad and it's unforgettable.
>
> (From the final interview with Student C)

Moreover, Table 6.2 reveals that the students all felt that teacher feedback on supporting evidence was very helpful. Students A and C both said that Teacher T concentrated her efforts on supporting evidence and gave a large amount of feedback on that issue. Student A said: *"Teacher T wrote not only in-text but also end comments about it. I feel this repetition was one of the most important reasons why it's helpful."* Student C said: *"Even if you can't understand it at the beginning, you can understand it eventually [because of teacher attention to it]."* In the final interview, once again Student B used how she accepted Teacher T's feedback on Michael Yu as an example to show the significant helpfulness of teacher feedback on supporting evidence (See Section 5.3.2 in Chapter 5 for more information), saying Teacher T's feedback on supporting evidence *"left a deep impression on my [her] mind."*

Teacher T was sure about the helpfulness of her feedback on supporting evidence. However, because *"the issues of supporting evidence and coherence were too difficult to address"*, she did not believe that the students had mastered the skills to deal with these issues after receiving her feedback on supporting evidence and coherence only several times. In the final interview, Students A, B, and C similarly mentioned that teacher feedback on supporting evidence helped them move toward greater self-regulation, but they still had not achieved full self-regulation to deal with the issue of supporting evidence in new writings. Student C believed that *"it depends on what the writing topic we're asked to write about."* In this sense, Teacher T and the students had a similar opinion about the helpfulness of teacher feedback on supporting evidence.

In the final interview, when Teacher T and the students were asked to evaluate the helpfulness of teacher feedback on cohesion and coherence, they mainly assessed Teacher T's feedback on connectives and coherence at different levels of their writing (e.g., intra-sentential coherence and overall coherence). Teacher T reported that she was confident that her feedback on connectives, as well as her feedback on thesis statements and topic sentences, was very helpful. According to Teacher T,

> This is because it's much easier for the students to accept your [their teachers'] feedback on connectives and topic sentences. It's a little bit like error feedback. When you point out their problems with connectives and topic sentences [in your feedback], they can understand whether they were right or wrong. Comparatively, the issues like conjunctions and topic sentences are less difficult to address.
>
> (From the final interview with Teacher T)

Teacher T believed that Students A, B, and C all developed their ability to deal with connectives, topic sentences, and thesis statements because of teacher feedback. She said:

> If I could use marks to indicate their development, I'd like to give Student B 50 points for her ability to deal with these issues before feedback. After feedback I'd like to give her 70 points. Students A and C could get 80 points after feedback (60 points before feedback). Although they still can't write perfectly, I think at least there're topic sentences and thesis statements in their writing.
>
> (From the final interview with Teacher T)

Teacher T's opinions about the great helpfulness of her feedback on connectives, topic sentences, and thesis statements were shared by Student C. Student C pointed out that the teacher feedback on connectives, topic sentences, and thesis statement *"made a notable impression"* on her. In Student C's view, Teacher T's connectives feedback helped her completely understand that direct transfer of Chinese conjunctions into English did not work. Also, Student C felt that Teacher T's feedback on these issues was *"easy to understand"* and *"actionable"*. She said in the final interview: *"Now, if I were asked to read my classmates' writing, I would unconsciously look at whether there were topic sentences in their work."*

However, Student C believed that her use of connectives in new writing tasks was still problematic. In the interview, she said:

> I'd be at a loss as to what to do in a longer piece of writing where there were several body paragraphs to be structured and more connectives to be used. I want to use 'firstly, secondly, and thirdly' in every paragraph. In my W3, to avoid repetition, I used 'firstly, secondly, and thirdly' in one paragraph, and "on the one hand

and on the other hand" in the other paragraph. But I didn't know whether my use of them was right or wrong when writing. Teacher T explained its usage in class, but I forgot exactly how to use it.

(From the final interview with Student C)

By comparison, Students A and B were confident in their ability to deal with English connectives before receiving teacher feedback. As such, they considered that Teacher T's feedback led to no great changes for them. In the final interview, Student A insisted that Teacher T's feedback on connectives provided her with no further insight but "*coherence is important.*" She said that she "*had already realized this and understood the use of conjunctions can't guarantee your writing is coherent before receiving the feedback.*" Student B felt that Teacher T always gave her positive connectives feedback. She said: "*I don't have a big problem with it [use of connectives], and I paid a lot of attention to this issue when writing as well since I feel it's important.*"

Student A also believed that she had gained deep insight into the issues of topic sentences and thesis statements and had the ability to deal with these issues before feedback. So, according to Student A, Teacher T's feedback on those issues was helpful, but it just slightly helped her improve. Differently, Student B felt that she benefitted greatly from Teacher T's feedback on topic sentences and topic statements since she "*used to write long, indirect topic sentences and introduction.*" Student B also agreed with Teacher T and Student C that teacher feedback on topic sentences and thesis statements was "*actionable.*"

As mentioned above, Teacher T felt that her feedback on coherence was not overly helpful because the issue of coherence was difficult to address. In the final interviews, Teacher T, and Students B and C all felt the application of teacher feedback on coherence was not easy and it was not that helpful. Among the participants, only Student A felt that coherence feedback was very helpful because it conveyed useful insights to her about how to organize sentences and texts in a logical and coherent order. Furthermore, Student A said that Teacher T's feedback on coherence showed her the criteria and standards to evaluate a piece of written text. She said:

> Now, I'll consider whether my sentences are coherent and whether my writing is logical when I'm writing my assignments. Teacher T's feedback on coherence taught me how to evaluate whether my sentences and my writing are good or bad. Her feedback gave me criteria and standards.
>
> (From the final interview with Student A)

In conclusion, the students in my study all believed that, as the result of Teacher T's direct, negative EA feedback, they became better writers and acquired better abilities to deal with the issues of supporting evidence, cohesion and coherence, topic sentences, and topic statements. Students A and B even felt that they had acquired self-regulation skills to deal with the issue of connectives.

6.4 Chapter Summary

This chapter reported the following results stemming from the ongoing and the concluding interview data. First, it presented the findings about the teacher and the students' overall evaluations of the effectiveness of the feedback processes over a semester. In the ongoing interviews, all participants reported that the feedback process was effective. Findings derived from the final interview data indicated that the student participants felt that sometimes teacher-student miscommunication happened over the course of the semester, but the feedback-and-interpretation was effective overall. Second, the student s all perceived the teacher-student interactions via EA feedback helped them become better writers and feedback receivers. Finally, this chapter reported the participants' assessment of the helpfulness of various types of EA feedback. Results showed that the participants' perceptions varied. However, the students all considered that teacher feedback on supporting evidence was very helpful and they benefitted a lot from Teacher T's direct, negative feedback.

6.5 Summary of All Findings

Generally, the findings my study obtained paint an interactional complex picture of the feedback-and-interpretation dynamic. During feedback provision, Teacher T interacted with student writing, the students (treated as feedback receivers, writers, classroom participants, and people who have emotion), herself (as a feedback provider, a critic, an instructor, and an emotional decision-maker), and various levels of contexts (e.g., classroom instruction context, sociocultural context) to decide upon feedback focus and feedback delivery approaches. Overall, Teacher T's cognitive, behavioral, and affective involvement interacted in feedback provision and her decision-making did not vary greatly from one student to another. To decide whether to accept and incorporate teacher feedback, Students A, B, and C worked through the interaction of their cognitive, behavioral, and affective engagement with teacher feedback, and various types of student-context interactions (i.e., student-feedback interaction, student-writing interaction, student-self interaction, student-teacher interaction and student-context interaction). Generally, as communication problems often arose during the feedback process, findings from my study showed that the interactional feedback process was not always smooth. However, despite the feedback-and-interpretation process sometimes being difficult, my study still found that feedback-led learning occurred and an alignment between the teacher and the student, to some extent, had been achieved.

Chapter 7   Discussion and Conclusion

7.0   Introduction

Apart from this introduction section (7.0), there are five sections in this chapter. Sections 7.1 and 7.2 provide a brief review of the aims, the methodology, and the main findings of my study reported in this book. Section 7.3 presents the empirical, theoretical, methodological and pedagogical discussion of my findings and their contributions. Section 7.4 focuses on the limitations inherent in my study and their implications for future and further studies. Finally, this chapter concludes with my closing remarks (7.5).

7.1   Aims and Methodology of the Study

My study, focusing on Chinese EFL teachers' non-error EA feedback, investigated the feedback-and-interpretation process and teachers'/students' evaluation of this process. Specifically, the following key issues related to the feedback process were examined in my study:

- what EA-related concerns teachers focus on,
- how teachers deliver EA feedback,

- how teachers make decisions regarding their feedback foci and feedback delivery approaches,
- to what extent students accept and incorporate EA feedback,
- how students make decisions regarding their acceptance and incorporation of EA feed back, and
- how teachers/students evaluate the helpfulness of feedback interactions.

As argued in the Literature Review Chapter, my study aimed to
- (empirically) extend the research base on the feedback process and non-error feedback,
- (theoretically) deepen our understanding of teacher written feedback, and
- (practically) deal with the doubts and questions stemming from my own feedback practices.

Methodologically, my study utilized a case study approach. In this case study research, three teacher-student pairs constituted three cases. It was conducted at KEY university in China, an EFL educational context where more research on teacher feedback is still needed. To ensure data richness, my study collected the teacher's and students' documents (teacher comments on student writing and the notes students took down in response to teacher feedback), along with think-aloud data and data from interviews (background interview, retrospective interview, ongoing interview, and final assessment interview).

7.2 Summary of Key Findings

Findings on RQ1: Teachers' Feedback Foci/Delivery Approaches and Decision-Making

With regards to teachers' feedback foci, my study found that Teacher T focused on EA issues and she constantly provided comments on thesis statement, topic sentence, supporting evidence, cohesion and coherence, conclusion, and overall organization of student writing. As to how Teacher T decided to focus on these issues, my study found that her decisions were informed by her feedback beliefs and her heightened awareness of student difficulties/problems. Furthermore, the interaction among sociocultural contexts (e.g., the examination culture of China), classroom instruction and teacher role also greatly influenced Teacher T's decision-making to focus on these issues.

Teacher T's feedback delivery approaches were identified from four perspectives in my study. From the perspective of its orientation, Teacher T provided evaluator-response comments (e.g., problem/strength-oriented feedback), instructor-response comments (e.g., explanatory feedback), and reader-response comments (e.g., feedback about the student writer's learning and learning/writing process); from the perspective of its degree of scaffolding, two thirds of Teacher T's EA feedback were combination comments (e.g., a praise-criticism-explanation-revision quaternity) and one third were single-statement comments. From the perspective of the language channel Teacher T used, her comments were delivered half in English and half in Chinese. Moreover, from the perspective of changes, Teacher T provided more positive and hedged feedback and less explanatory feedback with the passage of time.

As to Teacher T's feedback delivery approaches, her decision-making was found to be associated with the interaction among her cognitive, behavioral, and affective engagement during feedback (e.g., reading and interpreting student writing; consulting online dictionaries/resources; articulating her emotional state aroused by responding to student writing). Also, Teacher T's decisions were found to be mediated by her intensive interactions with the students (i.e., social cognitive engagement) and the interactions between teacher and contextual factors.

Findings on RQ2: Students' Acceptance and Incorporation of EA Feedback and Decision-Making

My study found that Students A, B, and C went through different experiences during their feedback interpretation. Student A's self-regulated, deep-level acceptance and incorporation of Teacher T's EA feedback occurred when she interpreted it on her W1 and W2; but as she interpreted Teacher T's EA feedback on her W3, she barely incorporated any of it and her emotional acceptance of it shifted from appreciation of the feedback to dissatisfaction with it. Compared with Student A, Student B's acceptance and incorporation of Teacher T's EA feedback was slow and superficial (e.g., memorization of genre/rhetorical knowledge contained in EA feedback). In fact, she did not cognitively, behaviorally, and affectively accept and incorporate teacher feedback until she dealt with it on her W3. Student C generally semi-accepted and semi-incorporated Teacher T's EA feedback; but emotionally, she did not begin to accept it until she interpreted it on her W2.

With regards to how Students A, B, and C decided to accept and incorporate Teacher T's EA feedback, my study found that it was related to ① the level at which the students cognitively processed it, ② the interaction among their cognitive, affective and behavioral engagement with it, and ③ various student-context interactions (e.g., student-feedback interactions, student-self interactions, student-teacher interactions).

Findings on RQ3: Helpfulness of Constructing and Interpreting EA Feedback

In my study, the students and Teacher T were asked to evaluate whether

Teacher T's EA feedback was helpful and whether students had achieved the self-regulation required to deal with various EA issues after feedback. Overall, they believed that the students became better writers and feedback receivers as the result of teacher feedback. Concerning the helpfulness of Teacher T's feedback on various EA issues (supporting evidence, thesis statement and topic sentence, cohesion, coherence, conclusion, and overall organization), what the students reported varied. However, they all believed that teacher feedback on supporting evidence led to the improvement of their writing. As to the usefulness of hedged feedback and positive feedback, generalizations cannot be claimed based on my study.

The Feedback-and-Interpretation Process: A Summary

A summarized account of the feedback-and-interpretation process is presented in Section 6.5 (Chapter 6). The full picture of the feedback process emerging from my study showed that the feedback-and-interpretation processes Teacher T and the students were involved in either started well and became difficult (Teacher T and Student A) or started out as difficult, but became easier as time progressed (Teacher T and Students B and C). Overall, the feedback-and-interpretation processes Teacher T and the students participated in were interactional, interactive, dynamic and complex.

7.3 Contributions of the Findings

This section discusses the contribution of my findings. It begins with a discussion of their empirical and theoretical contributions from the perspective of research aims (7.3.1), and then moves on to an empirical and theoretical discussion from the perspective of RQs (7.3.2). After that, the methodological implications for teacher feedback research (7.3.3) and the pedagogical implications for responding practices are identified and discussed (7.3.4).

7.3.1 The Empirical and Theoretical Contributions: A Discussion from the Perspective of Research Aims

Below, from the perspective of research aims, the empirical and theoretical contributions my study made are formulated respectively (7.3.1.1 & 7.3.1.2).

7.3.1.1 Empirical Contributions: From the Perspective of Research Aims

In the Literature Review Chapter, four most researched strands of feedback research were identified:

1) student perspectives on teacher feedback (e.g., student perceptions and preferences concerning teacher feedback),
2) the feedback itself (e.g., effectiveness of feedback),
3) teacher cognition (e.g., teachers' feedback beliefs), and
4) the feedback-and-interpretation/revision process.

My study followed the trend started by Hyland and Hyland (2006a) to investigate the feedback-and-interpretation process. As reviewed in Section 7.2, my study showed that the key characteristics of this process is its "interactional" nature. This result enhances and complements Hyland and Hyland's interpersonal view of the feedback process in the following ways.

Enhancement and Complement: Teacher-Student Interaction and Teacher/ Student Decision-Making

First, my study supports Hyland and Hyland's (2006a) argument that how teachers express their feedback is greatly influenced by their considerations of student factors. In Hyland and Hyland's words, when teachers write feedback on student essays, they tend to "conceptualize" (p.213) students first. What they meant is that teachers usually draw on students' personalities, needs, expectations, problems and difficulties, past experiences as writers and recipients of feedback, and possible response to teacher feedback, to name a few, to tailor their feedback on student writing.

In my study, Teacher T "conceptualized" students to decide how to deliver feedback as well. She evaluated students' abilities, students' writing attitude, and students' efforts devoted to the writing task, to name a few, to choose her feedback delivery approaches (See Section 4.6.3). For example, as reported in Section 4.6.3, Teacher T often invested considerable effort into reading and interpreting student texts in order to provide an evaluator-response comment (e.g., problems/strengths-oriented feedback). Sometimes, she was also found to be engaged in deep-level interpretation operations to identify the student's writing intention so that she could couple her problem-oriented feedback with positive words. Teacher T's investment of time and effort in reading and interpreting student texts reveals how the formation of teachers' feedback-delivery-approach decisions result from their interaction with student texts. Her deep-level processing of student texts and the formation of her decisions to add positive feedback show, when teachers are writing feedback, they interact not only with student texts, but also with the student writers. In this example, by taking her students' writing intention into consideration, Teacher T decided to accompany her negative feedback with some positive words in order to soften the negativity of her feedback.

When teachers interact with/"conceptualize" student writers and experience a high level of social engagement to decide how to deliver feedback, it seems that they take various student factors into consideration. As pointed out above, in Hyland and Hyland's (2006a) study, the teacher participants considered students' strengths and weaknesses, needs, personalities, and possible

251

responses to teacher feedback, among others. In Wang's (2011) study, the teacher participant kept her students' expectations, affect, and motivation in mind and chose to deliver her EA feedback in a mitigated, indirect way. In my study, Teacher T evaluated students' abilities, students' writing attitude, and students' efforts devoted to the writing task, to name a few, to choose her approaches to deliver EA feedback. It is inevitable that teachers may take different student factors into account during feedback provision because each teaching, learning and responding context is unique. However, it can be generalized that, to decide how to deliver teacher feedback, teachers "interact" with students who are feedback users, classroom participants, writers, learners and people who have emotions.

Complementing Hyland and Hyland's (2006a) interactive view of "conceptualizing" students, my study also found that students' acceptance of teacher feedback was determined by their "conceptualization" of the teacher (See Sub-section 5.5.4.4). For example, Students A and B sometimes did not fully accept Teacher T's feedback on supporting evidence when they felt that Teacher T had either misunderstood their writing or her comments contradicted their ideas. Also, in my study, there were instances where Student A fully accepted Teacher T's feedback on supporting evidence because she felt that Teacher T read her writing in detail and undertook her responding work very seriously.

Second, Hyland and Hyland's (2006a) argument that teachers are aware of the interpersonal aspects of teacher feedback is borne out in my findings about the formation of Teacher T's decisions to add positive feedback. For example, Teacher T believed there was a high level of trust between herself and Student B, and felt their relationship was closest (See Section 4.1.4). As such, her explanation for one of her deliberate choices to give encouraging/positive EA comments on Student B's text was: *"Because it was her [Student B's] writing; I won't do it on others (See Section 4.6.4)."*

As a complement, my study presented a connection between teacher-student relationship and student decision-making to accept and incorporate teacher feedback. The example related to this connection is as follows. Student C felt it was easier to take up teacher feedback when Teacher T commented (on her W2) "like a kind friend" than when she commented (on her W1) in a direct way "as an authoritative figure" (See Sub-section 5.5.4.4). My finding about the influence of teacher-student relationships on the students' decision-making also lends support to Lee and Schallert's (2008a, 2008b) result that a trusting and caring relationship influenced teacher feedback and student revision.

Furthermore, my study complements Hyland and Hyland's (2006a) interpersonal view of teacher feedback by revealing the roles teachers and students play during the feedback process. My study showed that, when interacting with the students to decide how to deliver EA feedback, the roles teachers play included feedback giver, critic, instructor, and emotional decision maker (See Section 4.6.3). As to students, as indicated in Section 5.5.1, when interactively responding to Teacher T's EA feedback, they exercised agency and took on the role of a superficial/deep feedback receiver, a writer, a critic, a superficial/deeper learner, and a rational decision-maker.

Enhancement and Complement: The Interactions Among Teachers, Students, Texts and Contexts and Teacher/Student Decision-Making
As evidenced by the review of literature, Hyland and Hyland (2006a) only "briefly" (p.213 & p.220) reported how teachers constructed feedback and how students interpreted teacher feedback during the feedback process. However, it is worth mentioning that in their study they clearly delivered

the following argument: studies of teacher written feedback must take into account the interactions and connections between teachers, students, texts, and the pedagogic context.

My study strengthened and complemented Hyland and Hyland's (2006a) argument by providing empirical evidence of how the interaction among teachers, students, texts and contexts occurs during the feedback process. As reported in Section 4.6.3, to decide how to deliver feedback, Teacher T was found to spend time and effort on reading student writing, interpreting her students' writing intentions, identifying the exact ideas she intended to convey in her feedback, evaluating student writing according to what they needed to learn from class, selecting the most appropriate words to provide high-quality EA feedback, reflecting on her teaching and feedback practice, and reviewing her feedback points to see whether she or the student was satisfied with the comments she had written. It is quite apparent that, as Teacher T worked her way through feedback construction, how she brought the students, student texts, herself, and the pedagogic context together and how the connections between teachers, students, texts, and the pedagogic context contributed to the emergence of teacher feedback can be empirically observed in my study.

Also, my study found how the students accepted and incorporated EA feedback was mediated by student-context interactions (See Section 5.5.4). This is another line of evidence from my study that helps to explain Hyland and Hyland's (2006a) interactional view mentioned above. For example, as reported in Sub-section 5.5.4.5, the students' sociocultural background (i.e., the traditional examination culture in China), writing instruction background and knowledge gap simultaneously and interactively prevented them from accepting and incorporating Teacher T's conclusion feedback. In fact, according to Teacher T, the feedback she provided on the students' concluding paragraph was not sophisticated and clear (because of her cognitive fatigue, See Section 6.3). Student A believed that Teacher T disregarded the concluding paragraph when commenting on student writing.

Clearly, the example set out above gives substance to Hyland and Hyland's (2006a) view on the coordinated interaction of teachers, students, feedback and contexts and its consequence. Since the students' sociocultural background and the conclusion feedback Teacher T wrote on their writing did not provide good learning opportunities and the students' insufficient knowledge and ability (shaped by their sociocultural background and instruction background) hindered them from fully engaging with the teacher feedback, it is valid to conclude the students' acceptance and incorporation of Teacher T's conclusion feedback did not take place because the interplay of the teacher, the student, the text and the macro/micro-level contexts occurred.

Apart from the pedagogic context, Hyland and Hyland (2006b) did emphasize the interactional effect of historical and sociocultural contexts. In my study, the contextual forces of society and culture operated on Teacher T as well. The following is an example. As reported in Section 4.6.3, Teacher T made great efforts to write high-quality EA feedback to model for the students what good writing looked like. According to Hyland and Hyland (2006a), how teachers deliver their feedback evokes images of themselves as teachers. My findings about the great efforts Teacher T made to write high-quality EA feedback indicated her wish to create a positive teacher image. In the retrospective interview, Teacher T also explained that she felt afraid of "losing face" for responding inappropriately to student writing. It is generally believed in Western society that people are less concerned about the face-saving/losing issues (Ting-Toomey & Kutogi, 1998) while people from collective societies (like the Chinese) are more concerned with loss of face (Waterman, 1984). As such, this example offers a picture that links the interactions among Teacher T's role as an instructor and feedback writer, her image, her consideration of students as writers and learners, and the contextual factor of society and culture with her feedback-delivery-approach decisions. In accord with Hyland and Hyland's view, it provides empirical evidence of how the interaction of teacher feedback, teachers, students, and sociocultural contexts occurs and how the joint interactions influence the teacher's construction of feedback.

Complement: The Cognition-Affect-Behavior Interaction and Teacher/ Student Decision-Making

My study produced new, complementary findings and highlighted the interactional nature of teacher feedback. A new line of findings my study presented is that Teacher T's/the students' decisions about how to construct/interpret EA feedback were the result of the interaction among their cognitive, affective, and behavioral engagement in the feedback process (See Sections 4.6.2 & 5.5.3). For example, although the percentage values of Teacher T's affective engagement (about 7% of the process to respond to EA issues; including her affective response to student writing, her emotional states aroused by responding to student texts, and her attitude towards her own comments) were low, my study showed that teacher affect was deeply interwoven with teacher cognition (including interpretation operations, evaluation operations, identification and selection operations, review operations, reflection operations, and planning and monitoring operations) and teacher behavior (including typing feedback into computer and consulting online dictionary/resources). As shown in Section 4.6.2, my study found that it was the cognition-behavior-affect interaction that led to the formation of Teacher T's feedback-delivery-approach decisions.

My study also found Students A, B, and C's acceptance and incorporation of Teacher T's EA feedback was closely related to the interaction among their cognitive, affective and behavioral engagement with it (See Section 5.5.3). So far, there is a limited amount of empirical work on the inseparability of students' cognitive, affective and behavioral engagement with error feedback (i.e., corrective feedback) and its contribution to students' use of error feedback (e.g., Han, 2016). As far as non-error feedback is concerned, researchers (Brice, 1995; Kumar, 2012; Kumar & Kumar, 2009; Kumar, Kumar, & Feryok, 2009) related students' acceptance and incorporation of teacher feedback mainly to their cognitive operations themselves. My study showed it is not only the students' cognitive operations but the cognition-affect-behavior interaction that contributes to the formation of students' decisions as to what feedback to accept and incorporate and how to accept and incorporate it. The key characteristics of teacher feedback my study identified is its "interactional" nature.

Complement: The Dynamic Feedback Interactions

Complementing Hyland and Hyland's (2006a) findings, my study exposed the dynamic nature of the feedback-and-interpretation process that both the teacher and the student participate in. For example, my study found, with the passage of time, Teacher T came to realize the EA issues in the students' expository writing were more problematic than she had thought previously and her feedback beliefs about focusing on EA issues were heightened. Informed by her increased awareness, she decided to give EA issues more attention when providing feedback. This finding suggests that teacher beliefs/ cognition are evolving and dynamic in nature (Borg, 2015), which accordingly makes dynamics one of the key features of teacher feedback. In my study, apart from Teacher T' feedback beliefs changing over time, Students A, B, and C went through different, changing experiences during feedback interactions, which also contributes supporting evidence about the dynamics of teacher feedback.

To summarize what has been discussed so far, my study amplifies the research trend started by Hyland and Hyland (2006a) to investigate the feedback-and-interpretation process and confirms many of Hyland and Hyland's (2006a, 2006b) findings and arguments. Presenting a picture and an evaluation of the feedback process affords us a window into the interactional, the interpersonal, the dynamic, and the complexity aspects of teacher feedback.

7.3.1.2 Theoretical Contributions: From the Perspective of Research Aims

On the theoretical level, to the research base of L2 teachers' feedback, my study contributes a perspective (a sociocognitive perspective of teacher feedback) and empirical evidence that can support and better understand this perspective. As elaborated in Sub-section 2.2.1.6, underlying the sociocognitive perspective of teacher feedback my study advocated are Atkinson's inseparability, adaptivity, and alignment principles. The forthcoming theoretical discussion is thus provided in relation to these three basic principles.

As argued in the Literature Review Chapter, thus far, the past four decades of research on teacher feedback have witnessed the following main trends in viewing teacher feedback: ① a product-oriented, textual perspective (focusing on the feedback itself), ② a contextualized perspective (emphasizing a consideration of the varying layers of contexts in which teacher feedback is given and taken), ③ a social-oriented perspective (defining feedback as teacher-student conversation), and ④ a sociocultural perspective (equating feedback with sociocultural scaffolding, or using activity theory to define it). Based on the latest research trend toward focusing on the complex, dynamic feedback process from the sociocultural perspective, my study

Chapter 7   Discussion and Conclusion

adopted Atkinson's sociocognitive theory of learning and development to conceptualize teacher feedback. This sociocognitive perspective is illuminating because the three basic principles underlying it (the inseparability, adaptivity, and alignment principles) allow us to see ① how the teacher offers feedback through the workings of his/her "mindbodyworld", ② how the student attends to teacher feedback through the workings of his/her "mindbodyworld", ③ how the teacher, the student, the feedback (as the text-level context), and the context interact and integrate with each other, and ④ how student learning and development occur through the interactions among the teacher, the student, the feedback and the context.

Adopting a sociocognitive perspective to view teacher feedback is not completely innovative. Han (2016) has already applied it to her doctoral thesis study on error/corrective feedback. However, Han's study focused on the students' engagement with error feedback. As such, on the theoretical level, Han mainly made clear ① how the learner deals with error feedback and ② how learning via error feedback occurs. From the perspective of sociocognitive theory, my study comprehensively revealed the role both teachers and students play in ecosocial interactions/feedback and the occurrence of student learning/development during it.

It is true that, in my study, Teacher T's feedback provision and the students' feedback interpretation is predominately cognitive (70% of Teacher T's total engagement when constructing EA feedback and 80% of the students' total engagement when interpreting EA feedback on average); however, my findings about the inseparability of Teacher T's/the students' cognitive, affective and behavioral engagement indicate that merely taking a cognitive perspective to look at teacher feedback is not enough. This viewpoint parallels what Ellis (2010) and Han (2016) argued for in the field of error/corrective feedback. They believed that leaving out the affective and behavioral dimensions of error feedback would make a complete understanding of error feedback impossible. They suggest that it is necessary to take a sociocognitive perspective, a perspective that integrates cognitive, behavioral, and affective dimensions, to define and research error feedback. Now, by bringing studies related to error feedback and my study about non-error feedback together, it can be said that taking a sociocognitive lens to view teacher written feedback (including both error feedback and non-error feedback) is theoretically plausible.

Before turning to the contributions my study made to the sociocognitive perspective of teacher feedback, let us review Atkinson's sociocognitive theory of learning and development first to ensure clarity of terminology and the forthcoming discussion. Simply put, sociocognitive theory of learning views learning as a social construction in which the cognitive and the social are dialectically inseparable (Guerrero & Villamil, 2002) and it advocates the inseparability, adaptivity, and alignment principles. According to Nishino and Atkinson (2015), **the inseparability principle** holds that the mind, body, and ecosocial world are inseparable contributors in ecosocial interaction (i.e., ecological and social interaction between human beings and between human beings and non-human environments) and human development/learning. From the sociocognitive perspective, to construct and maintain ecosocial interactions and to develop/learn throughout ecosocial interactions, the mind, body, and world are functionally integrated, instead of separated (Atkinson, 2014). To understand the ecosocial interaction processes and human development/learning, the mind, body, and world need to be considered together. As to **the adaptivity principle**, it holds that ecosocial interactions require the mutual, continuous and dynamic adaptation, adjustment and coordination of the individuals with each other or the high-skilled adaptation, adjustment and coordination between the individuals and their non-human environments (Nishino & Atkinson, 2015). With regards to **the alignment principle**, Atkinson (2014) metaphorically explained that it means that the ecosocial interaction where learning opportunities lie is like a cooperative (not competitive) ping pong game, in which two or more partners coordinate or align their activities sensitively and moment by moment to come to "common ground" (i.e., "a common understanding of the nature, procedures, and goals of the activity in which they are engaged", Batstone, 2010, p.7) and share knowledge.

Theoretical Contributions: A Better Understanding of the Inseparability Principle

In my study, the inseparability principle stated that the teacher/student works as a "mindbodyworld" (i.e., the inseparability of mind/cognition, body/affect, body/behavior, and world/contextual background) ecology during the feedback process (See Sub-section 2.2.1.6). The following is an example of how the sociocognitive inseparability principle is reflected in my study. As reported in Section 4.4, the formation of Teacher T's decisions about what to focus on was dependent of the interaction between teacher factors (e.g., her belief about feedback foci, her heightened awareness of what to focus on, her role as a test assessor) and contextual factors (e.g., her sociocultural background and pedagogical objective in class). For one thing, Teacher T's feedback beliefs informed her decision-making and her decision-making in turn raised her awareness of feedback foci (the inseparability of mind and body). For another, when Teacher T was constructing EA feedback, her decision-making was closely bound up with her sociocultural background (i.e., the examination culture of China she was rooted in). As such, it can be clearly seen that Teacher T based her decisions about feedback foci on the workings of the inseparable and interrelated mind (e.g., her feedback beliefs), body (e.g., her actions) and world (e.g., the examination culture of China).

In my study, how the students decided to accept and incorporate Teacher T's EA feedback was also found to be the result of various indivisibilities (i.e., the inseparability of their cognitive, affective and behavioral engagement with EA feedback and the student-context integration, See Section 5.5 to look at findings and Sub-section 7.3.1.1 to look at analysis of examples). That is to say, the students, like Teacher T, also participated in the feedback process through the workings of their "mindbodyworld".

Theoretical Contributions: A Better Understanding of the Adaptivity and Alignment Principles

In my study, there is also clear evidence to illustrate the other two principles that underlay my sociocognitive approach to teacher written feedback: the adaptivity and alignment principles. For example, in my study, Teacher T employed a variety of cognitive operations to construct feedback/interaction, such as reading at a deeper level to identify the students' writing intention (to accompany her negative feedback with positive words), evaluating students' affective reactions to teacher feedback (to comment less directly), making efforts to select a better word to express her feedback (to write quality feedback), and so forth. These operations Teacher T carried out when writing feedback clearly show that she was devoted herself to situating her students within a textual context of feedback/interaction that can help them more easily achieve adaptivity and teacher-student alignment.

In addition, the roles the students played during feedback process can also be used to understand the adaptivity and alignment principles of teacher feedback. For example, when attending to EA feedback, Student A usually processed it at a deep level. Also, my study found that sometimes she tried to regulate her negative emotions, and sometimes she self-initiated help-seeking behaviors. In other words, during feedback, Student A cognitively, affectively, and behaviorally adapted herself to the feedback/interaction Teacher T constructed and made great efforts to align with the feedback/context/"world" in the course of interaction.

In my study, Student B felt difficult to interpret Teacher T's EA feedback on her W1. However, according to Teacher T, in her W2 Student B mechanically applied what Teacher T said in her W1 although she did not seem to understand it. As such, on Student B's W2 which was not very well-written (for her mechanical use of teacher feedback), Teacher T provided more positive feedback and a larger amount of EA feedback to show encouragement (See Section 4.5.4). As Student B noticed these changes in Teacher T's feedback, she cognitively and affectively became more receptive to it. Meanwhile, when processing teacher feedback on her W2, Student B had developed some familiarity with Teacher T's feedback delivery approaches and gained some awareness of her own problems with argumentation. By such kind of adaptivity (e.g., her mechanical use of teacher feedback) and coordination, Student B's slow, increasing acceptance and incorporation of EA feedback occurred.

Theoretical Contributions: Genre Approach
Insights from the sociocognitive perspective on teacher feedback provide a valuable way forward in understanding the genre approach to writing instruction. According to Hyland (2007), L2 writing genre instructors play the role of planning, sequencing, supporting, and assessing learning in teaching practice. Enlightened by sociocognitive theory, we can also assume that, when

planning, sequencing, supporting, and assessing learning in the genre-based classroom, the teacher plays her role in "mindbodyworld", and his/her goal is to achieve teacher-student alignment.

In summary, this sub-section (7.3.1.2) presents a theoretical discussion related to the feedback-and-interpretation process Teacher T and the students were involved in. It shows that my study contributes to the theorization of teacher feedback by providing empirical evidence and enriches our understanding of the sociocognitive perspective of teacher feedback by giving substance to its principled basis (inseparability, adaptivity and alignment principles).

7.3.2 The Empirical and Theoretical Contributions: From the Perspective of RQs

In the following six sub-sections (7.3.2.1–7.3.2.6), the empirical contributions of the findings in response to each RQ (feedback focus, feedback delivery approach, teacher decision-making, students' acceptance and integration of feedback, student decision-making, feedback-linked student learning/development), together with their contributions to theories (the sociocognitive perspective of teacher feedback and SFL-informed genre pedagogy), are presented. In each sub-section, the empirical discussion usually follows a general to specific order. The theoretical discussion is provided from the sociocognitive perspective of teacher feedback to genre pedagogy if both are discussed. At the end of this section, the contributions my study made from the perspective of RQs are summarized (7.3.2.7).

7.3.2.1 Empirical and Theoretical Contributions: Feedback Focus

Empirical Contribution: Feedback Focus
As indicated in Sub-section 7.3.1.1, so far, four main strands of research on teacher feedback have been identified: ① student perspectives on teacher

feedback, ② the feedback itself, ③ teacher cognition, and ④ the feedback-and-response process. My findings about the EA issues Teacher T focused on made some contributions to the second strand of **research on the feedback itself**.

In my study, finer-grained findings were reported. As indicated in the Literature Review Chapter, most of the available research on feedback itself only roughly reported the extent to which teacher feedback focused on content, organization, vocabulary and grammar. For example, Li's (2016) study showed that 31% of teacher feedback was focused on content, 26% on vocabulary, and 14% on organization. My study went one step further and investigated the subcategories that fell under Teacher T's EA feedback (i.e., the feedback related to the organization of students' expository writing), finding that she wrote feedback mainly on *thesis statement, topic sentence, supporting evidence, cohesion and coherence,* and *the concluding paragraph* of her students' expository writing (See Section 4.3 for finer-grained details about each feedback focus). More studies like mine, together with the error feedback research that has already offered a detailed way of analyzing the various errors L2 teachers usually focus on (e.g., Bitchener, Young, & Cameron, 2005), can build a detailed picture of L2 teachers' feedback focus.

In Hyland and Hyland's (2006a) paper, the researchers chose to use the terminology "idea feedback" to refer to teacher feedback on argumentation. Based on the analytical samples given by Hyland and Hyland (e.g., "I would have liked you to give some examples of countries which have one or the other system as the material is rather difficult to grasp/understand without concrete/real life examples." p.217), it can be determined that it referred to teacher feedback on argumentation of ideas/points or supporting evidence. Hyland and Hyland's study indicated that the major concerns of the experienced ESL teachers were how to effectively develop ideas with supporting evidence and how to explicitly create a coherent, logical argument when they provided feedback on students' expository writing. They found that experienced teachers focus on argument construction when they provide feedback on expository writing (i.e., EA-related issues). As such, my data is consistent with this finding of Hyland and Hyland.

According to Min (2013), even experienced teachers struggle with how to comment on argumentation and supporting evidence. When thinking aloud during feedback provision, Teacher T, who had seven years of teaching experience, also experienced difficulties with delivering feedback on supporting evidence. As reported in Chapter 4, when commenting on supporting evidence, she sometimes articulated her feelings about the difficulty in giving good revisions. Here, my point is that to help the teachers provide argumentation feedback more easily and effectively, teacher feedback on supporting evidence is clearly an issue requiring continued investigation.

My study also reported some findings that are largely nonexistent in literature. Concerning teacher feedback on cohesive devices, my study found that Teacher T concentrated on connectives and referential pronouns (See Section 4.3). As cohesion may be realized through different devices, such as metatext (e.g., an advanced organizer clarifying links between ideas/parts), transitions, reference, and other ways (e.g., substitution, ellipsis, synonyms, etc.), in-depth studies devoted wholly to cohesion feedback are needed in order to produce a thorough picture of teacher feedback on each type of cohesion. In previous studies, Bitchener and Basturkmen (2010) and Wang (2011) reported ESL and EFL teachers provided feedback on *metatext*, an important cohesive device that is used less in Chinese writing than in English writing (Kim & Lim, 2013). Considering that it may be very difficult for some Chinese EFL writers, it is important for researchers to focus their attention on teacher feedback on metatext.

My study particularly reported that Teacher T commented on thesis statements and topic sentences from the perspective of the rhetoricality of style (i.e., direct and concise statement of thesis and arguments in the opening paragraph and in topic sentences). So far, only a limited number of L2 feedback/ assessment studies has ever mentioned teachers'/test raters' focus on the rhetoricality of style (e.g., Junqueira & Payant, 2015). However, researchers' inadequate attention does not mean that the issue of style is unimportant. According to Hinds (1990), the oriental style involves a delayed introduction of purpose, and Chinese EFL students' indirect thesis statements and topic sentences are often buried somewhere in the texts. That is to say, although ineffective style is often viewed as an error issue (Bitchener & Basturkmen, 2010), it should not be automatically diagnosed as symptomatic of problems on a surface level. As it may be a cultural issue, it needs Chinese EFL teachers' particular attention and it should not be ignored by researchers either.

Most prior feedback studies did not look at the cross-assignment and cross-student changes of teachers' foci. My study found that Teacher T's feedback foci across student assignments were relatively stable. Best's (2011) and Clements' (2008) studies yielded different findings. However, as Best and Clements investigated novice teachers' feedback practices and Teacher T in my study had seven-year teaching experience, one of the reasons for the different results is likely to be teachers' experience. Ferris, et al. (1997) found that less non-error feedback was provided on narrative assignments than on other genres of writing assignments (e.g., argumentative writing assignments). By implication, the other possible reason why Teacher T's feedback foci remained comparatively stable was that she provided feedback only on one genre (exposition) in a semester.

My study reported a relative cross-student stability in Teacher T's feedback foci. This result seems to suggest that Teacher T's feedback foci were not greatly influenced by the students' writing ability (Students A and C identified by Teacher T as higher-level writers). As such, this finding appears not to corroborate the finding obtained in Cohen's (1991) study, which showed the EFL teacher provided more argumentation-related comments on lower performers' writing than on the higher and intermediate performers' writing. However, the inconsistent finding can be explained by how "student ability" is evaluated in the two studies. In Cohen's study, the students' writing abilities (higher, intermediate, and lower performers) were judged according to their control of argumentation-related issues. As such, Cohen's lower performing participant, whose writing exhibited more argumentation problems, tended to receive more teacher feedback on logical reasoning issues. In my study, Teacher T evaluated Students A, B, and C's writing abilities in a general way (control of organization, ideas, and language). That is to say, although Students A and C were considered to be better writers, they still might have had some major EA issues and, therefore, needed many EA comments. In this sense, Teacher T's feedback, though appearing to be stable across students, was indeed adaptive to student abilities to deal with EA issues. Cohen's study and mine reveal that, in future studies, the specific information about how students' abilities are judged and evaluated must be clearly provided.

Theoretical Implications for the Sociocognitive Perspective of Teacher Feedback and SFL-Informed Genre Pedagogy: Feedback Focus

In my study, from the sociocognitive perspective, teacher feedback was defined as a complex, dynamic system (See Sub-section 2.2.1.6). My study highlighted the complexity of teacher feedback. The above empirically-based discussion reveals it is virtually impossible to talk about the feedback itself without talking about what teachers/students bring to the feedback process (e.g., teacher experience, student ability), the teaching/learning contexts (e.g., the genre of writing tasks), and the sociocultural background (e.g., the oriental writing style).

My findings about Teacher T's feedback focus have theoretical implications for genre pedagogy too. Literature on genre pedagogy has shown that this instructional approach aims to help student writers to acquire and apply rhetorical and discursive knowledge (e.g., how to organize writing, how to begin/end writing, how to write in an appropriate style). As in the background interview Teacher T considered that there are rhetorical and discursive differences between Chinese and English, insights from these data are that EFL teachers may comment from the perspective of Chinese-English differences and look at genre pedagogy from the orientation of contrastive rhetoric. However, it is highly suggested that the teacher who uses the genre-based approach be reminded not to oversimplify genre approach and equate it with rhetorical differences.

As repeated several times, genre pedagogies include four components: planning learning (e.g., gathering sample texts), sequencing learning (e.g., determining the most critical skills relevant to students' immediate needs), scaffolding learning (e.g., analysing and modelling good expository texts for students), and assessing learning (e.g., assessing student writing against clear and agreed upon performance criteria). My findings about Teacher T's feedback foci, as well as the similar findings from L2 writing contexts (e.g., Clements, 2008; Conrad & Goldstein, 1999; Hyland & Hyland, 2006a; Wang, 2011), suggest the following: in expository writing class, at the stages of planning, sequencing, scaffolding, and assessing learning, the issues of thesis statement, topic sentence, supporting evidence, cohesion and coherence, and the concluding paragraph should become L2 genre teachers' central focus. For example, at the stage of planning learning, when L2 genre teachers gather sample texts for their expository writing class, the criteria on which to base their selection of the sample texts should be whether the materials can draw students' attention to the key EA issues identified in my study.

7.3.2.2 Empirical and Theoretical Contributions: Feedback Delivery Approaches

Empirical Contribution: Feedback Delivery Approaches
My findings about Teacher T's feedback delivery approaches (See Section 7.2 for the review of findings) also make a contribution to the line of **research on the feedback itself**.

According to the Literature Review Chapter, there are currently two main traditions of research on the feedback itself. In the tradition of Ferris, teachers' feedback delivery approaches are studied mainly from the perspective of their pragmatic functions (e.g., statement, imperative, and question; Conrad & Goldstein, 1999); in the tradition of Hyland and Hyland (2001), teachers' feedback delivery approaches are studied according to their orientation (e.g., praise, criticism, and suggestion). Largely, my study continued the research tradition Hyland and Hyland's studies established, and supported quite a number of their findings (e.g., L2 teachers' provision of similar amounts of positive and negative feedback).

Empirical Contribution: Strength/Problem-Oriented Feedback and Suggestions
As Section 7.2 summarized, Teacher T's feedback delivery approaches were

typically categorized from four perspectives: orientation, scaffolding degree, language channel, and changes. Concerning the approaches L2 teachers usually use to deliver non-error feedback (from the perspective of orientation), the findings available at present appear not to be completely consistent. Hyland and Hyland's (2001, 2006a) results indicated the teachers provided **a similar amount of positive and negative feedback**, but one teacher gave more suggestions than her colleague. My study found that Teacher T, in general, used a similar amount of problems-indication feedback (negative comments), strengths-indication feedback (positive comments), explanations, advice/ suggestions, and revisions when commenting on EA issues (each about 20%). Wang (2011) reported 96% of teacher feedback on EA was **negative**, 11% of which were suggestions (classified by Wang as a type of negative feedback). Clements' (2008) case study teacher preferred to provide **positive** comments and became more positive with the passage of time; but he did not manage to provide suggestions other than pointing out the strengths/problems of his EFL students' writing.

Although the empirical evidence on L2 teachers' feedback delivery approaches does not to paint a consistent picture, there appears to be similar thinking behind the way teachers provide non-error feedback. That is, all the teachers in the above-mentioned studies were aware of the interpersonal effects of feedback. In Wang's (2011) study, the teacher comments were overwhelmingly negative (96%), but the teacher took student expectations, affect and motivation into consideration and mitigated her negative feedback most of the time (89% mitigated negative feedback). Clements' (2008) teacher participant emphasized on the strengths of student writing, which also reflects his sense of the students' affective needs. In my study, Teacher T usually began her combination comments with positive-oriented feedback. These available studies about feedback delivery approaches, though yielding seemingly inconsistent findings, support Hyland and Hyland's (2006a) argument that teachers have awareness of the interpersonal and affective aspect of feedback and they have a desire to construct a better teacher-student relationship and a more supportive teaching environment when writing comments.

As to the different results regarding L2 teachers' provision of suggestions, there may be two main reasons for the differences. First, teachers utilized different techniques to give feedback. In Wang's (2011) study, the teacher used both written and oral feedback to respond to student writing. When giving oral feedback, she was found to move from pointing out problems to finding solutions together with her students. As such, we can assume that the teacher might save suggestions and explanation for her oral feedback and this is the reason why there were fewer written suggestions reported in Wang's study. According to Hyland and Hyland (2001), the teacher's use of a feedback sheet caused a much higher number of suggestions to be provided by teachers. In addition, it might be closely related to teacher beliefs and teacher experience. For instance, in my study, Teacher T strongly believed that suggestions must be provided, otherwise teacher feedback cannot be considered effective. In Clements' (2008) study, the lack of suggestions could be explained by the teacher's limited experience in providing feedback.

Empirical Contribution: Combination Feedback
From the perspective of scaffolding degree, my study found Teacher T mainly provided combination feedback (more than 65% of her EA feedback), which usually began with something positive and consisted of feedback pointing out strengths and problems, feedback explaining problems, and feedback providing suggestions/solutions. Similarly, Hyland and Hyland (2001) reported teachers' provision of praise-criticism pairs, criticism-suggestion

pairs, and "the praise-criticism-suggestion triad" (p.196) as well. Min's (2013) study reported her use of combination feedback that clarified the writers' intentions, identified writing problems, explained problems, and made specific suggestions. However, Hyland and Hyland's and Min's studies chiefly related the teachers' provision of combination feedback to the affective aspect of teacher feedback (e.g., the teacher's probing and collaborative reader stance), rather than to its pedagogic effect. In my study, according to Teacher T's report in the background interview, her combination comments allowed a high degree of pedagogic helpfulness. In light of these findings, L2 teachers probably could do better if they keep both the pedagogic and affective effects of their written feedback in mind when deciding how to deliver EA feedback.

Empirical Contribution: Feedback in English/Chinese/Both and Use of Emoticons

To my knowledge, so far, no feedback studies in the field of L2 writing have ever touched upon the language channel of feedback (e.g., feedback in Chinese/English/both) and teachers' use of emoticons (e.g., ☺; ☹). According to Forman (2008), in bilingual L2 classrooms the local teachers' use of the L1 can be seen as scaffolding to build knowledge. In my study, Teacher T also believed that commenting in Chinese or in both Chinese and English provided a scaffold for teachers' efforts to write feedback and students' efforts to attend to it. Considering my study found that the use of comments in Chinese and emoticons triggered different reactions from the students (e.g., Student A felt feedback language did not matter while Students B and C preferred feedback in Chinese), teachers' choice of language channel for EA feedback and use of emoticons warrant a thorough investigation.

Empirical Contribution: Teacher Revision

My study found that *revision* was a type of feedback Teacher T provided rather frequently. Teacher T took the affective aspect of feedback into consideration when revising student writing as well. For instance, she usually used mitigation strategies and preceded her revisions with words like "*Here, a possible revision can be: ...*" to mitigate the imposition of her revisions. However, whether it is appropriate for teachers to provide students with a number of revisions is still an open question. One reason is that, when offering such guidance, the teacher is considered to be in danger of appropriating students' writing and becoming a critic rather than a coach (Sprinkle, 2004).

Empirical Contribution: Cross-assignment and Cross-student Differences
Similar to the cross-assignment and cross-student changes of teachers' foci, most prior feedback studies did not look at the cross-assignment and cross-student changes of teachers' feedback delivery approaches. My study found that, across writing assignments, there was a constant increase of positive and hedged feedback and a decrease of explanations and direct feedback. A reasonable explanation of these changes is that they are a consequence of student improvement over time. In Ferris et al.'s (1997) study, one possible explanation the researchers provided for such cross-assignment differences was "student improvement and greater shared knowledge" (p.172). Similarly, according to Hyland (2007), genre teachers gradually reduce their direct explanations of genre issues, their guidance, and their control over time because, with the passage of time, the students' competence and knowledge in the target genre grow and their confidence in genre writing increases. To a large extent, it seems that Teacher T's situation was such a case.

In my study, Teacher T provided a larger amount of EA feedback and more positive comments to Student B, whom she considered to have a relatively lower level of expertise in English writing and lower-level English proficiency. This result is somewhat inconsistent with Ferris et al.'s (1997) finding that "teachers take a more collegial, less directive stance when responding to stronger students, while focusing more on surface-level problems with weaker students" (p.177). However, in their study, Ferris et al. also pointed out how teachers deliver their feedback might be influenced by students' interaction with the teacher. My finding shows that this claim of Ferris et al. could be true. As the example in Sub-section 7.3.1.1 illustrates, in my study Teacher T also felt she had a better relationship with Student B and the teacher-student relationship was a reason why she wrote more positive feedback on Student B's writing.

Theoretical Contribution to the Sociocognitive Perspective of Teacher Feedback and SFL-Informed Genre Pedagogy: Feedback Delivery Approaches
The empirical contribution discussed above reveal a striking factor that greatly influences teacher decisions about how to deliver EA feedback, that is, teachers' affective considerations. It once again mirrors Hyland and Hyland's (2006a) argument about the importance of the interpersonal and affective aspect of teacher feedback. Moreover, once again, it reveals the interactional, complex picture of teacher feedback. In other words, it is impossible to isolate the teacher's feedback delivery approaches from teacher factors (e.g., teacher experience, teachers' affective considerations), as well as student factors (e.g., student improvement and development), the affect and effect of teacher feedback, and contextual factors (e.g., supportive teaching environment).

In the Literature Review Chapter, from the sociocognitive perspective, the feedback itself is considered as the text-level context the teacher constructs in the feedback process, and students' interaction with it offers potential for their learning and development. In my study, the findings about Teacher T's feedback delivery approaches unveiled the details of the text-level context L2 teachers construct in practice: a similar amount of positive/

negative comments, explanations, advice/suggestions, and revisions; and most of EA feedback was combination feedback. From Teacher T's frequent acknowledgement of the strengths of student writing and her frequent provision of combination feedback to scaffold her students' understanding of teacher feedback there is an indication that the text-level context teachers constructed had two typical layers: the interpersonal layer and the pedagogic layer.

Moreover, my study shows, to better understand teacher feedback, a systematic, finer-grained model for characterizing teachers' feedback delivery approaches is still needed. As repeatedly mentioned, my study used various perspectives (orientation, scaffolding degree, and language channel) to identify Teacher T's feedback delivery approaches. It mainly followed Hyland and Hyland's (2001) tradition to group teacher feedback into praise, criticism, and suggestion, but moved beyond it since more categories characterizing Teacher T's feedback delivery approaches emerged from my data (e.g., teacher revisions, feedback in Chinese). These various categories used in earlier studies and my study seem to indicate that we can broadly categorize feedback according to its internal (e.g., feedback orientation like positive/ negative responses, pragmatic function of feedback) and external (e.g., the language used to provide feedback) qualities.

Generally, it seems that underlying Teacher T's feedback delivery approaches were the principles of product-oriented teaching and genre teaching. On the one hand, the evidence that the bulk of Teacher T's EA feedback was evaluator-response comments (74%) reflects that it is very likely that Teacher T's instruction occurred in a product-oriented evaluative environment. This is because in the product-oriented environment, the teacher usually takes the stance of an evaluator and assumes the role of evaluating the single draft of students' assignments. On the other hand, Teacher T provided a large amount of combination comments (65%) to point out and analyze the students' EA problems/strengths and to provide the students with explanations, suggestions, and revisions. Her frequent use of combination comments implies that, when providing EA feedback, Teacher T seemed to emphasize the importance of supportive, explicit instruction and she applied the most typical principle of the genre-based pedagogical approach (i.e., The teacher helps to scaffold the students' understanding of how to explain argumentatively and why it should be explained argumentatively in the ways it is.). In general, the findings about Teacher T's feedback delivery approaches suggest that she might apply a combination of genre-and product-oriented perspectives to her teaching and an aggregation of pedagogies might be underlying her feedback practices. In some situations, to maximize the learning opportunities, an eclectic combination of methods and activities may be necessary.

7.3.2.3 Empirical and Theoretical Contributions: How Teachers Decide What to Focus on and How to Deliver EA Feedback

Empirical Contribution: Teacher Decision-Making

As reviewed in Section 7.1, behind Teacher T's decisions about her feedback foci and feedback delivery approaches, teacher belief/cognition stands out. On the one hand, my study found that Teacher T's decisions about feedback foci were mainly informed by her beliefs about what EA issues to focus on. On the other hand, my study found that Teacher T's decisions about feedback delivery approaches were not always informed by her beliefs. For example, she believed that she would mainly provide direct EA feedback, but in reality, she provided more hedged comments with the passage of time. Simply put, my study indicated that Teacher T's actual practices were both consistent and inconsistent with her feedback beliefs.

It is obvious that my findings about the belief-practice consistency and inconsistency contributed new empirical evidence to the line of **research on teacher cognition**. So far, feedback studies on teacher cognition have reported three main types of findings: belief-practice inconsistency (e.g., Lee, 2008a), belief-practice consistency (e.g., Min, 2013), and both belief-practice consistency and inconsistency (e.g., Ferris, 2014). Here, it is not possible to say that my study offered further evidence to the studies that shared findings (e.g., Ferris, 2014). This is because, in Ferris' (2014) study, teachers felt they frequently used *questions* while they actually used more statements and imperatives and the belief-practice inconsistency was related to questioning feedback. In my study, the belief-practice inconsistency was related to direct/ hedged EA feedback. Clearly, there is still a need for further, detailed research on teacher cognition and beliefs to explain mixed results and generalize findings.

Theoretical Contribution to Understanding the Sociocognitive Perspective of Teacher Feedback and Genre Pedagogy: Teacher Decision-Making

The evidence related to Teacher T's decision-making points to the dynamics of teacher feedback. My study contributes two types of supporting evidence about this dynamic quality. First, as discussed earlier in Sub-section 7.3.1.1, Teacher T's developing and increasing awareness of student problems with EA shows that her feedback beliefs evolved (though slowly) during my study and teacher feedback is inherently dynamic. Second, Teacher T's decision-making was context-sensitive. For example, because of the influence of the traditional Chinese examination culture, one objective Teacher T set for her writing assignments was to prepare her students for the coming CET-4 test at the end of semester. In this sense, my study found that it is greatly due to the forces of the inseparable sociocultural and pedagogic contexts that Teacher

T decided to provide feedback on EA issues (See Section 4.4). This finding corroborates Lee's (2008a) report that the Chinese EFL teachers' feedback beliefs and practices were deeply affected by the examination orientation in the education system and culture, and it also highlights the susceptibility of teacher feedback to the contexts and its dynamic/changing nature.

In fact, from the above-mentioned inseparability of the sociocultural and pedagogic contexts, more theoretical implications arise. First, as can be seen in Sub-section 2.2.1.6 (about the sociocognitive perspective of teacher feedback), my study acknowledged the importance and the value of **structured** contexts. A glimpse of the layers of the contexts laid out in my study (e.g., the sociocultural and pedagogic contexts at the macro and the micro level respectively) can make us more aware of what the "structured" contexts at the macro-, meso-, and micro-level look like. Moreover, as it is the interrelated sociocultural and instructional contexts that explain how teacher feedback is provided, the interrelatedness of the layered contexts contributes to broadening our understanding of the inseparability principle that underlay the sociocognitive perspective of teacher feedback my study adopted.

According to Hyland (2007), genre teachers are encouraged to take a critical, reflective look at their work so as to make informed decisions. In Teacher T's case, she usually spent considerable time and energy reflecting on her feedback practices (See Sub-section 4.6.3 about Teacher T's review and reflection operations). As teachers in previous studies (e.g., Best, 2011; Feuerherm, 2011/2012; Min, 2013) often used action research to recognize and develop their feedback beliefs, genre teachers are also encouraged to do action research to increase awareness of their feedback beliefs and improve their feedback practices.

7.3.2.4 Empirical and Theoretical Contributions: Students' Acceptance and Incorporation of EA Feedback

Empirical Contribution: A General Discussion

As already mentioned, one of the research strands in focus explores **feedback from the perspective of students**. My findings about students' acceptance and incorporation of EA feedback made three major contributions to this strand of research. First, my findings and results were much broader in scope. As pointed out in the Literature Review Chapter, the amount of empirical work on students' cognitive, affective, and behavioral acceptance and incorporation of EA feedback at the feedback-interpreting stage is still very limited and the available findings were mainly related to whether students had difficulties in understanding teacher feedback or its intention. My findings, going beyond that, help to show whether the students cognitively, affectively, and behaviorally understood, agreed with, and incorporated teacher feedback when they were in the act of processing it.

Second, because of my study, the generalizability of findings about students' acceptance and incorporation of teacher feedback becomes complicated. As to the students' understanding of, agreement with, and incorporation of EA feedback, my study found that Students A, B, and C were unique individuals. For example, as to teacher feedback on supporting evidence, Student A could understand it by turning to online resources for help; Student B could gradually understand it over time; and Student C often could understand it but still had some questions about how to act on it. Now, findings from previous studies about students' understanding of teacher feedback are diverse (e.g., having difficulty, not having difficulty, and sometimes having difficulty in understanding teacher feedback). Due to the uniqueness of my findings, it seems hard to say my findings supported any of these three positions.

However, it seems that my study is capable of supporting some studies that touched upon students' emotional acceptance of teacher feedback. In my study, Students A, B, and C all experienced a change in terms of emotional acceptance and incorporation of EA feedback (Student A: from emotional acceptance to dissatisfaction; Students B and C: from emotional non-acceptance to acceptance/satisfaction). Although no changes were reported in Clements' (2008) study, my study seems to lend some support to his findings that each of his student participants was a unique case (either emotionally accepted teacher feedback or felt overwhelmed by and unsatisfied with it). My study also supports Mahfoodh's (2017) report that students' emotional acceptance of teacher feedback varied from one student to another.

Empirical Contribution: A Specific Discussion of Students' Variations and Individual Cases

In my study, Students A, B, and C varied greatly in their acceptance and incorporation of EA feedback. As such, my findings about these cross-student variations provide support to Hyland and Hyland's (2006b) caution that we should not lump students "as an undifferentiated group" (p.11) when we seek to understand how teacher feedback is structured and interpreted.

In L2 teaching and learning literature, Chinese as well as Asian students are often labelled "as an undifferentiated group" and considered as passive, obedient learners. To a large extent, this is because in the traditional Eastern education culture the teacher is viewed as the authority figure (e.g., Kumaravadivelu, 2003; Pennycook, 1998). My findings about the cross-student variations show that there may be great individual differences among Chinese EFL students and some students may diverge greatly from the image that the unrefined cultural stereotypes have imposed on them. As a simple example, Student A's self-regulated, deep-level acceptance and incorporation of Teacher T's feedback shows that she brought agency to the feedback process and, instead of being a passive learner, she could take control of her own learning. Kumar, Kumar, and Feryok's (2009) feedback study also provided a counter-example to the general image that Chinese students are mostly passive who accept whatever their teachers tell them.

Similar to the case of Student A, Ene and Upton (2014) reported that students' use of teacher feedback on the development of ideas dropped within a two-semester time period. According to Ene and Upton, one of the reasons behind this drop was that students' writing abilities developed with the passage of time and then their uptake of such feedback became unnecessary. It seems that this reason can be used to explain Students A and B's decreasing and increasing cognitive and behavioural acceptance and incorporation of EA feedback as well. After Student A internalized the genre/rhetorical knowledge from Teacher T's supporting evidence-related feedback and improved her writing ability, it is not surprising that she did not incorporate similar feedback any more. As Student B's ability to understand Teacher T's feedback on supporting evidence improved over time, it is natural that she began to accept and incorporate more of it.

The other reason Ene and Upton (2014) gave for the students' declining uptake of teacher feedback on the development of ideas was the increasing complexity of writing tasks in the second semester (more advanced writing stage). The researchers considered that the increased complexity made it harder for students to implement the feedback. In my study, the complexity of writing tasks did not change greatly from W1 to W3 (about practicing cause-and-effect, exemplification, and freely-chosen argumentation techniques respectively). This lack of change in the complexity of writing tasks can probably explain Student C's relative stability in her cognitive and behavioural acceptance and incorporation of Teacher T's EA feedback. However, Students B and C felt that they had problems with the technique of cause-and-effect, which implies that this technique could have been somewhat more difficult.

In my study, Students B and C encountered the following problems in relation to their acceptance and incorporation of EA feedback: inability to understand and agree with teacher feedback (e.g., Student B), inaccurate understanding of teacher feedback (e.g., Student B), and uncertainty about their understanding of the intention of the teacher (e.g., Student C). These findings show that, when processing EA feedback, students may encounter various understanding-related problems. If this were the case, there is a need for future research to raise attention to the understanding-related issue.

In fact, there are two other reasons why the issue related to student understanding of teacher feedback deserves attention. One is that the available findings about students' understanding of teacher feedback are diverse. For instance, in Ferris's (1995) study, nearly 50% of participants emphasized that they never had any problems understanding teacher comments while Lee's (2008b) interviews showed only 11% of highly proficient students said they could understand teacher feedback. Nazif, Biswas, and Hilbig (2004) and Zacharias (2007) found that students "sometimes" had difficulty in understanding teacher feedback or its intention. Another reason is that learners' understanding of feedback is an issue that is equally as important as learners' use of feedback (Zhao, 2010). According to Zhao, feedback that is used/copied but not understood does not necessarily support the development of learners' long-term writing proficiency.

My study also found that Student B sometimes disagreed with Teacher T's feedback on supporting evidence, and then she refused to accept and incorporate it. Similar teacher-student disagreement has been reported in previous studies. In Cohen's (1991) study, when teacher feedback reminded the high performer to provide examples, the student argued that she purposely wrote concisely for fear that she was too repetitive. In Brice's (1995) study, the student responded to teacher feedback about the irrelevance of supporting evidence with the following disagreement and justification: he wrote the way he wrote for the purposes of meeting task requirements and his teacher's expectation that stories were used as explanations. To a large extent, as teacher feedback, especially teacher feedback on supporting evidence, may lead to such teacher-student disagreement, it seems that feedback providers need to have a better reading of student writing and try to provide comments from the perspective of students' writing intentions.

Theoretical Implications for the Sociocognitive Perspective of Teacher Feedback and SFL-Informed Genre Pedagogy: Students' Acceptance and Incorporation of EA Feedback

Theoretical Implications: The Sociocognitive Perspective of Teacher Feedback

As explained in the Literature Review Chapter and in this chapter, the adaptivity and alignment principles are two basic principles underlying the sociocognitive theory of student learning and development. To borrow Atkinson's (2014) metaphor, during the feedback cycle (one type of social interaction), the teacher and the student, like the cooperative ping pong players, are sensitively and continuously aligning their thoughts, affect, and actions moment by moment so that student-teacher shared/aligned thoughts, affect, and actions are created, and teacher feedback can be successfully accepted, incorporated, and used by students. The cross-case discussion presented above indicates that Students A, B, and C's cognitive, behavioural, and affective interpretation of teacher feedback was constantly **"changing"** and **"shifting"**, which is clear evidence of the student's adaptation and alignment for learning during the social interaction/feedback.

As discussed in Section 7.3.1, findings from teacher data support the sociocognitive perspective on teacher feedback, which conceptualizes it as a complex, dynamic system. The above empirical discussion in this sub-section (7.3.2.4), which encompasses attention to student factors (e.g., student agency, individual differences, student affect) and contextual factors (e.g., the genre of writing tasks), once again shows the inseparability of "mindbodyworld" and the complexity of teacher feedback. Moreover, the above-reviewed results in relation to the changes of Students A, B, and C's cognitive and emotional acceptance of teacher feedback depict the dynamics of teacher feedback.

Theoretical Implications: Genre Pedagogy
My findings about the students' acceptance and incorporation of EA feedback inform L2 genre teachers what is necessary when they sequence learning and scaffold learning. As already mentioned in this sub-section (7.3.2.4), in my study, the students experienced difficulties in interpreting and understanding EA feedback. When sequencing learning, as genre teachers need to determine the most critical skills relevant to students' immediate needs, the difficulties pinned down in my study make the instruction related to EA issues in general and supporting evidence in particular central to the teaching of exposition writing. Hyland (2007) pointed out that the degree and the forms of scaffolding play a key role in helping students reach a higher level of performance. When L2 genre teachers provide scaffolding to help students deal with the difficult EA issues, it seems that direct, deep, and long-term scaffolding is needed and diversified forms of scaffolding are necessary.

According to genre theorists (e.g., Hyland, 2007), genre pedagogy emphasizes student learning through teacher support/scaffolding. However, this pedagogy also points out that students need teacher scaffolding less and less as their competence in writing targeted genres and their confidence in writing grow. In my study, a good case in support of this position (about decreasing scaffolding) is that Student A processed Teacher T's EA feedback on her W3 in a simple way. This is because she considered she could not gain new insights from Teacher T's EA feedback on her W3 and she confidently felt that she had acquired the genre/rhetorical knowledge provided in Teacher T's previous comments. Hyland (2007) pointed out that ongoing diagnostic assessments are needed in the genre-oriented classroom since they can help teachers identify areas where learners need extra practice and allow teachers to target the areas that need additional teaching. My study suggests that teachers need to integrate ongoing assessments into their teaching to identify when to decrease or remove scaffolding/feedback.

According to Hyland (2007), a genre-based writing course usually begins with doing needs analysis and seeking information about learners' current proficiencies, perceptions, and ambitions. Considering the occurrence of learning in the inseparability of student cognition, affect and behavior, it is probably also necessary for genre teachers to assess students' emotional needs and consider how to best serve their emotional needs before the course unfolds.

7.3.2.5 Empirical and Theoretical Contributions: How the Students' Acceptance and Incorporation of EA Feedback were Decided

Empirical Contribution: Student Decision-Making
As to the decision-making processes students engage themselves in as they process teacher feedback, this is a novel area of research that holds particular

Chapter 7   Discussion and Conclusion

promise (Hyland & Hyland, 2006a), but which so far has been explored by only a handful of researchers. As such, one important contribution my study made was presenting some similar and novel findings about how the students' acceptance and incorporation of EA feedback were produced (i.e., the depth of the students' cognitive processing of EA feedback, the integration of the students' cognitive, affective, and behavioural engagement with EA feedback, and the mediation of student-context interaction).

In my study, Students A, B, and C varied in the depth of their processing of Teacher T's EA feedback. My study related Student A's self-regulated, deep-level acceptance and incorporation of Teacher T's EA feedback to her deep processing of it. As to Student B's slow acceptance and incorporation of Teacher T's EA feedback, my study connected it to her superficial cognitive engagement with it. For Student C, her other-regulated acceptance and incorporation of Teacher T's EA feedback was linked to her processing of feedback at a moderately deep level.

To my knowledge, apart from Brice's (1995), Kumar's (2012), Kumar and Kumar's (2009), and Kumar, Kumar, and Feryok's (2009) studies, there seems to be no other work that related the students' acceptance and incorporation of teacher feedback to the depth of their cognitive operations. In Brice's (1995) study, the researcher reported two cases similar to Students A and B. One of them, like Student A, processed his teacher's feedback deeply by **describing the teacher comments, explaining his understanding of those comments**, and **responding to teacher comments** and he had little trouble understanding his teacher's feedback on content and organization. The other student, similar to Student B, could not understand his teacher's feedback on supporting evidence since he just spent time and energy explaining and arguing why he wrote the way he wrote but did not analyze the teacher feedback.

Kumar and her colleagues' (2009) studies reported similar findings, which also revealed the depth of students' cognitive engagement is closely related to students' acceptance and incorporation of teacher feedback. In these studies, the researchers reported that their student participants' acceptance and use of teacher feedback resulted from their interpretation and evaluation of it, their consideration of and reflection on the issues highlighted in it, and their justification and explanation of their own work. In Kumar and Kumar's (2009) opinion, the effort the student spent on justifying and explaining her own work deepened her thinking about teacher feedback and pushed her to accept and incorporate it.

Although studies that are now available reported similar results, research into students' actual thought processes as they attend to teacher feedback is still limited (Hyland & Hyland, 2006a; Kumar, 2012; Kumar & Kumar, 2009; Kumar, Kumar & Feryok, 2009) and empirical evidence is obviously still lacking. As such, there is a need for future research to continue to describe and elucidate such thought processes. Teachers need to understand them so that they can help students learn to process teacher feedback at a deep level and accept and incorporate teacher feedback more easily.

Previous studies have so far identified a number of factors that influenced students' processing and use of teacher feedback (e.g., student motivation; Goldstein, 2006). Generally, my study confirmed the importance of the factors identified in previous studies. For example, to some degree, the decisions Student A made about accepting and incorporating teacher feedback were built upon her motivation to deal with teacher feedback. This result largely supports Goldstein's (2006) claim that motivation is particularly important in understanding how students might use their teachers' commentary.

In fact, Goldstein (2006) claimed that it is the interaction of context- and student-related factors that may greatly influence how students attend to feedback. The influential interplay of student and contextual factors was similarly identified in my study (See Section 5.5.4). For example, it is clear from the discussion in Sub-section 7.3.1.1 that it is the interplay of the sociocultural context, teacher fatigue, simplicity of teacher feedback, and students' insufficient writing knowledge and ability that led to Students B and C's non-or semi-acceptance of teacher feedback on conclusion.

Theoretical Contributions to the Sociocognitive Perspective of Teacher Feedback and SFL-Informed Genre Pedagogy: Student Decision-Making
As elaborated in Sub-section 7.3.1.1, my findings about student decision-making provide evidence for the sociocognitive perspective of teacher feedback which rested on the inseparability, adaptivity, and alignment principles. The following analysis of the depth of the students' cognitive processing of EA feedback and their decision-making explains how student learning takes place successfully or unsuccessfully, which makes a contribution to a better understanding of the sociocognitive adaptivity principle and genre pedagogy.

According to the adaptivity principles of sociocognitive theory, animals evolve nervous systems to "enable them to adapt to, function in, and coexist with the ecosocial environments" (Nishino & Atkinson, 2015, p.39). That is to say, humans' learning (i.e., nervous/cognitive evolvement) is largely a process of better adapting to the contexts and humans' learning is adaptive (Atkinson, 2010b). In this sense, human beings who can better adapt themselves to the context probably learn faster. In my study, Student A evaluated, analyzed, and reviewed Teacher T's EA feedback and her writing problems, and she processed Teacher T's EA feedback at a deep level. In other words, Student

A was able to well adapt herself to the text-level context (i.e., Teacher T's EA feedback), which naturally brought about her quicker and better acceptance and incorporation of EA feedback.

My findings related to student decision-making make students' learning in the genre-based classroom concrete. According to Hyland (2007), genre teachers need to prepare opportunities for students to **engage in, explore, explain, extend, and evaluate their learning** (See Section 2.2.2). In my study, when dealing with EA feedback, only Student A could carry out the explanation, exploration, extension, and evaluation operations and then decided on her acceptance and incorporation of EA feedback. As shown in Chapter 5, when processing Teacher T's EA feedback, Student A made great effort to identify and summarize the focus, key points, and implications of Teacher T's EA feedback (i.e., to perform analyzing operations). That is to say, when interacting with teacher feedback, Student A could **explain** teacher feedback in her own words (e.g., summarizing teacher feedback) and **explore** in great depth the things behind teacher feedback (e.g., identifying the implications of teacher feedback). Furthermore, when she found that she still had questions about how to use evidence to support topic sentences, she adaptively **extended** the range of her learning opportunities to critically read, evaluate, and analyze a model text she found online. In addition, when processing Teacher T's EA feedback, Student A also critically analyzed her own writing problems (analyzing operations) and kept **evaluating** her own work. Then, due to her **deep-level cognitive engagement** with Teacher T's EA feedback, it is doubtless that she could effectively understand it and fully accept and incorporate it, and as a result, she learnt and developed relatively faster than the other two students.

Student C, like Student A, could explain the focus and key points of Teacher

T's EA feedback, and explore the implications. However, as she usually did not go further to find answers to her questions about teacher feedback, her engagement with teacher feedback did not involve **sufficient exploration and extension operations**. So, it is not surprising that Student C could not accept and incorporate teacher feedback on supporting evidence as fully as Student A did. Student B's superficial-level processing of Teacher T's EA feedback merely involved her reading of Teacher T's EA feedback and her own work (reading operations) and her simple evaluation of Teacher T's EA feedback (evaluating operations). That is to say, her engagement with teacher feedback barely involved higher-level thinking operations such as explanation, exploration, extension, and evaluation of teacher feedback. As such, Student B could not understand Teacher T's EA feedback very well, let alone accept it immediately.

It is generally believed that students bring agency to the feedback process (or learning process). There is one possible reason why Students B and C failed to exercise agency and could not adequately engaged in processing feedback. That is, between the students and Teacher T, the common ground is significantly lacking. This assumption is made because when Student B began to develop some familiarity with Teacher T's EA feedback and gained some awareness of her problems with argumentation, she began to accept and incorporate Teacher T's feedback. In other words, when the common ground between Teacher T and Student B started to expand, Student B's acceptance and incorporation of teacher feedback emerged. In this sense, the significant lack of teacher-student common ground deprived Students B and C of opportunities to exercise agency, so it was impossible for them to accept and incorporate Teacher T's EA feedback easily.

7.3.2.6 Empirical and Theoretical Contributions: Students' and Teachers' Evaluation of the Feedback Process

Empirical Contribution: Evaluation of the Feedback Process

As explained in the Methodology Chapter, to answer RQ3 (*According to the student and the teacher, to what extent does the process of constructing and interpreting EA feedback help students improve, if it is considered effective?*), interviews with the students and Teacher T were conducted. Interview data led to the following findings:

- effective feedback processes;
- student growth as writers and feedback receivers; and
- mixed opinions about the helpfulness of positive/negative EA feedback and hedged feedback.

Apparently, my findings about the students' evaluation of the feedback-and-interpretation process also make empirical contributions to the research strand on students' perspectives on teacher feedback. The major contributions can be outlined from two perspectives: generalizability of findings and novel findings.

Empirical Contribution: Generalizability of Findings

First, my findings about the students' acknowledgement of the helpfulness of EA feedback increase the likelihood of the generalizability of existing literature. So far, a number of studies have found that ESL and EFL university students generally felt that their teachers' feedback helped them progress as writers (e.g., Clements, 2008; Enginarlar, 1993; Ferris, 1995; Hedgcock & Lefkowitz, 1994; Li, 2016; Seker & Dincer, 2014; Yang, 2013; Zhang & Hyland, 2022). When commenting in a general sense on the effectiveness of the feedback interactions, Students A, B and C also said that it was effective

Chapter 7 Discussion and Conclusion

and they became better writers and better feedback receivers because of it. By far, it seems that a generalizable result about the helpfulness of teacher feedback can be tentatively established. Largely, previous studies and my study verify Ferris' (2003), Ferris and Hedgcock's (2014), and Hyland and Hyland's (2006b) assertion that students feel teacher feedback is valuable to them and it can help them improve their writing.

However, it is necessary to point out, in my study, although the teacher and the students shared the opinion that EA feedback was effective, the students all reported that some communication problems occurred during the feedback interactions. Student A felt that sometimes she was misunderstood by Teacher T; Students B and C felt they could not understand what Teacher T was communicating or they could not communicate very well with Teacher T (especially when they dealt with teacher feedback on their W1). It seems that my findings support Hyland's (1998) argument that "the feedback situation has great potential for miscommunication and misunderstanding" (p.255). They are also consistent with Clements' (2008) result that the students felt teacher comments were helpful for them, but sometimes the feedback-revision process was not "a smooth one" (p.207).

In my study, as to the helpfulness of positive feedback and direct, negative feedback, mixed results were obtained. On the one hand, Students A and B did not deny the helpfulness of positive feedback; on the other hand, they both acknowledged the helpfulness of direct, negative feedback. In her final interview, Student C firmly expressed her belief in the helpfulness of direct, negative feedback and reported that hedged, positive feedback did not work in the long run. Generally, as Students A, B, and C expressed mixed opinions about the helpfulness of positive feedback, it is hard to generalize the results of student report. However, the findings of my study seem to align with

Hyland and Hyland's (2006a) results. In their study, the students similarly expressed reservations regarding the usefulness of positive teacher feedback.

Empirical Contribution: Novel Findings

To date, few studies have ever asked the students to evaluate the extent to which each type of EA feedback was helpful for them to become better writers. As a result, my study contributes the following novel findings to the literature about students' perspectives on teacher feedback.

One is that my study reported conflicting findings about the helpfulness of hedged feedback. As listed in the Literature Review Chapter, previous studies diverged in their findings about the helpfulness of hedged feedback (e.g., useful, harmful, or unclear). According to Hyland and Hyland (2006b), it is dangerous to use mitigated comments. In my study, the findings were not very clear. For example, in the ongoing interviews, Student C reported that hedged feedback enhanced her motivation to deal with teacher feedback and it was more helpful than direct feedback; but in the final interview, when Student C made further comparison, she reported that she benefitted more from direct feedback in the long run. Given that the findings about the helpfulness of hedged feedback are as yet inconclusive, there is certainly a need for future research to continue to investigate it.

The students in my study felt they had become better feedback receivers after all the feedback sessions in a semester. Students A and C reported that they could quickly identify teacher intent in EA feedback. Student B said she could better deal with teacher feedback. Students B and C also reported that they had started to develop more accepting and less defensive attitudes toward teacher feedback. These reports suggest that the feedback interactions facilitated the development of the students' cognitive abilities and the students

Chapter 7   Discussion and Conclusion

seemed to be able to deal with EA feedback more rationally. Considering critical thinking skills are part of cognitive repertoires and students need to exercise critical thinking skills to judge and determine whether to accept, disregard, or reject EA feedback, the three students' development of cognitive abilities shows that there might be an improvement in their critical thinking skills because of their interpretation of teacher feedback. In this sense, the evidence from my study sheds some light on the question Ferris (2001, 2003) has repeatedly raised in her publications: *"Can teacher feedback foster the development of critical thinking skills without any tangible evidence of this development on student revisions?"*.

In contrast to the above-discussed positive findings, Student B did not think she had more strategies to attend to teacher feedback after my study. Considering the students were not afforded ample opportunities to attempt feedback strategies (Teacher T did not require revision or rewriting and the students as study participants were only asked to cognitively process teacher feedback), it is natural the students felt their feedback-handling strategies were still limited after several feedback sessions. In any event, my study indicates that Cohen's (1987) suggestion that students need training about strategies to handle teacher feedback is reasonable. However, whether feedback-handling strategies can be provided in teachers' feedback comments is still a question without clear answers (Conrad & Goldstein, 1999).

Theoretical Contribution to Better Using Genre Pedagogy: Student Evaluation
My findings are useful for genre teachers to facilitate the effectiveness of EA feedback for student development. For example, in my study, Students A, B, and C all felt that teacher feedback on supporting evidence could guide them to an awareness of the rhetorical expectations of the English readers and help them move toward greater self-regulation. According to the students' reports,

teacher feedback on supporting evidence was helpful because they felt that Teacher T repeatedly provided feedback on supporting evidence and devoted most of her effort to it. The reasons Students A, B and C stated provide Chinese EFL genre teachers with more insight into feedback intensity and teacher engagement.

7.3.2.7 The Contributions My Study Made from the Perspective of RQs: A Summary

In brief, as the result of my findings about Teacher T's constructing of feedback (RQ1), the students' processing of EA feedback (RQ2), and student/teacher evaluation of EA feedback (RQ3), my study expanded scholarship on three strands of feedback research: ① students' perspectives on teacher feedback, ② the feedback itself, and ③ teacher cognition. However, it seems that my research findings increase the complexity of our understanding of the previous results since each student in my study was found to be unique and their acceptance and incorporation of EA feedback differed and changed over time. It seems that my findings often cannot improve the generalizability of the inconsistently-reported existing results.

Theoretically, the above elaboration (7.3.2.1–7.3.2.6) makes the interactional, interpersonal, dynamic, and complex nature of teacher feedback become clearer and my findings support taking a sociocognitive perspective to conceptualize teacher feedback. As far as genre pedagogy is concerned, the contribution of my findings lies in their implications for the role L2 genre teachers and students play in the classroom that teaches expository writing and provides EA feedback (e.g., teachers' role in designing and maintaining class focus, teachers' role in ongoing assessment of students' emotional needs and student learning).

7.3.3 Contributions of My Study to Methodological Insights

As pointed out in the Methodology Chapter, my study was a case study and replicated the main methods (think-alouds and retrospective interviews) Hyland and Hyland (2006a) used in their study about the feedback-and-interpretation dynamic. Considering the RQs addressed in my study were adequately answered, the methods chosen were suitable for providing the best possible answers to my RQs. Furthermore, a closer examination of how my study was conducted yields some methodological insights regarding collection, analysis, and report of data.

First, since it is often considered that the use of think-alouds carries a risk of increased attention and deeper processing (Jourdenais, 2001), it is necessary to highlight the insight derived from my application of the think-aloud method. To a large extent, my study did not clearly show that the use of think-alouds increased attention and processing. In my study, Students A, B, and C cognitively processed EA feedback at a deep, a superficial, and a moderately deep level. It seems that Student B was not stimulated to engage herself in longer and deeper information processing because of thinking aloud. In my study, the student participants did not seem to have great difficulties with the think-aloud tasks either. Certainly, the main reason for this is that, when the students were verbalizing their thoughts, they were not faced with the dual task like composition writing and thought-verbalizing at the same time. Instead, they only needed to interpret EA feedback and verbalize their thought processes, which might be much less cognitively demanding.

Teacher T could produce long think-aloud protocols. However, in her view, the tasks of typing in comments on the difficult EA issues and verbalizing her thoughts at the same time were cognitively demanding. Due to cognitive overload, she felt tired for thinking aloud and constructing feedback on the concluding paragraph simultaneously. As such, she usually only provided very brief comments on the concluding paragraph and often chose not to provide "revision" on it. To some extent, this finding highlights a limitation of my study because the teacher probably did not provide rich data concerning commenting on the concluding paragraph. In future studies that design to use the think-aloud method, how to reduce the possible cognitive demands on the participants should be considered in advance.

Second, my findings about the belief-practice consistency and inconsistency contributed some methodological knowledge to studying teachers' feedback beliefs. In my study, in terms of Teacher T's feedback foci and feedback delivery approaches, belief-practice consistency and belief-practice inconsistency were both observable. By implication, when teacher belief is studied, breaking it down according to whether it is related to feedback foci or feedback delivery approaches can make the issue of belief-practice consistency/inconsistency much easier to operationalize and study. Borg (2015) also claimed that deconstructing teacher belief into different foci could better study teacher belief.

Third, my study makes a significant contribution to research on non-error feedback by offering a system of codes to analyze the verbal report data (See Appendices G and H for the codebook). So far, although there have been a handful of research studies investigating the teacher/student decision-making thought process during feedback (e.g., Hyland & Hyland, 2006a; Kumar, 2012), there is not a set of codes readily available in previous literature. According to Nunan (1993), to report teachers' classroom decision-making (in a 43-page research paper), he spent hours going through the data and constructing the analytical codes and categories. The construction of my codes and categories was rather demanding too. Even with the aid of the NVivo software, it still took me months to (re)decipher and (re)code data. Although the code system created in my study might not be fully applicable in future/further studies, at least some insights can be gained from it when it is referred to.

Fourth, the other methodological contribution my study makes lies in its data reporting. According to Yin (2014), case study reports can be presented in the traditional narrative form or in the alternative question-and-answer form. Generally, the presently available case studies are mainly reported in the narrative form (e.g., Clements, 2008; Goldstein, 2006). In Yin's view, presenting case study reports in the question-and-answer form is clearer, and readers can directly examine the answers related to each RQ. In my own experience with reporting case study evidence in the question-and-answer format, using this format made the complicated, messy feedback process easier to report and this style of report is suitable for novice researchers.

7.3.4 Recommendations for Responding Practice

From the findings about the teacher's cognitive, behavioural, and affective involvement in feedback provision, student learning and development, feedback foci and feedback delivery approaches, my study yields the following practical insights.

On the whole, my study reassures EFL genre teachers that feedback and EA feedback on student writing are worthwhile investments of time and effort. Also, the findings of my study (about the helpfulness of EA feedback for students **as feedback receivers**) imply that EA feedback may facilitate students' development of critical thinking abilities. However, commenting on EA issues is a tremendous struggle (Min, 2013). There are two main reasons for this difficulty in providing EA feedback. First, my study found that

Teacher T provided EA feedback in "mindbodyworld" (Atkinson, 2014) and it usually came at a high cognitive, emotional, and behavioral cost. Second, my findings show that there may be great individual differences among students. This adds another layer of difficulty to feedback writing since it is necessary for teachers to know their students and customize their feedback to each student's writing and language abilities, his/her motivation for learning English and writing in English, his/her insights into EA issues and English writing, and his/her needs, to name a few.

To resolve the difficulty that giving EA feedback is costly, teachers may need to be selective (Ferris, 2003), responding each time only to the issues that have been covered in class and helping the students focus on a limited number of issues in their writing (Andrade & Evans, 2013). My study seems to suggest that, an easier provision of EA feedback may depend on whether teachers have availed themselves of some cost-saving (meta)cognitive and concrete resources before writing EA comments. For example, my study was aware that teacher response is essentially about the ways in which teachers read student writing and add notes to it. Hence, a good, deep-level reading of student writing can provide teachers with good cognitive resources. That is to say, a good, deep-level reading of student writing can help teachers accurately capture the weakness in student writing and identify its reasons, which can help teachers suggest alternatives more easily.

In my study, Teacher T's affective involvement with feedback writing included her emotional response to student writing, her emotional states aroused by responding to student texts, and her (dis)satisfaction with her own comments. Teachers' pre-knowledge of the types of their emotional investments may help them develop some conscious metacognitive strategies in advance and write EA feedback more efficiently.

Moreover, in my study, Teacher T often used online resources (i.e., one type of her behavioral operations) to ensure that the revised version she provided to the students greatly improved the original. Considering Teacher T often searched the widely-used Chinese search engine *Baidu* or consulted online dictionaries developed by some Chinese companies (e.g., *Youdao)*, the use of corpora and corpus-based tools for writing instruction (e.g., the British National Corpus, the Corpus of Contemporary American English) can be introduced to Chinese EFL teachers. The use of corpora and corpus-based tools can help teachers save the time and efforts they spend on judging and analyzing the random, unmoderated collection of materials available on search engines.

Certainly, the provision of feedback should be attuned to the students' needs and developmental levels. As to how to do it, Ferris (2003) suggested that teachers diagnose rhetorical and grammatical problems during the first week of class and create more opportunities to get to know the students' ability, personality, and attitudes toward writing and the writing course (e.g., asking students to write a journal about themselves and reading it). Moreover, as pointed out in Sub-section 7.3.2.4, my study pinned down some difficulties students may encounter in accepting and incorporating EA feedback. The difficulties identified in my study provide a good starting point for teachers' responding practices.

Specifically, in my study, Students A, B, and C all believed that Teacher T's feedback on the concluding paragraph was not very helpful. As such, Chinese EFL teachers are advised to be particularly careful when providing feedback on this aspect. According to Students B and C, what was deeply rooted in their writing of the concluding paragraph was indeed a set format their high school teacher asked them to strictly follow and they did not know how to write the concluding paragraph. If this were the case, how to solve this deeply-rooted problem probably should be important considerations for Chinese EFL teachers.

In my study, the helpfulness of Teacher T's feedback on the specific issues related to thesis statement and topic sentence, cohesion, and coherence varied across students. For example, Students A and B did not consider feedback on connectives (a type of cohesion feedback) particularly helpful while they felt that teacher feedback on referential pronouns (another type of cohesion feedback) was useful. Accordingly, to best intervene in EA issues (thesis statement and topic sentence, cohesion, coherence, and supporting evidence), it seems necessary for teachers to identify the sub-issues that fall under each EA issue first (e.g., Cheung & Lee, 2018) and then selectively and purposefully focus their comments on the specific issues based on students' needs and developmental readiness.

Students A, B, and C took a variety of feedback-related factors into consideration when interacting with teacher feedback (e.g., feedback content, feedback clarity, feedback intensity, feedback actionability; See Sub-section 5.5.4.1). Hence, it is natural to point out that informative, clear, interactive, and actionable feedback are possibly the most effective responding method choices. According to Ferris and Hedgcock (2014), no matter what type of feedback is delivered, it is important that students are informed of the teachers' philosophies and intentions in advance.

7.4 Limitations and Future/Further Research

Inevitably, concerning what was studied (e.g., study scopes) in my research and how my research was conducted (e.g., research methods), there are a number of limitations. Each limitation acknowledged below is accompanied by my comments about how it can be alleviated in future or further research.

Chapter 7   Discussion and Conclusion

First (scope limitation), my study did not distinguish between e-feedback (teacher feedback delivered electronically via the computer) and handwritten feedback (feedback in pen and paper format). As mentioned in the Methodology Chapter, in my study, Teacher T preferred delivering e-feedback since she felt it was more legible, efficient, and convenient. However, as Teacher T did not consider it was functionally different from handwritten feedback, my study neglected this aspect of her feedback. In recent years, there has been a growing interest in investigating e-feedback (e.g., Ene & Upton, 2014; Ene & Upton, 2018). Studies have reported that e-feedback either shared many of the characteristics of handwritten feedback (Ene & Upton, 2014) or it better led to students' uptake of it (e.g., Cheung, 2015; Tuzi, 2004). The mixed results in the literature on e-feedback imply that electronically-delivered feedback may influence both teachers and students. Informed by my study, future/further studies are suggested to take the feedback delivery mode (handwritten feedback or e-feedback) into consideration and identify how it interacts with the other factors in the feedback process.

Apart from the feedback delivery mode, my study reveals a research gap. Conrad and Goldstein's (1999) study and Treglia's (2009) study showed that it was not the feedback delivery approach but the problem a teacher's comment focused on that determined students' use of teacher feedback. However, in my study, Students A, B and C's acceptance and incorporation of Teacher T's EA feedback were connected with whether there were explanations, models/ revisions, and hedges in teacher feedback (See Sub-section 5.5.4.1). As such, to what extent the interaction between feedback delivery approaches and feedback foci influences student decision-making is a topic for future research.

Second (scope limitation), my findings indicated that my study, aiming to paint a picture of the feedback-and-interpretation process, was somewhat broad in scope. In fact, to avoid the problem that the research scope was too broad, my topics were limited to the teacher's foci and delivery approaches related to **EA feedback**, the teacher's decision-making thought process while she was **constructing** EA comments, and the student's **acceptance and incorporation** of EA feedback while she was **processing** EA feedback. However, as the teacher's/student's decision-making thought process is complicated, it was difficult to cover all the components of it in detail. For example, when analyzing data, I found that Students A, B, and C's affective engagement with EA feedback could be specifically coded as surprise, (dis) satisfaction, joy, and pride, to name a few. As it was difficult to cover all these details in depth, my categorization of the students' affective engagement with EA feedback had to be made from a wide angle (i.e., emotional feeling aroused by processing feedback, affective evaluation of self-written text, and affective evaluation of teacher feedback). To address this limitation, future researchers can perhaps focus their attention on one of the key aspects of teacher feedback, be it the affective, interactional, interpersonal, or dynamic aspect.

Third (scope limitation), my study failed to look into "the interface between L2 writing and SLA [second language acquisition]" (Hyland, Nicolas-Conesa, & Cereza, 2016, p.443). In my study, 15% of Teacher T's feedback was provided on error issues and the students did spend some time and effort on it. Considering one of the typical characteristics of the feedback process is its interactional aspect, whether and how the students' engagement with the error feedback and non-error feedback interact with each other are questions that need to be considered by researchers. Moreover, in my study, Student A's deep-level engagement with the feedback helped her internalize the genre/ rhetorical knowledge included in Teacher T's EA feedback. Then, another question arises: is it possible that Student A's engagement with error feedback contributes to her acquisition of genre/rhetorical knowledge, and vice versa? These two unexplored questions probably merit future research.

Fourth (scope limitation), my study was conducted in a single draft classroom. In my study, the pedagogic context was reported as a key interactional factor that influenced not only how Teacher T expressed feedback but also how the students interpreted EA feedback. In this case, whether the study is conducted in the single-draft or multiple-draft context could produce different results. In future, comparative studies and replicative studies in other types of pedagogic contexts can be conducted.

Fifth (methodological limitation), one of the obvious methodological limitations of my study is the relatively small number of participating students and teachers. As indicated in the Methodology Chapter, my study was an embedded case study (including both the teacher and the students), in which three teacher-student pairs constituted three cases. Considering the complexity of my research question (about the participants' decision-making thought process), a three-case study was adequate and my exploratory work provides a foundation for future/further investigation. Still, four teacher-student pairs/cases (two teachers and two students of each teacher) might be ideal for my study. Under such a condition, the complex and dynamic picture of the feedback-and-interpretation process might be better presented. In short, for future/further research that chooses to use multiple cases, "how many cases?" (Creswell, 2013, p.101) will continue to be an issue that needs to be carefully considered by researchers.

Sixth (methodological limitation), another methodological limitation of my study is its data variety. According to an anonymous scholar, in a case study, "everything is data" (as cited in Hood, 2009, p.76). In retrospect, it might have been illuminating if I had collected the following types of data: the email messages Teacher T and the students sent to each other when the writing assignments were submitted and returned, the students' subsequent treatment of Teacher T's feedback after thinking alouds, the students' use of the web-based automatic feedback (*www.pigai.org*), and classroom observation. These types of data would supply additional contextual information and facilitate a greater understanding of the feedback-and-interpretation process. Generally, case study researchers probably need to bear in mind that no form or source of data is off limits if it contributes to a better understanding of the case (Hood, 2009).

7.5 Final Remarks

Generally speaking, as a result of my findings, I had clear answers to the questions that preoccupied my mind when I was teaching *College English*.

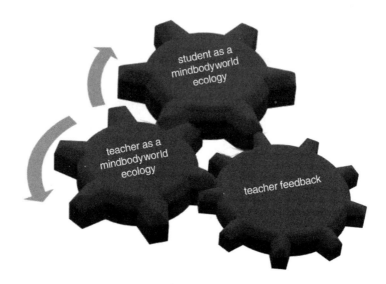

Chapter 7 Discussion and Conclusion

Empirically and theoretically, my study achieved the aim to gain a better understanding of the feedback-and-interpretation process and the construct *"teacher written feedback"*. My study this book reports found that teacher feedback has several typical features (interactional, interactive, dynamic, and complex), which can be shown by the above-given diagram.

Today, according to Manchón (2016), there is a need "to look into the role of technology in the domain of feedback studies" (p.11). In fact, due to the rapid growth of the use of electronic devices in language classes, e-feedback, computer-generated feedback, and web-based automatic feedback have already attracted the attention of researchers (e.g., Zhang & Hyland, 2018). Despite this, as it has been found that students value teachers' non-error feedback (e.g., feedback on organization and content) more highly than that comes from computers (Zhang & Hyland, 2018), there is certainly a need for future research to continue to provide insights into the process during which the teacher provides non-error feedback and the student attends to non-error feedback.

References

Ahmed, A. M., Troudi, S., & Riley, S. (2020). *Feedback in L2 English writing in the Arab world: Inside the Black Box*. Cham, Switzerland: Palgrave Macmillan.

Allison, D. (1999). Key concepts in ELT. *ELT Journal, 53*(2), 144.

Andrade, M. S., & Evans, N. W. (2013). *Principles and practices for response in second language writing: Developing self-regulated learners*. New York, NY: Routledge.

Arndt, V. (1993). Response to writing: Using feedback to inform the writing process. In M. Brook & L. Walters (Eds.), *Teaching composition around the Pacific rim: Politics and pedagogy* (pp.90-116). Clevedon, England: Multilingual Matters.

Ashwell, T. (2000). Patterns of teacher response to student writing in a multiple-draft composition classroom: Is content feedback followed by form feedback the best method? *Journal of Second Language Writing, 9*(3), 227-257. https://doi.org/10.1016/s1060-3743(00)00027-8

Atkinson, D. (2002). Toward a sociocognitive approach to second language acquisition. *The Modern Language Journal, 86*, 525-545. https://doi.org/10.1111/1540-4781.00159

Atkinson, D. (2010a). Extended, embodied cognition and second language acquisition. *Applied Linguistics*, 31, 599-622. https://doi.org/10.1093/applin/amq009

Atkinson, D. (2010b). Sociocognition: What it can mean for second language acquisition. In R. Batstone (Ed.), *Sociocognitive perspectives on language use and language learning* (pp.24-39). Oxford, England: Oxford University Press.

Atkinson, D. (2011). Sociocognitive approach to second language acquisition: How mind, body, and world work together in learning additional languages. In D. Atkinson (Ed.), *Alternative approaches to second language acquisition* (pp.143-166). Oxford, England: Routledge.

Atkinson, D. (2012). Cognitivism, adaptive intelligence, and second language acquisition. *Applied Linguistic Review*, 3, 211-232. https://doi.org/10.1515/applirev-2012-0010

Atkinson, D. (2014). Language learning in mindbodyworld: A sociocognitive approach to second language acquisition. *Language Teaching*, 47, 467-483. https://doi.org/10.1017/S0261444813000153

Atkinson, D., Churchill, E., Nishino, T., & Okada, H. (2007). Alignment and interaction in a sociocognitive approach to second language acquisition. *The Modern Language Journal*, 91, 169-188. https://doi.org/10.1111/j.1540-4781.2007.00539.x

Batstone, R. (2010). Issues and options in sociocognition. In R. Batstone (Ed.), *Sociocognitive perspectives on language use and language learning* (pp.3-23). Oxford, England: Oxford University Press.

Bazeley, P., & Jackson, K. (2013). *Qualitative data analysis with NVivo* (2nd ed.). Los Angeles, CA: SAGE Publications.

Best, K. (2011). Transformation through research-based reflection: A self-study of written feedback practice. *TESOL Journal, 2*(4), 492-509. https://doi.org/10.5054/tj.2010.271901

Best, K., Jones-Katz, L., Smolarek, B., Stolzenburg, M., & Williamson, D. (2015). Listening to our students: An exploratory practice study of ESL writing students' views of feedback. *TESOL Journal, 6*(2), 332-357. https://doi.org/10.1002/tesj.152

Bitchener, J. (2010). *Writing an applied linguistics thesis or dissertation: A guide to presenting empirical research*. Houndsmill, England: Palgrave Macmillan.

Bitchener, J., & Basturkmen, H. (2006). Perceptions of the difficulties of postgraduate L2 thesis students writing the discussion section. *Journal of English for Academic Purposes, 5*(1), 4-18. https://doi.org/10.1016/j.jeap.2005.10.002

Bitchener, J., Basturkmen, H., & East, M. (2010). The focus of supervisor written feedback to thesis/dissertation students. *International Journal of English Studies, 10*(2), 79-97. https://doi.org/10.6018/ijes.10.2.119201

Bitchener, J., & Ferris, D. (2012). *Written corrective feedback in second language acquisition and writing*. New York, NY: Routledge.

Bitchener, J., & Storch, N. (2016). *Written corrective feedback for L2 writing*. Bristol, England: Multilingual Matters.

Bitchener, J., Young, S., & Cameron, D. (2005). The effect of different types of corrective feedback on ESL student writing. *Journal of Second Language Writing*, 14, 191-205. https://doi.org/10.1016/j.jslw.2005.08.001

Bogdan, R. C., & Biklen, S. K. (2011). *Qualitative research for education: An introduction to theories and methods* (5th ed.). Boston, MA: Allyn and Bacon.

Borg, S. (2003). Teacher cognition in language teaching: A review of research on what language teachers think, know, believe and do. *Language Teaching*, *36*(2), 81-109. https://doi.org/10.1017/S0261444803001903

Borg, S. (2015). *Teacher cognition and language education: Research and practice* (2nd ed.). London, England: Bloomsbury Academic.

Bowles, M. A. (2010). *The think-aloud controversy in second language research*. New York, NY: Routledge.

Brice, C. (1995). ESL writers' reactions to teacher commentary: A case study. ERIC Document Reproduction Service No. ED394 312. https://files.eric.ed.gov/fulltext/ED394312.pdf

Carless, D., Salter, D., Yang, M., & Lam, J. (2011). Developing sustainable feedback practices. *Studies in Higher Education*, *36*(4), 395-407. https://doi.org/10.1080/03075071003642449

Casanave, C. P. (2004). *Controversies in second language writing: Dilemmas and decisions in research and instruction*. Ann Arbor, MI: University of Michigan Press.

Casanave, C. P. (2010). Case studies. In B. Paltridge & A. Phakiti (Eds.), *Continuum companion to research methods in applied linguistics* (pp.66-79). London, England: Continuum.

Chapin, R., & M. Terdal. (1990). Responding to our response: Students' strategies for responding to teacher written comments. ERIC Document Reproduction Service No. ED328098.

Chen, Y. (2002). The problems of university EFL writing in Taiwan. *The Korea TESOL Journal*, *5*(1), 59-79.

Cheung, Y. L. (2015). A comparative study of paper-and-pen versus computer-delivered assessment modes on students' writing quality: A Singapore study. *The Asia-Pacific Education Researcher*, *25*(1), 23-33. https://doi.org/10.1007/s40299-015-0229-2

Cheung, Y. L., & Lee, J. P. A. (2018). The influence of coherence-creating mechanisms on the development of coherence in expository essays: A case study. *The Asian EFL Journal*, *20*(4).

Clements, P. (2008). Instructors' written comments on students' compositions in an intensive English program: International standards, local pressures. *Bulletin of Faculty of Education*, Shizuoka University, Kyoka Kyoiku Series, 39, 199-212.

Cohen, A. D. (1987). Student processing of feedback on their composition. In A. L. Wenden & J. Rubin (Eds.), *Learner strategies in language learning* (pp.57-69). Englewood Cliffs, NJ: Prentice-Hall.

Cohen, A. D. (1991). Feedback on writing: The use of verbal report. *Studies in Second Language Acquisition*, 13, 133-159.

Cohen, A. D., & Cavalcanti, M. C. (1990). Feedback on compositions: Teacher and student verbal reports. In B. Kroll (Ed.), *Second language writing: Research insights for the classroom* (pp.155-177). Cambridge, England: Cambridge University Press.

Connors, R. J. (1985). The rhetoric of explanation: explanatory rhetoric from 1850 to the present. *Written Communication, 2*(1), 49-72. https://doi.org/10.1177/0741088385002001004

Connors, R. J., & Glenn, C. (1987). *The St. Martin's guide to teach writing.* New York, NY: St. Martin's Press.

Conrad, S., & Goldstein, L. (1999). ESL student revision after teacher written comments: Texts, contexts and individuals. *Journal of Second Language Learning, 8*, 147-180. https://doi.org/10.1016/S1060-3743(99)80126-X

Creswell, J. W. (2013). *Qualitative inquiry and research design: Choosing among five approaches* (3rd ed.). Thousand Oaks, CA: SAGE Publications.

Cumming, A., Kantor, R., & Powers, D. E. (2002). Decision making while rating ESL/EFL writing tasks: A descriptive framework. *The Modern Language Journal, 86*(1), 67.

Diab, R. L. (2005a). Teachers' and students' beliefs about responding to ESL writing: A case study. *TESL Canada Journal, 23*, 28-43.

Diab, R. L. (2005b). EFL university students' preferences for error correction and teacher feedback to writing. *TESL Reporter, 38*(1), 27-51.

Dörnyei, Z. (2007). *Research methods in applied linguistics: Quantitative, qualitative, and mixed methodologies.* Oxford, England: Oxford University Press.

Duff, P. (2008). *Case study research in applied linguistics*. New York, NY: Lawrence Erlbaum Associates.

Eddington, A. (2005). "What are you thinking?": Understanding teacher reading and response through a protocol analysis study. *Journal of Writing Assessment, 2*(2), 125-148.

Edlund, J. (2003). Non-native speakers of English. In I. Clark & B. Bamberg (Eds.), *Concepts in composition: Theory and practice of the teaching of writing* (pp.363-387). Mahwah, NJ: Lawrence Erlbaum Associates.

Ellis, R. (2010). Cognitive, social, and psychological dimensions of corrective feedback. In R. Batstone (Ed.), *Sociocognitive perspectives on language use and language learning* (pp.151-165). Oxford, England: Oxford University Press.

Elwood, J. A., & Bode, J. (2014). Student preferences vis-à-vis teacher feedback in university EFL writing classes in Japan. *System, 42*, 333-343. https://doi.org/10.1016/j.system.2013.12.023

Ene, E., & Upton, T. A. (2014). Learner uptake of teacher electronic feedback in ESL composition. *System, 46*, 80-95. https://doi.org/10.1016/j.system.2014.07.011

Ene, E., & Upton, T. A. (2018). Synchronous and asynchronous teacher electronic feedback and learner uptake in ESL composition. *Journal of Second Language Writing, 41*, 1-13. https://doi.org/10.1016/j.jslw.2018.05.005

Engeström, Y. (1987). *Learning by expanding: An activity theoretical approach to developmental research*. Helsinki, Finland: Orienta-

Konsultit.

Enginarlar, H. (1993). Student response to teacher feedback in EFL writing. *System*, 21, 192-203. https://doi.org/10.1016/0346-251X(93)90041-E

Ericsson, K. A., & Simon, H. A. (1993). *Protocol analysis: Verbal reports as data*. Cambridge, MA: MIT Press.

Fathman, A., & Whalley, E. (1990). Teacher response to student writing: Focus on form versus content. In B. Kroll (Ed.), *Second language writing: Research insights for the classroom* (pp.178-190). Cambridge, England: Cambridge University Press.

Ferris, D. R. (1995). Student reactions to teacher response in multiple-draft composition classrooms. *TESOL Quarterly*, 29, 33-53.

Ferris, D. R. (1997). The influence of teacher commentary on student revision. *TESOL Quarterly*, *31*(2), 315-339. https://doi.org/10.2307/3588049

Ferris, D. R. (2001). Teaching written for academic purposes. In J. Flowerdew & M. Peacock (Eds.), *Research perspectives on English for academic purposes* (pp.298-314). Cambridge, England: Cambridge University Press.

Ferris, D. R. (2003). *Response to student writing: Implications for second language students*. Mahwah, NJ: Lawrence Erlbaum Associates.

Ferris, D. R. (2007). Preparing teachers to respond to student writing. *Journal of Second Language Writing*, 16, 165-193. https://doi.org/10.1016/j.jslw.2007.07.003

Ferris, D. R. (2013). *Writing in a second language*. Shanghai, P. R. China: Shanghai Foreign Language Education Press.

Ferris, D. R. (2014). Responding to student writing: Teachers' philosophies and practices. *Assessing Writing*, 19, 6-23. https://doi.org/10.1016/j.asw.2013.09.004

Ferris, D. R., & Hedgcock, J. (1998). *Teaching ESL composition: Purpose, process, and practice*. Mahwah, NJ: Lawrence Erlbaum Associates.

Ferris, D. R., & Hedgcock, J. (2005). *Teaching ESL composition: Purpose, process, and practice* (2nd ed.). Mahwah, NJ: Lawrence Erlbaum.

Ferris, D. R., & Hedgcock, J. (2014). *Teaching L2 composition: Purpose, process, and practice* (3rd ed.). New York, NY: Routledge.

Ferris, D. R., Brown, J., Liu, H., Eugenia, M., & Stine, A. (2011). Responding to L2 students in college writing classes: Teacher perspectives. *TESOL Quarterly*, 45, 207-234.

Ferris, D. R., Liu, H., and Rabie, B. (2011). "The job of teaching writing": Teaching views of responding to student writing. *Writing & Pedagogy*, 3, 39-77. http://dx.doi.org/10.1558/wap.v3i1.39

Ferris, D. R., Pezone, S., Tade, C. R., & Tinti, S. (1997). Teacher commentary on student writing: Descriptions & implications. *Journal of Second Language Writing*, 6(2), 155-182. https://doi.org/10.1016/s1060-3743(97)90032-1

Feuerherm, E. (2011-2012). Written feedback, student writing, and institutional policies: Implications for novice teacher development. *CATESOL Journal*, 23(1), 132-154.

Flowerdew, J., & Peacock, M. (2001). *Research perspectives on English for academic purposes*. Cambridge, England: Cambridge University Press.

Forman, R. (2008). Using notions of scaffolding and intertextuality to understand the bilingual teaching of English as a foreign language. *Linguistics and Education, 19*(4), 319-332. http://dx.doi.org/10.1016/j.linged.2008.07.001

Freedman, S. W. (1987). *Response to student writing* (Vol. 23). Urbana, IL: NCTE.

Gao, X. (2010). *Strategic language learning: The roles of agency and context*. Bristol, England: Multilingual Matters.

Goldstein, L. M. (2001). For Kyla: What does the research say about responding to ESL writers. In T. Silva & P. K. Matsuda (Eds.), *On second language writing* (pp.73-89). Mahwah, NJ: Lawrence Erlbaum Associates.

Goldstein, L. M. (2004). Questions and answers about teacher written commentary and student revision: Teachers and students working together. *Journal of Second Language Writing, 13*(1), 63-80. https://doi.org/10.1016/j.jslw.2004.04.006

Goldstein, L. M. (2005). *Teacher written commentary in second language writing classrooms*. Ann Arbor, MI: University of Michigan Press.

Goldstein, L. M. (2006). Feedback and revision in second language writing: Contextual, teacher, and student variables. In K. Hyland & F. Hyland (Eds.), *Feedback in second language writing: Contexts and issues* (pp.185-205). New York, NY: Cambridge University Press.

Goldstein, L. M. (2016). Making use of teacher written feedback. In R. M. Manchón & P. K. Matsuda (Eds.), *Handbook of second and foreign language writing* (pp.407-430). Boston, MA: De Gruyter.

Han, Y. (2016). *Learner engagement with teacher written corrective feedback in Chinese tertiary-level EFL classrooms: A sociocognitive perspective*. Unpublished doctoral dissertation. The University of Hong Kong, Hong Kong SAR, China.

Hattie, J., & Timperley, H. (2007). The power of feedback. *Review of Educational Research, 77*(1), 81-112. https://doi.org/10.3102/003465430298487

Hedgcock, J., & Lefkowitz, N. (1994). Feedback on feedback: Assessing learner receptivity to teacher response in L2 composing. *Journal of Second Language Writing*, 3, 141-163. https://doi.org/10.1016/1060-3743(94)90012-4

Hedgcock, J., & Lefkowitz, N. (1996). Some input on input: Two analyses of student response to expert feedback in L2 writing. *The Modern Language Journal*, 80, 287-308. https://doi.org/10.1111/j.1540-4781.1996.tb01612.x

Hinds, J. (1990). Inductive, deductive, quasi-inductive: Expository writing in Japanese, Korean, Chinese, and Thai. In U. Connor and A. Johns (Eds.), *Coherence in writing* (pp.87-109). Washington, DC: TESOL Publications.

Hood, M. (2009). Case study. In J. Heigham & R. A. Croker (Eds.), *Qualitative research in applied linguistics: A practical introduction* (pp.66-90). Basingstoke, England: Palgrave Macmillan.

Huang, J., & Shi, W. (2010). Policies and practices of lifelong learning in China. In W. Zhang (Ed.), *Theories, policy, and practice of lifelong learning in East Asia* (pp.3-12). Abingdon, England: Routledge.

Huot, B. (2002). *(Re)Articulating: Writing assessment for teaching and learning*. Logan, UT: Utah State University Press.

Hyland, F. (1998). The impact of teacher written feedback on individual writers. *Journal of Second Language Writing*, 7, 255-286. https://doi.org/10.1016/S1060-3743(98)90017-0

Hyland, K. (2002). *Teaching and researching writing*. Harlow, England: Longman.

Hyland, K. (2003). *Second language writing*. New York, NY: Cambridge University Press.

Hyland, K. (2007). Genre pedagogy: Language, literacy and L2 writing instruction. *Journal of Second Language Writing*, *16*(3), 148-164. https://doi.org/ 10.1016/j.jslw.2007.07.005

Hyland, K. (2004). *Genre and second language writing*. Ann Arbor, MI: University of Michigan Press.

Hyland, F., & Hyland, K. (2001). Sugaring the pill: Praise and criticism in written feedback. *Journal of Second Language Writing*, 10, 185-212. https://doi.org/ 10.1016/S1060-3743(01)00038-8

Hyland, K., & Hyland, F. (2006a). Interpersonal aspects of response: Constructing and interpreting teacher written feedback. In K. Hyland & F. Hyland (Eds.), *Feedback in second language writing: Contexts and issues* (pp.206-224). New York, NY: Cambridge University Press.

Hyland, K., & Hyland, F. (2006b). *Feedback in second language writing:*

Contexts and issues. New York, NY: Cambridge University Press.

Hyland, F., Nicolas-Conesa, F., & Cereza, L. (2016). Key issues of debate about feedback on writing. In R. M. Manchón & P. K. Matsuda (Eds.), *Handbook of second and foreign language writing* (pp.433-452). Boston, MA: De Gruyter.

Hyon, S. (1996). Genre in three traditions: Implications for ESL. *TESOL Quarterly, 30*(4), 693-722. https://doi.org/10.2307/3587930

Johns, A. M. (1990). L1 composition theories: Implications for developing theories of L2 composition. In B. Kroll (Ed.), *Second language writing: Research insights for the classroom* (pp.24-36). Cambridge, England: Cambridge University Press.

Johnson, D. M. (1992). *Approaches to research in second language learning*. New York, NY: Longman.

Johnston, L. (2006). Software and method: Reflections on teaching and using QSR NVivo in doctoral research. *International Journal of Social Research Methodology*, 9(5), 379-391. https://doi.org/10.1080/13645570600659433

Jourdenais, R. (2001). Cognition, instruction and protocol analysis. In P. Robinson (Ed.), *Cognition and second language instruction* (pp.354-375). New York, NY: Cambridge University Press.

Junqueira, L., & Payant, C. (2015). "I just want to do it right, but it's so hard": A novice teacher's written feedback beliefs and practices. *Journal of Second Language Writing*, 27, 19-36. https://doi.org/10.1016/j.jslw.2014.11.001

Kaplan, R. B. (1967). Contrastic rhetoric and the teaching of composition. *TESOL Quarterly*, 4, 10-16.

Kasper, G. (1998). Analyzing verbal protocols. *TESOL Quarterly*, *32*(2), 358-362.

Keh, C. (1990). Feedback in the writing process: A model and methods for implementation. *ELT Journal*, *44*(4), 294-304. https://doi.org/10.1093/elt/44.4.294

Kim, L. C., & Lim, J. M. (2013). Metadiscourse in English and Chinese research article introductions. *Discourse Studies*, *15*(2), 129-146. https://doi.org/10.1177/1461445612471476

Knoblauch, C. H., & Brannon, L. (1981, Fall). Teacher commentary on student writing: The state of the art. *Freshman English News*, 10, 1-4.

Kroll, B. (1990). *Second language writing: Research insights for the classroom*. Cambridge, England: Cambridge University Press.

Kroll, B. (2003). *Exploring the dynamics of second language writing*. New York, NY: Cambridge University Press.

Kumar, M. (2012). Insights from verbal protocols: A case study. *International Journal of Applied Linguistics and English Literature*, *1*(5), 25-34. https://doi.org/10.7575/ijalel.v.1n.5p.25

Kumar, V., & Kumar, M. (2009). Recursiveness and noticing in written feedback: Insights from concurrent think aloud protocols. *European Journal of Social Sciences*, 12, 97-103.

Kumar, M., Kumar, V., & Feryok, A. (2009). Recursiveness in written feedback. *New Zealand Studies in Applied Linguistics*, *15*(1), 26-37.

Kumaravadivelu, B. (2003). Problematizing culture stereotypes in TESOL. *TESOL Quarterly*, *37*(4), 709-716.

Larsen-Freeman, D. (2012). Complex theory. In S. M. Gass, & A. Mackey (Eds.). *The Routledge handbook of second language acquisition* (pp.73-87). Abingdon, England: Routledge.

Lee, I. (2008a). Understanding teachers' written feedback practices in Hong Kong secondary classrooms. *Journal of Second Language Writing*, 17, 69-85. https://doi.org/10.1016/j.jslw.2007.10.001

Lee, I. (2008b). Student reactions to teacher feedback in two Hong Kong secondary classrooms. *Journal of Second Language Writing*, 17, 144-164. https://doi.org/10.1016/j.jslw.2007.12.001

Lee, I. (2011). Feedback revolution: What gets in the way? *ELT Journal*, *65*(1), 1-12.

Lee, I. (2014). Revisiting teacher feedback in EFL writing from sociocultural perspectives. *TESOL Quarterly*, 48, 201-213.

Lee, I. (2016). Putting students at the center of classroom L2 writing assessment. *Canadian Modern Language Review*, *72*(2), 258-280. https://doi.org/10.3138/cmlr.2802

Lee, I. (2017). *Classroom writing assessment and feedback in L2 school contexts*. Singapore: Springer.

Lee, G., & Schallert, D. L. (2008a). Constructing trust between teacher and students through feedback and revision cycles in an EFL writing classroom. *Written Communication*, *25*(4), 506-537. https://doi.org/10.1177/0741088308322301

Lee, G., & Schallert, D. L. (2008b). Meeting in the margins: Effects of the teacher– student relationship on revision processes of EFL college students taking a composition course. *Journal of Second Language Writing*, *17*(3), 165-182. https://doi.org/10.1016/j.jslw.2007.11.002

Leki, I. (1990). Coaching from the margins: Issues in written response. In B. Kroll (Ed.), *Second language writing: Research insights for the classroom* (pp.57-68). Cambridge, England: Cambridge University Press.

Leki, I. (1992). *Understanding ESL writers*. Portsmouth, NH: Boynton/Cook Heinemann.

Leki, I., Cumming, A. H., & Silva, T. (2008). *A synthesis of research on second language writing in English*. New York, NY: Routledge.

Leont'ev, A. N. (1978). *Activity, consciousness, and personality*. Englewood Cliffs, NJ: Prentice-Hall.

Li, Z. (2016). Written teacher feedback: Student perceptions, teacher perceptions, and actual teacher performance. *English Language Teaching*, *9*(8), 73-84.

Liamputtong, P. (2009). *Qualitative research methods* (3rd ed.). South Melbourne, Australia: Oxford University Press.

Loewen, S., & Reinders, H. (2011). *Key concepts in second language acquisition*. Basingstoke, England: Palgrave Macmillan.

Ma, J. (2010). Chinese EFL learners' decision-making while evaluating peers' texts. *International Journal of English Studies*, *10*(2), 99-120. https://doi.org/10.6018/ijes.10.2.119221

Ma, J. (2012). *Chinese EFL university students' decision-making in peer review of second language writing*. Unpublished doctoral dissertation. The University of Hong Kong, Hong Kong SAR, China.

Mackey, A., & Gass, S. M. (2005). *Second language research: Methodology and design*. Mahwah, NJ: Lawrence Erlbaum Associates.

Mahfoodh, O. A., & Pandian, A. (2011). A qualitative case study of EFL students' affective reactions to and perceptions of their teachers' written feedback. *English Language Teaching*, 4, 14-25.

Mahfoodh, O. A. (2017). "I feel disappointed": EFL university students' emotional responses towards teacher written feedback. *Assessing Writing*, 31, 53-72. https://doi.org/10.1016/j.asw.2016.07.001

Manchón, R. M. (2011). *Learning-to-write and writing-to-learn in an additional language*. Amsterdam, the Netherlands: John Benjamins.

Manchón, R. M. (2012). *L2 writing development: Multiple perspectives*. Berlin, Germany: De Gruyter.

Manchón, R. M., & Matsuda, P. K. (2016). *Handbook of second and foreign language writing*. Boston, MA: De Gruyter.

Martin, J. R. (1989). *Factual writing: Exploring and challenging social reality*. Oxford, England: Oxford University Press.

Marshall, C., & Rossman, G. B. (1999). *Designing qualitative research* (3rd ed.). Thousand Oaks, CA: Sage Publications.

McKay, S. (1984). *Composing in a second language*. Rowley, MA: Newbury House. McKay, S. (2006). *Researching second language classrooms*. Mahwah, NJ: Lawrence Erlbaum Associates.

McKay, S. (2009). Introspective techniques. In J. Heigham & R. A. Croker (Eds.), *Qualitative research in applied linguistics: A practical introduction* (pp.220-241). Basingstoke, England: Palgrave Macmillan.

Merriam, S. B. (2009). *Qualitative research: A guide to design and implementation*. San Francisco, CA: Jossey-Bass.

Merriam, S. B., & Tisdell, E. J. (2016). *Qualitative research: A guide to design and implementation*. San Francisco, CA: Jossey-Bass.

Montgomery, J. L., & Baker, W. (2007). Teacher-written feedback: Student perceptions, teacher self-assessment, and actual teacher performance. *Journal of Second Language Writing*, 16, 82-99. https://doi.org/10.1016/j.jslw.2007.04.002

Min, H. (2013). A case study of an EFL writing teacher's belief and practice about written feedback. *System*, 41, 625-638. https://doi.org/10.1016/j.system.2013.07.018

Ministry of Education. (2007). College English curriculum requirements. Beijing, P. R. China: Department of Higher Education, Ministry of Education.

Murphy, L., & de Larios, J. R. (2010). Feedback in second language writing: An introduction. *International Journal of English Studies*, *10*(2), i-xv.

Murray, H. G. (1985). Classroom teaching behaviors related to college teaching effectiveness. *New Directions for Teaching & Learning*, 23, 21-34. https://doi.org/10.1002/tl.37219852305

Murray, N., & Beglar, D. (2009). *Inside track: Writing dissertations and theses.* New York, NY: Pearson Longman.

Mustafa, R. F. (2012). Feedback on the feedback: Sociocultural interpretation of Saudi ESL learners' opinions about writing feedback. *English Language Teaching*, 5(3), 3-15.

Nazif, A., Biswas, D., & Hilbig, R. (2004). Towards an understanding of student perceptions of feedback. *Carleton Papers in Applied Language Studies*, 21(22), 166-192.

Ng, C. H., & Cheung, Y. L. (2018). Mediation in a socio-cognitive approach to writing for elementary students: Instructional scaffolding. *Education Sciences*, 8(3), 1-13.

Nishino, T., & Atkinson, D. (2015). Second language writing as sociocognitive alignment. *Journal of Second Language Writing*, 27, 37-54. https://doi.org/ 10.1016/j.jslw.2014.11.002

Nunan, D. (1992). *Research methods in language learning.* Cambridge, England: Cambridge University Press.

Nunan, D. (1993). *Teachers interactive decision-making.* Sydney, Australia: National Centre for English Language Teaching and Research, Macquarie University.

Nunan, D., & Bailey, K. M. (2009). *Exploring second language classroom research: A comprehensive guide.* Boston, MA: Heinle, Cengage

Learning.

Nurmukhamedov, U., & S. H. Kim. (2009). "Would you perhaps consider ...": Hedged comments in ESL writing. *ELT Journal*, 64, 272-282.

Pennycook, A. (1998). *English and the discourses of colonialism*. London, England: Routledge.

Pessoa, L. (2008). On the relationship between emotion and cognition. *Nature Reviews Neuroscience*, 9, 148-158. https://doi.org/10.1038/nrn2317

Polio, C. (2017). *Teaching second language writing*. London, England: Routledge.

Qi, L. (2007). Is testing an efficient agent for pedagogical change? Examining the intended washback of the writing task in a high-stakes English test in China. *Assessment in Education: Principles, Policy & Practice*, *14*(1), 51-74.

Radecki, P., & Swales, J. (1988). ESL student reaction to written comments on their written work. *System*, 16, 355-365. https://doi.org/10.1016/0346-251X(88)90078-4

Ravand, H., & Rasekh, A. E. (2011). Feedback in ESL writing: Toward an interactional approach. *Journal of Language Teaching and Research*, *2*(5), 1136-1145. https://doi.org/10.4304/jltr.2.5.1136-1145

Reid, J. (1993). *Teaching ESL writing*. Englewood Cliffs, NJ: Regents/Prentice Hall.

Reid, J. (1994). Responding to ESL students' texts: The myths of appropriation. *TESOL Quarterly*, 28, 273-292. https://doi.

org/10.2307/3587434

Remenyi, D. (2012). *Case study research*. Reading, England: Academic Publishing International Limited.

Richards, K. (2003). *Qualitative inquiry in TESOL*. Basingstoke, England: Palgrave Macmillan.

Richards, L. (2005). *Handling qualitative data: A practical guide*. London, England: Sage Publications.

Richards, K. (2009). Interviews. In J. Heigham & R. A. Croker (Eds.), *Qualitative research in applied linguistics: A practical introduction* (pp.182-199). Basingstoke, England: Palgrave Macmillan.

Saito, H. (1994). Teachers' practices and students' preferences for feedback on second language writing: A case study of adult ESL learners. *TESL Canada Journal*, 11, 46-70. https://doi.org/10.18806/tesl.v11i2.633

Seker, M., & Dincer, A. (2014). An insight to students' perceptions on teacher feedback in second language writing classes. *English Language Teaching*, 7(2), 73-83.

Silva, T. (1988). Comments on Vivian Zamel's "Recent research on writing pedagogy". *TESOL Quarterly*, 22, 517-519. https://doi.org/10.2307/3587297

Silva, T. (1990). Second language composition instruction: Developments, issues, and directions in ESL. In B. Kroll (ed.), *Second language writing: Research insights for the classroom* (pp.11-23). Cambridge, England: Cambridge University Press.

Silva, T. (1993). Toward an understanding of the distinct nature of L2 writing: The ESL research and its implications. *TESOL Quarterly*, 4, 657-676. https://doi.org/10.2307/3587400

Silva, T., & Matsuda, P. K. (2001). *On second language writing*. Mahwah, NJ: Lawrence Erlbaum Associates.

Silva, T., & Matsuda, P. K. (2010). *Practicing theory in second language writing*. West Lafayette, IL: Parlor Press.

Silva, T., Thomas, S., Park, K., & Zhang, C. (2014, September). Scholarship on L2 writing in 2013: The year in review. *TESOL-SLWIS Newsletter*. Retrieved from http://newsmanager.commpartners.com/tesolslwis/issues/2014-09-24/6.html

Song, G., Hoon, L. H., & Alvin, L. P. (2017). Students' response to feedback: An exploratory study. *RELC Journal, 48*(3), 357-372. http://dx.doi.org/10.1177/0033688217691445

Sprinkle, R. S. (2004). Written commentary: A systematic, theory-based approach to response. *Teaching English in the Two-Year College, 31*(3), 273-286.

Straub, R. (2000). *The practice of response: Strategies for commenting on student writing*. Cresskill, NJ: Hampton Press.

Sugita, Y. (2006). The impact of teachers' comment types on students' revision. *ELT Journal, 60*(1), 34-41. https://doi.org/10.1093/elt/cci079

Tardy, C. (2014, November). Representations of professionalization in second language writing: A view from the flagship journal. Paper presented at the 2014 symposium on second language writing, Tempe, AZ.

Ting-Toomey, S., & Kurogi, A. (1998). Facework competence in intercultural conflict: An updated face-negotiation theory. *International Journal of Intercultural Relations*, 22, 187-225.

Treglia, M. (2008). Feedback on feedback: Exploring student responses to teachers' written commentary. *Journal of Basic Writing*, 27, 105-138.

Treglia, M. (2009). Teacher-written commentary in college writing composition: How does it impact student revisions? *Composition Studies*, 37(1), 67-86.

Tsui, A. (2003). *Understanding expertise in teaching: Case studies of second language teachers*. Cambridge, England: Cambridge University Press.

Tuzi, F. (2004). The impact of e-feedback on the revisions of L2 writers in an academic writing course. *Computers and Composition*, 21(2), 217-235. http://dx.doi.org/10.1016/j.compcom.2004.02.003

van Beuningen, C. (2010). Corrective feedback in L2 writing: Theoretical perspectives, empirical insights, and future directions. *International Journal of English Studies*, 10(2), 1-27. https://doi.org/10.6018/ijes/2010/2/119171

Van Lier, L. (2005). Case study. In E. Hinkel (Ed.), *Handbook of research in second language teaching and learning* (pp.195-208). Mahwah, NJ: Lawrence Erlbaum Associates.

Villamil, O. S., & Guerrero, M. C. M. (2006). Sociocultural theory: A framework for understanding the social-cognitive dimensions of peer feedback. In K. Hyland & F. Hyland (Eds.), *Feedback in second language writing: Contexts and issues* (pp.23-42). New York, NY:

Cambridge University Press.

Wang, Z. (2011). A case study of one EFL writing teacher's feedback on discourse for advanced learners in China. *University of Sydney Papers in TESOL*, 6, 21-42.

Wang, W., & Wen, Q. (2002). L1 use in the L2 composing process: an exploratory study of 16 Chinese EFL writers. *Journal of Second Language Writing*, 11, 225-246. https://doi.org/10.1016/S1060-3743(02)00084-x

Waterman, A. S. (1984). *The psychology of individualism*. New York, NY: Praeger.

Weissberg, R. (2006). Scaffolded feedback: Tutorial conversations with advanced L2 writers. In K. Hyland & F. Hyland (Eds.), *Feedback in second language writing: Contexts and issues* (pp.246-265). New York, NY: Cambridge University Press.

Welsh, E. (2002). Dealing with data: Using NVivo in the qualitative data analysis process. *Forum: Qualitative Social Research*, 3(2), Art. 26. http://nbn-resolving.de/urn:nbn:de:0114-fqs0202260

Wigglesworth, G., & Storch, N. (2012). Feedback and writing development through collaboration: A socio-cultural approach. In R. Manchón (Ed.), *L2 writing development: Multiple perspectives* (Vol. 6, pp.69-99). Berlin, Germany: De Gruyter.

Williams, J. (2005). *Teaching writing in second and foreign language classrooms*. New York, NY: McGraw-Hill.

Woods, D. (1996). *Teacher cognition in language teaching: Beliefs, decision-*

making, and classroom practice. Cambridge, England: Cambridge University Press.

Woods, D. (2006). Who does what in the 'management of language learning'? Planning and the social construction of the 'motivation to notice'. In S. Gieve, & I. K. Miller (Eds.), *Understanding the language classroom* (pp.115-135). New York, NY: Palgrave Macmillan.

Wood, D., Bruner, J. S., & Ross, G. (1976). The role of tutoring in problem solving. *Journal of Child Psychology and Psychiatry*, 17, 89-100. https://doi.org/10.1111/j.1469-7610.1976.tb00381.x

Yang, L. (2013). A case study of the impact of teacher written feedback on Chines EFL university student. *Shandong Foreign Language Teaching Journal*, 5, 12-18.

Yin, R. K. (2004). *The case study anthology*. Thousand Oaks, CA: Sage Publications.

Yin, R. K. (2009). *Case study research: Design and methods* (4th ed.). Los Angeles, CA: Sage Publications.

Yin, R. K. (2014). *Case study research: Design and methods* (5th ed.). Los Angeles, CA: Sage Publications.

Yu, S. (2021). Feedback-giving practice for L2 writing teachers: Friend or foe? *Journal of Second Language Writing*, 52, 1-14, https://doi.org/10.1016/j.jslw.2021.100798

Yu, S., Jiang, L., & Zhou, N. (2020). Investigating what feedback practices contribute to students' writing motivation and engagement in Chinese EFL context: A large scale study. *Assessing Writing*, 44, Article 100451.

https://doi.org/10.1016/j.asw.2020.100451.

Yu, S., Zhang, E., & Liu, C. (2022). Assessing L2 student writing feedback literacy: A scale development and validation study, *Assessing Writing*, 53,100643, https://doi.org/10.1016/j.asw.2022.100643.

Zacharias, N. (2007). Teacher and student attitudes toward teacher feedback. *RELC Journal*, 38, 38-52. https://doi.org/10.1177%2F0033688206076157

Zamel, V. (1985). Responding to student writing. *TESOL Quarterly*, 19, 75-101. doi: 10.2307/3586773

Zhang, Z., & Hyland, K. (2018). Student engagement with teacher and automated feedback on L2 writing. *Assessing Writing*, 36, 90–102. https://doi.org/10.1016/j.asw.2018.02.004

Zhang, M. (2000). Cohesive features in the expository writing of undergraduates in two Chinese universities. *RELC Journal*, *31*(1), 61-95. https://doi.org/10.1177/003368820003100104

Zhang, C., Yan, X., & Liu, X. (2015). The development of EFL writing instruction and research in China: An update from the International Conference on English Language Teaching. *Journal of Second Language Writing*, 30, 14-18. https://doi.org/10.1016/j.jslw.2015.06.009

Zhao, H. (2010). Investigating learners' use and understanding of peer and teacher feedback on writing: A comparative study in a Chinese English writing classroom. *Assessing Writing*, 15, 3-17. https://doi.org/10.1016/j.asw.2010.01.0

Appendices

Appendix A: Teacher Background Interview Guide

Thank you for joining me today and agreeing to take this interview. First, let me remind you about the purpose of this interview. This interview aims to obtain information concerning your usual way of providing feedback at the level of text. It will take about half an hour. Throughout the interview process, if you do not understand the question that I ask, just tell me and then I will explain. There are no right or wrong answers to these questions. All the information you provide is confidential. You and your school will not be identified in my final write-up for pseudonyms will be used in it. You can decline answering any question or stop participating at any time. There will be no loss of benefits to which you are otherwise entitled or any other negative consequence for it. During the interview, I will tape record our conversation and take notes in order to make sure I get everything you say correct.

1. Could you please tell me a little about yourself and your experience of teaching English and writing?
2. Could you please talk about your plan, objectives, and approaches of teaching English and writing in this semester?
3. Could you please share with me your ideas about teacher feedback on student writing?
4. On which aspects of student writing do you think you usually write feedback? Why?
5. In this semester, on which aspects of student writing are you going to

write feedback? Why?

6. Is it possible that you may make a change of feedback focus when writing comment on student writing this semester? If so, what might be the reasons and what changes might you make?
7. How do you usually write your feedback?
8. In this semester, how are you going to write your feedback? Why?
9. Is it possible that you may change your usual way of writing your feedback when actually writing feedback in this semester? If so, what changes might you make and what might be the reasons of the changes?
10. Could you please share with me your experience of teaching the three classes last semester?

Thank you very much for your time today and your support of this research project. I appreciate you taking the time to share your thoughts with me. If you happen to talk about this study with anyone, please remember not to mention any specific participant by name. If you have any other questions, please do not hesitate to contact me.

Appendix B: Student Background Interview Guide

Thank you for joining me today and agreeing to take this interview. First, let me remind you about the purpose of this interview. This interview aims to obtain information concerning your experience of processing of teacher feedback at the level of text. The interview will take about 30 minutes. Throughout the interview process, if you do not understand the question that I ask, just tell me and then I'll explain. There are no right or wrong answers to these questions. All the information you provide is confidential. You and your school will not be identified in my final write-up for pseudonyms will be used in it. You can decline answering any question or stop participating at any time. There will be no loss of benefits to which you are otherwise entitled or any other negative consequence for it. During the interview, I will tape record our conversation and take notes in order to make sure I get everything you say correct.

1. Could you please tell me a little about yourself and your experience of taking English and English writing classes?
2. How do you evaluate yourself as an English learner and your ability to write in English? Why?
3. What do you think of writing in English and in Chinese?
4. Questions concerning feedback processing (to be asked one by one): Did you get feedback from teachers on your writing before? If yes, what did the written feedback focus on (content, organization, style, grammar, etc.)? How did your teachers write feedback? Did you usually read teacher feedback carefully? How did you read teacher feedback?

For what purpose did you read teacher feedback? Did you take some actions to incorporate teacher feedback? When reading feedback, did you also consider how to use teacher feedback? To what extent do you usually base on teacher feedback to take action? Which type of feedback do you usually take and act on it? What actions do you usually take?

5. In this semester, will you respond to teacher feedback in the same way? If so, why? If not, how might you respond to teacher feedback?
6. Could you please share with me your ideas about teacher feedback?
7. Could you please share with me your experience of taking English class last semester?

Thank you very much for your time today and your support of this research project. I appreciate you taking the time to share your thoughts with me. If you talk about this interview with anyone, please remember not to mention any specific participant by name. If you have any other questions, please do not hesitate to contact me.

Appendix C: Think-Aloud Protocol in the Training Session

(Based on Procedures Proposed by Bowles in 2010)

1. Describing what is meant by think-aloud. Think-aloud is "a type of research method in which learners verbalize their thoughts as they perform an activity" (Loewen & Reinders, 2011, p.166). Its purpose is to "provide insight into the cognitive processes that learners experience when performing a task in question" (Loewen & Reinders, 2011, p.166). In think-aloud tasks, the researcher wants the participants to say out loud everything that they would say to themselves silently while working on a problem. When thinking aloud, participants do not need to explain or justify their thoughts.

2. Specifying participants can use the language that occurs in their mind to verbalize their thoughts. By using their first language—Chinese, participants can communicate their thoughts more effectively. Meanwhile, participants will be told that it would be fine for them to use English when necessary as they think aloud.

3. Demonstrating how to do think-aloud for each participant. According to Mackey and Gass (2005), there is a caution to be alerted to when modelling how to think aloud. That is, the researchers need to use a similar, or a completely different task (rather than the same target task) when demonstrating how to think aloud. Otherwise, it is possible that the learners will use the strategies that the researchers have used when the researchers model think-aloud for the learners. In this study, a similar task is to be used because "learners may be able to go from the

practice verbalization to the operational study more easily" (Bowles, 2009, p.117). I will follow Wang and Wen's (2002) way of instructing Chinese EFL student writers to do think-aloud. ① When modelling for the student participant, I will give a demonstration of thinking aloud while reading a student's English writing produced by one of my former students. Then the student participant will be asked to think aloud while reading the feedback I provided on a piece of English writing by one of my former students. The participant will be told to vocalize every single thought and use the language that occurs in his/her mind. When the student finishes the task, I will ask him/her to estimate his/her difficulty with the think-aloud method. I will also make further explanation to the student participant concerning the difficulties I find he/she has during he/she practices think-aloud. ② When modelling for the teacher participant, I will give a demonstration of thinking aloud while reading the comments I wrote on a piece of writing produced by one of my former students. Then the teacher participant will be asked to think aloud while writing feedback on a piece of English writing by one of my former students. She will be told to vocalize every single thought and use the language that occurs in her mind. When she finishes the task, I will ask her to estimate her difficulty with the think-aloud method. I will also make further explanation to the teacher participant concerning the difficulties I find she has during she practices think-aloud.

4. Answering the participants' questions concerning think-aloud to ensure that he/she is familiar enough and at ease with think-aloud protocols.

Appendix D: Teacher Retrospective and Ongoing Interviews Guide

Thank you for joining me today and agreeing to take this interview. First, let me remind you about the purpose of this interview. This interview aims to obtain information concerning your processing of teacher feedback at the level of text. The interview will take about less than 1 hour. Throughout the interview process, if you don't understand the question that I ask, just tell me and then I'll explain. There are no right or wrong answers to these questions. All the information you provide is confidential. You and your school will not be identified in my final write-up for pseudonyms will be used in it. You can decline answering any question or stop participating at any time. There will be no loss of benefits to which you are otherwise entitled or any other negative consequence for it. During the interview, I will tape record our conversation and take notes in order to make sure I get everything you say correct.

1. Before providing feedback this time, on what did you plan to write feedback for her? Why?
2. On what did you write feedback for her eventually? Why did you focus on each of these aspects?
3. Before providing feedback this time, did you have any plan as to how to write feedback for her? Why?
4. How did you write each feedback for her eventually? Why?
5. What were you thinking when you wrote down this piece of teacher comment (the one indicated by the interviewer)?
6. Do you think this piece of teacher comment (the one indicated by the

interviewer) is readily understandable and acceptable? Why do you think so?

7. Concerning each problem pointed out in your text-level feedback, do you think the student can deal with it independently next time? Why do you think so?

8. Do you think the students are better able to deal with feedback next time? Why do you think so?

9. What do you think of your communication with your students through your feedback? Why do you think so?

Thank you very much for your time today and your support of this research project. I appreciate you taking the time to share your thoughts with me. If you talk about this with anyone, please remember not to mention any specific participant by name. If you have any other questions, please do not hesitate to contact me.

Appendix E: Student Retrospective and Ongoing Interviews Guide

Thank you for joining me today and agreeing to take this interview. First, let me remind you about the purpose of this interview. This interview aims to obtain information concerning your processing of teacher feedback at the level of text. The interview will take about less than 1 hour. Throughout the interview process, if you don't understand the question that I ask, just tell me and then I'll explain. There are no right or wrong answers to these questions. All the information you provide is confidential. You and your school will not be identified in my final write-up for pseudonyms will be used in it. You can decline answering any question or stop participating at any time. There will be no loss of benefits to which you are otherwise entitled or any other negative consequence for it. During the interview, I will tape record our conversation and take notes in order to make sure I get everything you say correct.

1. For what purpose did you read your teacher's feedback on your writing this time? Why?
2. To what extent do you think you understood and accepted teacher feedback this time?
3. What were you thinking when you interpreted this piece of teacher comment (the one indicated by the interviewer)?
4. Concerning this piece of teacher feedback (the one indicated by the interviewer), do you think you understood and accepted it? Why do you think so? If you accepted this piece of teacher feedback, did you consider how to act on it? For example, did you consider how to revise

it in mind? Why do you think so?

5. Concerning the problem addressed by this feedback (the one indicated by the interviewer), do you think you can better deal with it when writing new essays? Why do you think so?
6. Do you think you are better able to deal with teacher feedback next time? Why do you think so?
7. What do you think of your communication with your teacher through feedback this time? Why do you think so?

Thank you very much for your time today and support of this research project. I appreciate you taking the time to share your thoughts with me. If you talk about this with anyone, please remember not to mention any specific participant by name. If you have any other questions, please do not hesitate to contact me.

Appendix F: Teacher/Student Final Interview Guide

Thank you for joining me today and agreeing to take this interview. First, let me remind you about the purpose of this interview. This interview aims to obtain information concerning your views about the feedback sessions in this semester. The interview will take about less than 1 hour. Throughout the interview process, if you don't understand the question that I ask, just tell me and then I'll explain. There are no right or wrong answers to these questions. All the information you provide is confidential. You and your school will not be identified in my final write-up for pseudonyms will be used in it. You can decline answering any question or stop participating at any time. There will be no loss of benefits to which you are otherwise entitled or any other negative consequence for it. During the interview, I will tape record our conversation and take notes in order to make sure I get everything you say correct.

1. What do you think of your communication with your students/teacher through feedback in a semester? Why do you think so?
2. Do you think that your students/you are better able to deal with teacher feedback now? Why do you think so?
3. Do you think that teacher feedback on each of the text-level issues helpful? Why do you think so?
4. Do you think that teacher feedback on positive and direct, negative feedback are helpful? Why do you think so?

Thank you very much for your time today and support of this research project. I appreciate you taking the time to share your thoughts with me. If you talk about this with anyone, please remember not to mention any specific participant by name. If you have any other questions, please do not hesitate to contact me.

Appendix G: Teacher Think-Aloud Data Codebook

(Themes, Categories, Sub-categories, and Codes)

Theme 1: Teacher involvement

    Category: Behavioural involvement

        feedback-typing operations

            type in feedback

            type in added/edited feedback

        help-seeking operations

            consult online dictionary/resources

            consult materials (e.g., model writing)

    Category: Affective involvement

        articulate affective response to student writing (e.g., (dis)satisfied, pleasant)

        articulate feelings aroused by feedback-writing (e.g., anguished)

        articulate (dis)satisfaction with comments provided on student writing (satisfied and dissatisfied)

    Category: Cognitive decision-making involvement

        planning and metacognitive operations

            articulate focus

            articulate delivery approaches

            articulate control of emotions

        interpretation operations

            read student writing (overall, overall introduction, local-level issues in the paragraph of introduction, overall body paragraph, local-level issues in the paragraph, overall conclusion)

interpret student writing (e.g., identify the student's writing intention)

evaluation operations
- point out strengths
- point out problems
- evaluate student writing
- evaluate student writing process
- evaluate student ability
- evaluate student writing attitude
- evaluate student efforts
- evaluate students' acceptance of and affective reactions to EA feedback
- evaluate students' application of classroom instruction to writing
- evaluate student improvement
- consider plagiarism
- compare writing (cross-student comparison, cross-writing comparison)

identification and selection operations
- identify how to phrase comments in English
- identify what to write
- identify how to revise student writing
- identify how to express feedback in English
- select lexis, sentence stems, language expressions, use of symbols, feedback style (direct/indirect) and feedback

positions
  review operations
    read student writing
    review student writing
    read comments provided on student writing
    review comments provided on student writing
    consider instruction purposes via feedback
    articulate (dis)satisfaction with comments provided
    consider student reactions to teacher feedback (e.g., understanding of feedback, incorporation of feedback)
    consider the improvement of the teacher-provided revisions
    consider plagiarism
    evaluate student ability
    evaluate student efforts
    compare student writing
  reflection operations
    consider how to deliver feedback
    consider what to teach in class
    consider student problems with dealing EA issues and the causes
    consider student progress in argumentation and the causes
    reflect on feedback purposes
    reflect on the effective feedback delivery approaches (e.g., confirmation of student strengths and progress)
    reflect on student affect, student acceptance of teacher feedback, and student application of classroom instruction concerning EA issues

Category: Interaction among affective, cognitive and behavioural involvement

Theme 2: Interactional factors influencing teacher decision-making

Category: Teacher factors

Category: Contextual factors

Appendix H: Student Think-Aloud Data Codebook

Labelling Think-Aloud Data from Students A, B, and C
(Themes, Categories, Sub-categories, and Codes)

Student A

Theme 1: Student engagement

    Category: Behavioural engagement

        seek online materials for help

        take notes

        make revision

        memorize/make mental note of the key points in teacher feedback (e.g., feedback on connectives)

        mark the key points

    Category: Affective engagement

        articulate affective evaluation of teacher feedback

        articulate affective evaluation of self-written text

        articulate emotional feelings aroused by responding to teacher feedback

        articulate difficulty in making revision

    Category: Cognitive engagement

        reading operations

            scan self-written text

            read self-written text

            read teacher comment

processing operations (process self-written text)
    identify key issues of self-written text
    evaluate self-written text
    review self-written text
    (re-)identify key issues of self-written text
    articulate confidence in writing cohesively and coherently
    consider writing process
evaluation operations (evaluate teacher feedback)
    articulate questions about teacher feedback
    articulate preference for teacher feedback
    compare self-written text and teacher revision
    articulate expectation for teacher feedback
    articulate agreement with teacher feedback
    articulate disagreement with the negative part
    articulate inspiration of other feedback
    evaluate teacher attitude
    evaluate teacher understanding of self-written text
justification operations
    justify self-written text
    re-justify self-written text
analysis operations
    interpret advice as negative feedback
    translate teacher feedback into L1
    reinterpret teacher feedback
    identify explanation and advice as acceptable feedback points
    identify key points of explanation
    identify the problem indicated in feedback
    identify the "how" and "why" of feedback, suggestions,

and revisions
    identify foci of teacher feedback
    justify teacher feedback
incorporation decisions
    consider how to write in new composition
    summarize key points of teacher feedback
    consider how to revise
review operations
    read self-written text
    interpret self-written text
    identify key issues and strengths of self-written text
    reinterpret self-written text
    reinterpret teacher feedback
    evaluate self-interpretation of feedback
    go through the most important teacher feedback
metacognitive operations

Student B

Category: Behavioural engagement
take notes
mark key points in teacher feedback
memorize/make mental of key points in teacher feedback

Category: Affective engagement
articulate emotional feelings aroused by teacher feedback
articulate affective evaluation of self-written texts

articulate affective evaluation of teacher feedback
articulate positive attitude towards revision
consider teacher revision meaningless
acknowledge appreciation of teacher feedback

Category: Cognitive engagement

reading operations
- read self-written text
- read teacher feedback
- scan self-written text

evaluation operations (evaluate teacher feedback)
- acknowledge notice of teacher feedback
- articulate questions about teacher feedback
- compare self-written text and teacher revision
- articulate agreement with teacher feedback
- articulate disagreement with the negative part of feedback
- acknowledge knowledge gaps
- make connections between feedback

analysis operations (analyze teacher feedback)
- interpret advice as vocabulary problem
- interpret revision from language perspective
- self-identify writing problems
- interpret revision from register perspective
- interpret revision as language problems
- make connection with in-class instruction
- acknowledge inability to understand teacher feedback
- consider writing process

justification operations
- justify self-written text

> > re-justify self-written text
> > incorporation decisions
> > > articulate summarization
> > review operations
> > > re-read self-written text
> > > re-read teacher feedback
> > > re-interpret teacher feedback
> > > re-justify self-written text
> > > evaluate self-written text
> > > self-identify writing problems
> > metacognitive operations

Student C

Category: Behavioural engagement
> consult dictionaries installed in mobile phone
> take notes
> make revision
> memorize/make mental note of the key points in teacher feedback
> mark the key points in teacher feedback

Category: Affective engagement
> articulate emotional feelings aroused by responding to teacher feedback
> articulate affective evaluation of self-written texts
> articulate affective evaluation of teacher feedback
> articulate appreciation of teacher feedback
> articulate trust of teacher

Category: Cognitive engagement
> reading operations

    scan self-written text
    read self-written text
    read teacher feedback

self-written text processing operations (process self-written text)
    identify problem of self-written text
    evaluate self-written text
    consider reasons for writing strengths

evaluation operations
    interpret teacher feedback from the teacher perspective
    articulate questions about teacher feedback
    articulate agreement with teacher feedback
    interpret teacher feedback as problem indication
    compare revision with self-written text
    acknowledge notice of teacher feedback
    evaluate teacher feedback
    evaluate teacher understanding of written text
    articulate notice of positive feedback

justification operations
    justify self-written text
    re-justify self-written text

analysis operations (analyse teacher feedback)
    identify the "why" of teacher feedback
    identify the "why" of positive teacher feedback
    identify the "how" of teacher revision
    identify the "what" of teacher feedback
    identify the exact meaning of EA feedback
    identify the writing problem
    identify connection between feedback

                identify the implication of teacher feedback
            incorporation decisions
                consider how to revise
                summarize key points in teacher feedback
            review operations
                identify writing problems
                re-interpret EA feedback
            metacognitive operations

    Category: Interaction among affective, cognitive and behavioural involvement

Theme 2: Interactional factors influencing student decision-making
    Category: Student factors
    Category: Contextual factors

Appendix I: Student Writing with Teacher Comments

(A Sample in Original Version)

The Campus Activity that benefits the most

Our lives at college cannot be colourful unless we gets rid of boring courses (写作中尽量避免消极的评论，尽量传递积极信息 your writing could reflect your state of mind or life attitude, and your writing would influence the reader) and take an active part in various activities, and among these different activities, social practice benefits the most.(This opening could get straight to the point, but not very attractive. Try this: Campus activities play an indispensable and active part in the college life. Among these various activities, social practice benefits me the most. 是否更加简洁些☺)

There are lots of reasons contributing to the trend that joining in social practice play increasingly crucial role in a student's life. (在段落之间有这样一个承上启下的主题句是非常必要的☺ 建议这一段与下面两段合并为第二段，主要讨论的是原因。结构会更清楚些。另外这句话表述有些不清楚，可以改为 Social practice plays an increasingly significant role in students' life and several reason contribute to that.)

Be involved in social practice found a platform for us to communicate and cooperate with others. (It's good to have a clearly expressed opinion as a sub-topic sentence。另外这句话可以再简洁些，改为 **The involvement in** social practice **provides** a platform for communication and cooperation with others.)We can obtain different friendships in the process. With different ideas and talents, the valuable experience makes us open-minded, flexible and easy-going, being a landmark during our growth.

(就这一部分而言，开头第一句话表达明确，即可以提供给我们交流和合作的平台，之后的句子应该围绕这层意思进一步展开，做到连贯性。The following sentences should provide details to further explain or illustrate about how or why it helps to communicate or cooperate. But, your following sentences fail to do that. Instead, you gives not that coherent ideas.)

There is no doubt that social practice can enhance our sense of responsibility and confidence, and a success practice after our efforts can give us a sense of achievement and pleasure, even a failure can still broaden our horizon and help us find what our weaknesses are and make a solid foundation for next trial. 这一部分论述的层次结构不清楚，是原因的罗列，没有进一步展开，建议只保留 2-3 个 causes 就可以，

再稍微展开写下。建议结构如下：

Social practice plays an increasingly significant role in students' life and several reason contribute to that.— 主题句

Cause 1 The involvement in social practice provides a platform for communication and cooperation with others.—supporting sentences

Cause 2 There is no doubt that social practice can enhance our sense of responsibility and confidence.—supporting details

Cause 3 broaden our horizon— 也可以不要

Considered the fact that our students' time at college is a period of translation to a world of work, it is necessary to make use of it to touch on some fields about what we are learning or interested. Inevitably, social practice can bring us meaningful experience and abundant knowledge which cannot be heard in the classroom. Now, as we know, many students, dreaming of having a bright career and promising future will find their hop from a classroom to a company or office delayed a bit, because many employers prefer those experienced employees who are full of knowledge about the work and ability to address practical issues. (这一段表述不清楚。貌似在说社会实践可以锻炼课堂学不到的实际应用能力，这也是今后工作所需要的能力。这一层意思仍然属于原因，作为结尾段不合适，应该归到第二部分。这层原因可以表述为：The social practice can improve the practical competence which cannot be provided in the classroom. 仍需要写一个比较完整的结尾。)

1. Pay attention to the paragraph setting. Three paragraphs would be acceptable. Too many paragraphs would make the writing unclear and not well structured. 注意文章结构，建议采取传统的三段模式，本文段落太多。

2. Generally, the coherence of the writing is fine. The choice of words is pretty impressive, such as platform, flexible, Inevitably, landmark, etc ☺

3. The general structure of the writing is not that sound since you need **a conclusion.** Also pay attention to the logic and structure of each paragraph.

Appendix J: Student Writing with Teacher Comments and Student-Written Notes

(A Sample in Original Version)

The Campus Activity that benefits the most

在英语中，好的结构往往可以引人入胜，比如好的反问句、反义疑问句，并不是在传递消极信息，而是用欲扬先抑的感觉去描述好处。

Our lives at college cannot be colourful unless we get rid of boring courses (写作中尽量避免消极的评论，尽量传递积极信息 your writing could reflect your state of mind or life attitude, and your writing would influence the reader) and take an active part in various activities, and among these different activities, social practice benefits the most.(this opening could get straight to the point, but not very attractive. Try this: Campus activities play an indispensable and active part in the college life. Among these various activities, social practice benefits me the most. 是否更加简洁些 ☺)

There are lots of reasons contributing to the trend that joining in social practice play increasingly crucial role in a student's life. (在段落之间有这样一个承上启下的主题句是非常必要的 ☺ 建议这一段与下面两段合并为第二段，主要讨论的是原因。结构会更清楚些。另外这句话表述有些不清楚，可以改为 Social practice plays an increasingly significant role in students' life and several reasons contribute to that.)

名词化的短语使用会显得很正式，也可以让多个句子合并在一个长句里，并且避免了好多动词出现在句子里，显得生硬。

Be involved in social practice found a platform for us to communicate and cooperate with others.

(It's good to have a clearly expressed opinion as a sub-topic sentence。另外这句话可以再简洁些，改为 **The involvement in** social practice **provides** a platform for communication and cooperation with others.)We can obtain different friendships in the process. 具体的展示遇到问题我们可以交流合作完成什么样的任务, when our peers meet obs with different ideas and talents, the valuable experience makes us open-minded, flexible and easy-going, being a landmark during our growth.（就这一部分而言，开头第一句话表达明确，即可以提供给我们交流和合作的平台，之后的句子应该围绕这层意思进一步展开，做到连贯性。The following sentences should provide details to further explain or illustrate about how or why it helps to communicate or cooperate. But, your following sentences fail to do that. Instead, you gives not that coherent ideas.)

There is no doubt that social practice can enhance our sense of responsibility and confidence, and a success practice after our efforts can give us a sense of achievement and pleasure, even a failure can still broaden our horizon and help us find what our weaknesses are and make a solid foundation for next trial. 这一部分论述的层次结构不清楚，是原因的罗列，没有进一步展开，建议只保留 2–3 个 causes 就可以，再稍微展开写下。**建议结构如下：**

Social practice plays an increasingly significant role in students' life and several reason contribute to that.—— 主题句

Cause 1 The involvement in social practice provides a platform for communication and cooperation with others.—supporting sentences

Cause 2 There is no doubt that social practice can enhance our sense of responsibility and confidence.—supporting details

Cause 3 broaden our horizon— 也可以不要

Consider the fact that our students' time at college is a period of translation to a world of work, it is necessary to make use of it to touch on some fields about what we are learning or interested. Inevitably, social practice can bring us meaningful experience and abundant knowledge which cannot be heard in the classroom. Now, as we know, many students, dreaming of having a bright career and promising future will find their hop from a classroom to a company or office delayed a bit, because many employers prefer those experienced employees who are full of knowledge about the work and ability to address practical issues. (这一段表述不清楚。貌似在说社会实践可以锻炼课堂学不到的实际应用能力，这也是今后工作所需要的能力。这一层意思仍然属于原因，作为结尾段不合适，应该归到第二部分。这层原因可以表述为：The social practice can improve the practical competence which cannot be provided in the classroom. 仍需要写一个比较完整的结尾。)

1. Pay attention to the paragraph setting. Three paragraphs would be acceptable. Too many paragraphs would make the writing unclear and not well structured. 注意文章结构，建议采取传统的三段模式，本文段落太多。

2. Generally, the coherence of the writing is fine. The choice of words is pretty impressive, such as platform, flexible, Inevitably, landmark, etc ☺

3. The general structure of the writing is not that sound since you need **a conclusion**. Also pay attention to the logic and structure of each paragraph.

主要问题：(1) 文章的结构，原因在构思时就要逻辑清晰，两三点不要有交叉，要独立，最好是多角度，有全面。总结，深化主题，最好用一些简洁有力的表达观点的句子，这样观点明确。（2）重中之重，段落内部的结构，主题句一出来，要跟有两三句支撑它的话起到细节补充的作用，从 how 和 why 的角度多考虑考虑，分成几个独立的句子来进一步论证，要真实有力。

Appendix K: Writing Prompts

Below the three writing prompts are presented in the order in which they were written over the course of the semester.

1. **Writing assignment 1 (W1)**

    Writing topic: The Campus Activity that Benefits the Most

    Directions: You should use the writing technique of **Cause-Effect** to illustrate your views. You can write about 250 words.

2. **Writing assignment 2 (W2)**

    Writing topic: The Importance of Reading Literature

    Directions: You should use **Examples** to support your views and you can write about 250 words.

3. **Writing assignment 3 (W3)**

    Writing topic: How to Reduce the Campus Waste

    Directions: You can use any writing techniques that we have ever discussed in class to support your views and you can write about 250 words.